THE WARREN COURT

THE WARREN COURT
A Critical Analysis

Editors
Richard H. Sayler
Barry B. Boyer
Robert E. Gooding, Jr.

Chelsea House
New York

LIBRARY
University of Texas
At San Antonio

CONTENTS

THE WARREN COURT
A Critical Analysis

THE WARREN COURT
AN EDITORIAL PREFACE

THE Supreme Court under Chief Justice Earl Warren destroyed one of the fundamental notions of the Court's role in American history. Political literature of this century has described the Court as a brake on the democratic process, thus preserving the institutions and concepts of the immediate past and delaying the efforts of the legislative and executive branches to implement a new political consensus. Most crises in the life of the Court—from John Marshall's defiance of Jefferson and Jackson through the *Dred Scott* case, the Income Tax case of 1894, and the New Deal controversies—had involved the Court in a fight against what appeared to be the will of the people. Over the years, no one had ever suggested that the Court itself could be a major instrument of change, that it could establish new goals for the nation, articulate a new moral sense for the people and, in effect, reorganize the political structure of the country itself. But the Warren Court did produce precisely that kind of revolution.

Many believed the Warren Court had moved too fast, and the controversy over the nomination of Abe Fortas as Chief Justice unleashed bitter feelings against the Court's decisions. Senatorial questioning of Justice Fortas focused on the emotional areas of crime and obscenity but ignored the main thrust of the Court's work in political reorganization and civil rights. Yet, behind the questions leveled at Fortas was an undercurrent of dissatisfaction with the Court for not abiding by the normal rules of political inertia that required the Justices to lag behind the legislative branch in reallocating political and economic power.

Chief Justice Warren understood what was important in the work of his Court. When asked the three most significant decisions during his tenure, he named *Baker* v. *Carr*, the reapportionment case: *Brown* v. *Board of Education*, the school desegregation case; and *Gideon* v. *Wainwright*, which established the right to counsel in a criminal proceding. The order of his response showed Warren's concern with the proper working of the political process. If we assume that social change should reflect the will of the people, then the political machinery must accurately reflect that will. Thus, reapportionment of the states' archaic rotten boroughs became a compelling requirement. If the legislative process was bogged down in the area of civil rights due to the special power of southern senators and committee chairmen, the Court should, and did, break through that logjam. Similarly, reform in criminal procedure required, in the first instance, legal assistance for the poor so that they would be able to protect themselves in the courts.

Chief Justice Warren's decision to retire at the end of the October, 1968 term, clearly created the need and the opportunity to analyze and evaluate the Court's work over the last fifteen years. The idea for this collection originated with the staff of the Michigan Law Review. The essays range over nine specific areas of the Court's work. Reapportionment is discussed by Robert B. McKay, Dean of the New York University Law School, Robert L. Carter examines desegregation; other articles include: criminal procedure by A. Kenneth Pye; religious liberty by Paul G. Kauper; free speech by Harry Kalven, Jr.; the press by John P. MacKenzie; labor by Theodore J. St. Antoine; antitrust by Thomas E. Kauper, and the political process by William M. Beaney. Philip Kurland contributes an analysis of the Warren myths. A biographical over-view of Warren by Anthony Lewis, formerly Supreme Court correspondent for *The New York Times*, weaves together many of the themes in the separate essays.

The book as a whole, therefore, gives an ordered and comprehensive view of the changes the Court has wrought in these widely diversified areas. It becomes evident too, that no matter how much theorizing one engages in about the institution itself, the men who wield the power do make a difference. The Court is the least dangerous or the most dangerous branch of the government, depending on whether or not its members are deeply devoted to the democratic principles of the Constitution and the human rights embodied in the first ten amendments. There can be no doubt of Chief Justice Warren's position in this regard. Shortly after he announced his intention to retire he said:

> Justice in individual cases is the basis of justice for everyone. A failure to protect and further anyone's individual rights leads to justice for no one.
>
> Many countries have provisions in their Constitutions similar to our own. In only a few countries do these provisions find effect in the actual operation of the law. The failure of these Constitutions is not in the concepts of their draftsmen but rather in the absence of an independent judiciary to uphold these rights or a professionally independent bar to assert and defend them.
>
> Justice will be universal in this country when the processes as well as the doors of the courthouse are open to everyone. This can

occur only as the institutions of justice, the courts and their processes are kept responsive to the needs of justice in the modern world. Such a goal will be accomplished only as all elements of the legal system, the law-makers, practicing attorneys, legal scholars and judges, recognize the ever-changing effects of the law on society and adapt to them within the principles which are fundamental to freedom.

This collection, then, is designed to show how far the Court under Chief Justice Warren has balanced the need for justice with the problems of twentieth-century America.

LEON FRIEDMAN

April, 1969
New York City

EARL WARREN

Anthony Lewis*

A REVOLUTION made by judges. It is an implausible idea, temperamentally and historically. But there is not much exaggeration in using such terms for the record of the Court over which Earl Warren presided for sixteen terms, so fundamental were the changes it made or initiated in American law and politics and social arrangements. In no other country could a court thus have functioned. Only once before in this country has the Supreme Court played so large a part in shaping the national destiny; and that was John Marshall's Court, writing on a clean slate.

The Warren Court set the United States on a new path in race relations, wiping out the legal basis for discrimination and, as it happened, helping to release long-suppressed emotional results of racism. By imposing the rule that all citizens must be represented equally in state legislatures and the national House the Court changed the character of American politics, eliminating the traditional rural bias. It wrote what amounted to a new constitutional code of criminal justice, one restraining the whole process of law enforcement from investigation through arrest and trial, and applied the code rigorously to state and local activities formerly outside federal standards. It greatly broadened the citizen's freedom to criticize public figures, and the artist's to express himself in unconventional and even shocking ways; it greatly restricted government authority to penalize the individual because of his beliefs or associations.

That astonishing record tended, in the popular mind, to be attributed personally to Chief Justice Warren. The paranoid rantings of the John Birch Society, with its demand to impeach Earl Warren, laid to him all the ills it saw in the Court's work; those who delighted in the judicial reshaping of society could be almost equally mindless in their adulation. But the role of the Chief Justice was not a solitary or dominant one, for good or ill. To appraise his personal part in the history made by the Warren Court is an elusive business.

It hardly needs saying that without the happenstance of other appointments to the Court, the Chief Justice might have expressed in dissent many of the views that became the law. Presidents Eisen-

---

* Formerly Supreme Court Correspondent, now Chief London Correspondent, *New York Times*, B.A., 1948, Harvard University.—Ed.

hower, Kennedy, and Johnson could easily have named as Justices men less legally adventurous, to use a neutral adjective, than a Brennan, a Goldberg, a Fortas; then the votes would simply not have been there for many of the great changes made in the law by the Warren Court. No Chief Justice can command his associates' beliefs, despite what Jefferson thought of Marshall. In Earl Warren's day the Court did not lack for strong personalities and rooted convictions.

If any member of the Court saw his philosophy become doctrine, in fact, it was not the Chief Justice but Justice Black. For years he had carried on a great intellectual struggle with Justice Frankfurter over such issues as freedom of speech for Communists, the application of the Bill of Rights to the states, constitutional limits on legislative apportionment. When his views at length prevailed on the Court, as so many of them did, it was natural for observers to believe that Justice Black, with his powerful intellect, long service, and deep beliefs, had been the main influence for change. The Chief Justice was not a philosopher and made no attempt, in opinions or otherwise, to propound a consistent theory of how a judge interpreting the Constitution should approach his task.

But the legal revolution could not have taken place without Earl Warren. He saw the movement and put behind it the weight of his character and position and public reputation; they were essential in converting what might have been lost legal causes into the wave of the future. That he was a man of political experience rather than a scholar—an ordinary man, a rather simple man—all this was part of his contribution. At a time when the Supreme Court was undertaking to change so much so quickly in American life, and thus had inevitably become the subject of the most bitter controversy, the paternal, old-fashionedly patriotic figure of the Chief Justice was crucial to public acceptance of the change.

The personality that he projected to the outside world was friendly, openhearted, but also a bit bland and remote—as if it were easier for him to be kind in general than warm to a particular human being. In fact, there were very few persons with whom Earl Warren was really on intimate human terms. Nor was he quite the easygoing outdoor type that his massive frame and unpretentious California manners made him seem. He was a proud man, and an intensely emotional one, who burned at any sensed lack of respect or lack of candor in others. The inner emotion burst out infrequently in the courtroom, as on three occasions when the Chief Justice took offense at Justice Frankfurter's oral version of a dissenting opinion and answered back extemporaneously. There was a revealing expression of his true feelings when President Kennedy was assassinated; putting aside the official prose that ordinarily marked his writing, the Chief Justice said: "What moved some misguided wretch to do this horrible deed may never be known to us, but we do know that such acts are commonly stimulated by forces of hatred and malevolence such as today are eating their way into the bloodstream of American life. What a price we pay for this fanaticism!" His deep feelings, and his patriotism, led him to accept the job of chairman of the commission to investigate the assassination, despite the tremendous physical burden and psychological strain it imposed.

The decisions that history may regard as the most far-reaching of the period, the Reapportionment Cases, most plainly required Chief Justice Warren's support to be possible; it is hard to believe that they could have happened under another kind of Chief Justice, no matter who else was on the Court. The movement against racial discrimination had begun in any event, but the Supreme Court's vital intervention—in *Brown* v. *Board of Education* in 1954—would not have come when and as it did without Earl Warren. Nor can one imagine, in his absence, the creation within a few years of a host of new rights for state criminal defendants. With one relatively minor exception, on the question of censorship, he favored every major change in constitutional doctrine undertaken by the Court. That cannot be explained as coincidence.

We have been taught for decades by the realists that the Supreme Court is a political institution. Earl Warren, then, was a great political leader. If he was not a creative thinker like Justice Black, he did have some of the essential qualities of a statesman: a sense of history, an understanding of people, firmness of character. No one could deny that he had courage. For all his political background, he recognized that a judge should not seek popular favor; he never hesitated in the face of opposition from Congress or the organized bar or public opinion. All this makes it certain that he will go down as one of the outstanding figures in the history of the Supreme Court.

He was more than a judge—(to the public in the United States and much of the world he became a symbol.) It was the School Segregation Cases that fixed him in the minds of people abroad; Earl Warren represented to them the hope of America, the promise of our society that it would raise up the downtrodden without rebellion. At home, he was a convenient symbol of hate for those who sought racial or political or conspiratorial explanations for their personal anxieties. For other Americans, for the majority, he was a reminder of what seemed lost American virtues: openness, optimism, idealism without ideology. (In an age of character assassination, he saw good in other human beings.)(In an age of governmental indecision, he was decisive.)

The critical question that history will ask is whether Chief Justice Warren—and his Court—strained the role that judges should play in a democracy, even in so legalized a democracy as ours. In the Warren years, attitudes toward law and the courts shifted radically in the United States. Some of the qualities valued in the judicial process—stability, intellectuality, craftsmanship—seemed to be put aside. It was as an instrument of social change that the process came to be seen. Where once it had been an event for the Supreme Court to overrule one of its own prior decisions, that became common coin. The Court sat, many said, as a permanent constitutional convention—and accordingly, in the view of its critics, felt less obligated to justify its decisions in the language of the Constitution or the persuasiveness of precedent or the intellectual force of experience. Even young teachers of law were surprised at how their students brushed aside all the nice questions about relationships between one decision and another. The important thing was the just result; the presumption was that any challenged governmental act was unconstitutional. That the Supreme Court should leave many questions to the discretion of the political branches of government—an idea once so treasured by liberal-minded legal thinkers—seemed forgotten.

For this shift in attitudes the Chief Justice bore considerable responsibility. For, far more than most other members of the Court, he evidently felt unconfined by precedent or by a particular view of the judicial function. The contrast with Justices Frankfurter and Black is instructive. Justice Frankfurter argued for "self-restraint" on the part of judges to let the elected leaders of government have more room for experiment. Justice Black scornfully rejected that position, but he had his own strictly defined view of the limits on judicial power. His limits were verbal—what he could find in the literal text of the Constitution. If the words were not there, it was beyond his power to hold a governmental action invalid, however unpleasant it might seem. Thus he could not find any constitutional restraints on official wiretapping or eavesdropping; they were simply not mentioned in the Fourth Amendment; *Berger* v. *New York,* 388 U.S. 41 (1967); *Katz* v. *United States,* 389 U.S. 347 (1967). Justice Harlan said in an appraisal of his great colleague (81 Harvard

Law Review 1) that Justice Black "rejects the open-ended notion that the Court sits to do good in every circumstance where good is needed." The statement almost invites contrast to the Chief Justice's attitude.

In Chief Justice Warren's opinions one does not find doctrinal threads of the kind that run familiarly through the works of a Frankfurter or Black, arguing a legal theory decade after decade. He seldom troubled to quote his own past positions. A Warren opinion, characteristically, is a morn made new—a bland, square presentation of the particular problem in that case almost as if it were unencumbered by precedents or conflicting theories, as it inevitably must be. Often the framework of the argument seems ethical rather than legal, in the sense that one expects the law to be analytical. Chief Justice Warren's opinions are difficult to analyze because they are likely to be unanalytical.

An early example was the Chief Justice's opinion for a plurality of the Court in *Trop* v. *Dulles,* 356 U.S. 86 (1958), holding unconstitutional a statute under which a native-born American had been deprived of his citizenship for deserting the armed forces in time of war. One leg of the Chief Justice's opinion took the novel view that the expatriation was a "cruel and unusual punishment" in violation of the Eighth Amendment. In one vague paragraph the opinion, gliding past much contrary legal history, found that the deprivation of citizenship was technically "punishment." Then, although conceding that the death penalty would not have been "cruel," the opinion concluded that expatriation was so because it brought about "the total destruction of the individual's status in organized society" and cost him, with the loss of citizenship, "the right to have rights." The opinion ended with a ringing statement of the Supreme Court's duty to judge congressional enactments "by the standards of the Constitution," a passage faintly reminiscent of Justice Roberts' famous statement in *United States* v. *Butler,* 297 U.S. 1 (1936), that in constitutional cases the Court "has only one duty— to lay the article of the Constitution which is invoked beside the statute which is challenged and to decide whether the latter squares with the former." The Chief Justice concluded: "When it appears that an Act of Congress conflicts with one of these provisions, we have no choice but to enforce the paramount commands of the Constitution." But of course the question remains whether there was any conflict with the Eighth Amendment.

An interesting insight into his views was given by a speech to the Jewish Theological Seminary in New York in 1962. The Chief

Justice spoke of law as floating "in a sea of ethics" but indicated that law did not go ethically far enough. He suggested development of the profession of "counselor in ethics." By way of example he said: "Our college campuses might look very different if such problems as the promotion of faculty members were subject to deliberation on moral grounds. And our political campaigns, our nominations and elections might be different, if political parties included experts in ethics among those deciding policies." To most lawyers the proposal must smack of astonishing naiveté. The point is that, in the absence of other formal methods of weighing ethical considerations in life, the Chief Justice evidently felt that law and the courts must do so to a significant degree.

On the Court, he seemed often in his opinions to merge technical issues that had traditionally been fought over in civil liberties cases into larger questions of fairness. This approach was reflected in the questions he put at oral argument. Government counsel would be arguing the legal authority for some course of action against an individual when the Chief Justice would interrupt to ask: "But was it fair?" (Sometimes, personalizing the question, he would ask a government lawyer who had first heard of the case when it reached the Supreme Court, "Why did you treat him this way?")

In 1959 the government was defending its industrial security program under which private employees in defense industries were deprived of their clearance and jobs on security grounds without an opportunity to cross-examine their accusers. The Chief Justice asked: "If my neighbor accuses me of anything else but this and they are going to put me in jail or deprive me of my livelihood, I have a right to confront him. Why is this different?" But in fact one does not have a "right"—at least a constitutional right, which was presumably the question at issue—to confront an accuser before being dismissed from an ordinary job; that is in the discretion of the employer or the subject of some contractual relationship with a union. The very difficulty of the security case was that it fell somewhere between a criminal charge, where the Constitution unquestionably governs, and a matter of private employment, where it does not. That was where the Supreme Court had to begin its analysis of the problem.

If Chief Justice Warren occasionally appeared to put analysis aside because he found something outrageous, it must be remembered that there *were* outrages in American life—official racism, abuse of police authority, an unbalanced political system, intolerance of free expression—and that no other arm of government was doing anything about them. The willingness of the Supreme Court to deal with them bluntly and untechnically in the Warren era made a great difference. If the Chief Justice's approach was often generalized and moralistic, if simple answers were sometimes unsatisfyingly given to complicated questions, then at least American society was made to face some basic problems that it had ignored.

But appraising Chief Justice Warren's record in terms of the usefulness of particular results only raises the larger philosophical question: Is that the proper standard to apply to the work of a judge? And here we may begin to get closer to the personal mystery—to the inner forces that motivated Earl Warren.

Generations of American law students have been taught that justice is a process. Chief Justice Warren, one must think, did not take that view. To him justice consisted not of providing a fair mechanism of decision but of seeing that the right side, the good side, prevailed in the particular case. Most often his sympathy lay with the individual victim of governmental restraints; but interestingly, when he saw the need for social control of some evil, such as gambling or obscenity, he voted to sustain the government despite cries of inconsistency. He really did believe, to use Justice Harlan's phrase, that he sat as a judge to do good where good was needed.

Earl Warren was the closest thing the United States has had to a Platonic Guardian[1], dispensing law from a throne without any sensed limits of power except what was seen as the good of society. Fortunately he was a decent, humane, honorable, democratic Guardian. But there were those—and not only niggling or illiberal spirits—who were troubled at the idea of a Supreme Court Justice, appointed for life and subject to no effective popular control, playing such a role in our system of government. Chief Justice Warren's great virtues, in an age of public cynicism and political sophistry, were his simplicity, his humanity, his courage; they are vital qualities on the most powerful of all courts, but do they make a whole judge without a philosophy of the law? Judges of another day, filled with their own sense of natural justice, outlawed paper money and prevented a state from limiting bakers to a ten-hour working day, and held unconstitutional a federal law against shipment of goods made by child labor. In their revulsion against such decisions, the liberals of the 1920's and 1930's may have taken too constricted a view of

---

1. The reference is of course to Judge Learned Hand's *Holmes Lectures* at Harvard in 1958, reprinted as The Bill of Rights: "For myself it would be most irksome to be ruled by a bevy of Platonic Guardians, even if I knew how to choose them, which I assuredly do not."

what judges may properly do. But if we should applaud without undue historical uneasiness when the contemporary Supreme Court reaches a right-minded result, we may still feel it important that the Court arrive at that result by a process that inspires confidence and with an opinion that awakes the public conscience.

The standard of the Supreme Court's performance is important not only in abstract intellectual terms but as a matter of self-preservation, and there again some who value the institution had criticism of the Warren Court's performance. As an unrepresentative body, the Court depends especially on consent to govern; its judgments are meaningful as its opinions persuade. If it attempts to impose on the country values that depart too far from basic contemporary beliefs, or if its opinions over time do not satisfy Americans that some new direction it is taking is morally and intellectually necessary, then the Court risks repudiation—the fate it suffered when it attempted to enshrine Spencerian economic notions in the Constitution. The Warren Court aroused public opposition of an intensity not seen for a generation, not only on the racial issue but among persons concerned about the level of crime in the United States and those uneasy about rebellious expression generally. Many of the Court's opponents were so unworthy that their criticism was a compliment. But toward the end of the 1960's the political storm, especially over the criminal law decisions, was so great that the most sympathetic observer might wonder whether the Court had acted wisely or well. There was serious danger that a punitive Congress or President might limit its jurisdiction or attempt drastically to reduce constitutional restraints on police power. It remained to be seen whether this heavy price would be paid.

It is a delicious irony that a President who raised inactivity to a principle of government, Eisenhower, should have appointed a Chief Justice for whom action was all. Many Presidents have been surprised by their appointees to the Supreme Court; one can hardly expect a man given the freedom and responsibility of that position to act altogether predictably. But could anyone have foretold in general terms the line that Earl Warren would follow? His life before going on the Bench gave some clues, but hardly ones free from ambiguity.

He was born in Los Angeles on March 19, 1891, the son of a Norwegian immigrant who worked for the Southern Pacific Railroad. He knew poverty and personal tragedy. As a young man he was a railroad callboy, waking up the gangs, and he saw men with their legs cut off in accidents carried in on planks. His own father was murdered, the murderer never found. He put himself through college and law school at the University of California, was in private practice briefly. From the year 1920 onward he served without interruption in public office: as a deputy in the Alameda County district attorney's office, as a crusading district attorney for thirteen years, as California attorney general for four, as governor—the first in the state's history to be elected three times. He was defeated in an election only once, as the Republican candidate for Vice-President, running with Thomas E. Dewey in 1948.

Through most of his career in California politics he was regarded as a regular Republican, a favorite of the heavily right-wing group that ran the party. William Randolph Hearst promoted him for the Republican presidential nomination in 1944. The Saturday Evening Post described him admiringly as an "ardent believer in states' rights." As attorney general he had denounced "communistic radicals," attacked his election opponent for opposing a bill to make school children salute the flag, blocked the nomination of a liberal-minded law professor, Max Radin, to the state supreme court and opposed a pardon for that old radical figure, Tom Mooney. As governor he was a leading proponent of the wartime federal order removing all persons of Japanese ancestry from the West Coast and putting them in concentration camps; opposing the return of the evacuees in 1943, he told a conference of governors: "If the Japs are released, no one will be able to tell a saboteur from any other Jap."

Then, in 1945, he astounded his political friends—and enemies—by proposing a state program of prepaid medical insurance. Over the next eight years he became an apostle of liberal Republicanism, embittering many of his former conservative backers but achieving an extraordinary nonpartisan political grip on the state. Once he won both the Republican and Democratic primaries, saving the effort of competing in the election. A later Democratic governor, Edmund G. (Pat) Brown, said of Earl Warren: "He was the best governor California ever had. He faced the problems of growth and social responsibility and met them head on. He felt the people of the state were in his care, and he cared for them."

As his third term as governor drew near its end, on September 3, 1953, Warren announced that he would not be a candidate for reelection. A few days later the Chief Justice of the United States, Fred M. Vinson, died. President Eisenhower picked Governor Warren to succeed him.

At that point, was there material to indicate what kind of judge he would be? President Eisenhower said he had picked Governor Warren for his "integrity, honesty, middle-of-the-road philosophy . . ." Much of the comment emphasized the middle of the road, the cliché later overtaken by "moderate." Warren was described as an "administrator." The pious hope was often expressed that he would bring more unity to the Supreme Court, calming its internal quarrels. Certainly he had few commitments on the actual issues due to reach the Court, indeed almost no experience of the kind of legal business with which he would have to deal. His experience was political, and even in that he seemed by Washington standards an unsophisticated man. Personally, he was a man of few pretensions and simple tastes, who preferred sports to intellectual disputation; a few years earlier he had toyed with the idea of becoming Commissioner of Baseball. Ideologically, it was hard to categorize a man who had vigorously supported the Japanese relocation program and, later, fought the medical interests for a form of state-insured medicine. He was not a man who thought in ideological terms. He had advocated health insurance not because of some philosophical conversion but because he had fallen ill and suddenly realized how catastrophic serious illness would be for the man without resources.

But perhaps, with hindsight, there was one unifying thread in his career—the commitment to action. Earl Warren was plainly a man born to act, not to muse, and very likely a man born to govern. Through all the apparent inconsistencies in his political life he exerted his powerful abilities in the way naturally open to him at any time. As district attorney he was the enemy of crime and corruption. As wartime attorney general and governor he was a patriot, worrying about the flag and Japanese spies. When the war ended and the social and physical problems of an expanding California emerged, he applied his energy to them through the means available. It was crucial that his mind was never closed. He learned from experience, and found new ways of applying to the problems of society his own strict morality and innate humanitarianism.

The difficulty, of course, was to know how such an instinct for action would be expressed in the narrow channels usually open to a judge. Now, after the event, it is possible to offer a theory: The great issues that came before the Warren Court called, in one sense, for a judicial choice between action and inaction—between exercising power for reform or allowing things to go on as they were. It was Earl Warren's natural inclination to act: to break the long deadlock on reapportionment, to attack local police abuses long considered outside the scope of federal restraints, to condemn official discrimination on account of race. Those were the opportunities open to the Supreme Court to make an impression on American life—that is to say, to govern. The instinct of government, and the sense of duty, did not depart Earl Warren when he put on a robe.

Whatever theories may be constructed after the event, after years of his development as a judge, it was not so clear at first where Chief Justice Warren would fit into the Supreme Court spectrum. During the early years observers felt that there was an implicit struggle going on between Justices Black and Frankfurter for the judicial soul of their new colleague; no impropriety was suggested, just an understandable desire to align him with what each urgently regarded as the right way of looking at the law. It is evident that, in the end, the Chief Justice found Black a more congenial personality: easier in manner, less awesome in intellectuality, more understanding of others' views if, underneath, just as relentlessly committed to his own. In terms of judicial outlook, the new Chief Justice at first seemed close to Justice Frankfurter in numerous cases but, before too long, unmistakably took a different path. The change can be seen in, among many other examples, cases decided four years apart in the field of immigration and nationality.

Galvan v. *Press,* 347 U.S. 522 (1954), came in the first Warren term on the Court. Petitioner was an alien who had been brought to the United States at the age of seven, in 1918, had resided in the country since then and had an American wife and four children. He had been a member of the Communist party from 1944 to 1946 or 1947. The party was legal at the time, but under the Immigration and Nationality Act of 1950 an alien's membership in the party at any time after entry was ground for deportation. A deportation order against this alien was upheld by the Supreme Court, Justice Frankfurter writing for the majority that he might be ready to find the harsh order unconstitutional if he were writing on a "clean slate" but that precedent had established Congress' plenary power over aliens. Justice Black, joined by Justice Douglas, dissented in an opinion saying that aliens, like citizens, were entitled to enjoy the First Amendment's protections of free speech and freedom of association without being penalized later. The dissent argued that deportation was a "punishment" and therefore was covered by all the constitutional protections surrounding criminal cases—the view rejected in the old cases cited by Justice Frankfurter. The Chief Justice joined silently in the majority opinion.

Four years later came *Trop* v. *Dulles,* the expatriation case mentioned above as an example of Chief Justice Warren's moral expansiveness in finding grounds to hold unpleasant governmental acts unlawful. His opinion found expatriation for deserting in time of war a cruel and unusual punishment. It noted in passing what it termed the "highly fictional" view that deportation was not, legally, punishment but said this could not determine the *Trop* situation. It was a five to four decision, and the dissent was written by Justice Frankfurter. To uphold this expatriation, he said, was "to respect the actions of the two branches of our government directly responsive to the will of the people and empowered under the Constitution to determine the wisdom of legislation. The awesome power of this Court to invalidate such legislation, because in practice it is bounded only by our own prudence in discerning the limits of the Court's constitutional function, must be exercised with the utmost restraint."

The now established division between the two men was dramatically displayed in the courtroom the day they read those opinions, March 31, 1958. The Chief Justice's opinion, anticipating the strictures of the dissent, ended with the statement that the Court's "ordeal of judgment cannot be shirked. In some eighty-one instances since this Court was established it has determined that congressional action exceeded the bounds of the Constitution. It is so in this case." When Justice Frankfurter then announced his dissent, he began by interpolating orally a direct answer to the Chief Justice's final point. Those eighty-one cases holding acts of Congress unconstitutional, he said bitingly, were nothing to boast about —many had been overruled.

The shift in attitude by the Chief Justice from his early days on the Court cannot accurately be described only in relation to the conflicting philosophies of Justices Frankfurter and Black. Two other decisions from his first term, involving no division between his two senior brothers, throw an even more revealing light on his outlook at that stage.

In *Irvine* v. *California,* 347 U.S. 128 (1954), the police had planted microphones in the bedroom of a California gambler. Records of his conversations were used in evidence in a gambling prosecution. The Supreme Court sustained the conviction, rejecting claims that the police eavesdropping violated Irvine's right to due process of law under the Fourteenth Amendment because the tactics either were generally unconscionable (as in *Rochin* v. *California,* 342 U.S. 165 [1952], where police pumping of a suspect's stomach to obtain evidence was disallowed) or were specifically a form of compulsory self-incrimination. The vote was five to four, with Justices Black, Frankfurter, Douglas, and Burton dissenting. Justice Jackson, for the majority, condemned what the police had done while finding no ground to reverse the conviction; he said that he and the Chief Justice, among the five voting to affirm, would direct the clerk to send the record of the case to the Attorney General for consideration of possible prosecutions of the police for violation of the federal Civil Rights Acts. Perhaps, in this last gesture, the new Chief Justice's moral outrage may be detected.

Barsky v. *Board of Regents,* 347 U.S. 442 (1954), was one of a series of cases arising from the hearings of the House Committee on Un-American Activities. Dr. Edward K. Barsky, a distinguished New York physician, had been convicted of contempt for refusing to produce the records of the Joint Anti-Fascist Refugee Committee. Thereafter the New York medical authorities suspended his license to practice. The Supreme Court, in an opinion by Justice Burton, dismissed the contention that New York had unconstitutionally deprived Dr. Barsky of his right to practice his profession, weighing matters unrelated to his fitness to practice. Justices Frankfurter, Black, and Douglas dissented.

How far away those decisions seem, how unlikely the Chief Justice's assent to them. And here there was no choice between those two most strong-minded of his colleagues. Justice Frankfurter's deep opposition to police intrusion on the citizen's privacy, especially by wiretapping or eavesdropping, outweighed his reluctance to impose federal restraints on local police activity; in the *Barsky* case there appeared his aversion to weaving irrelevant ideological rigidities into professional standards, a feeling expressed as to the bar in *Schware* v. *Board of Examiners,* 353 U.S. 232 (1957). It is not conceivable that either of the two challenged governmental acts would have survived scrutiny by the later Warren Court; a decade later the decisions would in all likelihood have gone unanimously the other way. The Chief Justice's position in 1954 must, then, have reflected a beginning uncertainty that led him to take a conventional, restricted view of his role. Most men grow more conservative with age. In the governorship, experience had made Warren increasingly more adventurous, more liberated from conventional views, and the same was to happen on the Supreme Court.

One way to chart his development as a judge is to examine his opinions in one field critically. The area of communism, including under that head all the varied legal problems arising from attempts to repress or penalize radical views or associations, is a useful one for study—not because those opinions had more effect on society than the ones on race or reapportionment, far from it, but because they reveal something of the Chief Justice's thinking. One certainty is that the thrust of all his opinions relating to communism is in the opposite direction from *Barsky*. After *Barsky* it is impossible to cite a case in which the Chief Justice was unresponsive to a claim by someone suffering for his political beliefs or associations. There is no single theme such as Justice Black's powerful, unswerving assertion of the inviolate character of First Amendment freedoms in all circumstances. The Warren opinions advance a wide variety of grounds, statutory and constitutional, procedural and substantive, for upsetting government restraints. They have to be read in a pragmatic way: as an effort to mitigate, by whatever means available, the excesses of American anti-communism in the 1950's and 1960's. And they must, finally, be compared with other cases, apparently similar, in which the Chief Justice reached a different result because he placed a higher personal value on the governmental interests involved.

Peters v. *Hobby,* 349 U.S. 331 (1955), was intended as a broad test of the government loyalty program's denial to accused employees of the right to confront their accusers. Counsel for both petitioner and the government urged the Court to decide whether there was a constitutional right of confrontation in such circumstances, but the Court declined to do so. A seven to two majority found that the administrators of the loyalty program had exceeded their authority under President Truman's executive order when they reopened proceedings against Dr. Peters, a Yale Medical School professor, after he had been cleared. Chief Justice Warren wrote the tightly circumscribed opinion that upset the finding against Dr. Peters on this narrow ground. Only Justices Black and Douglas, in concurring opinions, found the entire concept of being tested for one's loyalty without knowing the names of one's accusers unconstitutional. During the heyday of loyalty-security measures the Court never did settle the confrontation issue in constitutional terms. Four years after *Peters,* in *Greene* v. *McElroy,* 360 U.S. 474 (1959), a majority held that neither the President nor Congress had authorized the Defense Department to operate an industrial security program for defense plant employees without affording them the right of confrontation. The opinion was again by the Chief Justice; but this time he expressed so broadly in *obiter dictum* his belief in the importance of the right to confront accusers that Justice Frankfurter was unable to subscribe and concurred separately in the narrow holding of lack of authority.

In 1956, in *Pennsylvania* v. *Nelson,* 350 U.S. 497, the Court affirmed a Pennsylvania Supreme Court judgment that upset a conviction under the state sedition law for advocating the overthrow of the United States Government. The Chief Justice's opinion found that Congress, in the Smith Act of 1940, had occupied the field to the exclusion of state legislation.

In the spring of 1957 there came a series of decisions, all related in one way or another to communism, that startled the public and produced an angry reaction in Congress. The Supreme Court, with a surprising degree of unanimity, appeared to be putting belated but still important limits on the internal security proceedings that had agitated American society for the last decade. Investigation and prosecution, federal and state, were covered. Two major cases with opinions by others than the Chief Justice may be mentioned briefly. In *Yates* v. *United States,* 354 U.S. 298 (1957), a masterfully subtle opinion by Justice Harlan construed the Smith Act to permit prosecution of Communist party leaders not for speech advocating overthrow of the government as "abstract doctrine" but only for speech amounting to incitement to action. *Jencks* v. *United States,* 353 U.S. 657 (1957) only coincidentally involved communism. In a prosecution for falsification of a non-Communist oath under the Taft-Hartley Labor Act, Justice Brennan, for an eight to one majority, said that a defendant in a federal trial must be allowed to check the testimony of adverse witnesses against statements they had given to the prosecution before trial. This unexceptionable rule of fair procedure was greeted hysterically—a more accurate word might be politically—by the Attorney General, Herbert Brownell, Jr., and Congress quickly passed a statute that was designed to prevent defense fishing expeditions in government files but had little effect on the essential *Jencks* principle.

Watkins v. *United States,* 354 U.S. 178 (1957), attracted the most attention. John T. Watkins, a union official, refused to answer questions put by a subcommittee of the House Committee on Un-American Activities about the Communist affiliations of other persons. He was convicted under a statute punishing as contempt of Congress the refusal to answer "any question pertinent to the question under inquiry" by a committee of either house. The Supreme Court reversed the conviction by a vote of six to one. The opinion of the Court, by the Chief Justice, was a massive one, dealing at large with the history of legislative investigations and their significance. After World War II, he wrote, a new kind of congressional inquiry appeared, interested in "the threat of subversion" and involving a "broad-scale intrusion into the lives and affairs of private citizens." The very process of questioning a witness about his "beliefs, expressions or associations" could have "disastrous" effects on him and others and could make the public stick fearfully to "orthodox and uncontroversial views and associations." The opinion said that there was "no congressional power to expose for the sake of exposure" and stated that constitutional limits applied to congressional committees. It criticized the authorizing resolution of the House committee as "excessively broad." But after all this, the opinion came down in the end to what was really quite a narrow holding: The committee had never defined the "question under inquiry" or explained the pertinence to it of the questions asked Watkins, so that he could not be found guilty of failing to answer pertinent questions. In a brief separate statement Justice Frankfurter said he was joining the Chief Justice's opinion on the understanding that it held only that much.

Sweezy v. *New Hampshire,* 354 U.S. 234 (1957), arose from an inquiry into subversion authorized by the state legislature and carried out by the Attorney General as a "one-man legislative committee." Paul M. Sweezy declined to answer questions about lectures he had given at the University of New Hampshire or about the Progressive party; he was convicted of contempt. The Supreme Court reversed by a vote of six to two. There was no majority opinion. For himself and Justices Black, Douglas, and Brennan, the Chief Justice wrote an opinion that can only be called opaque. After extolling academic freedom and saying that "we do not now conceive of any circumstance wherein a state interest would justify its infringement," the opinion concluded that the contempt conviction could not stand because there was no showing that the New Hampshire legislature "wanted the information the attorney general attempted to elicit from petitioner." Justice Frankfurter, in an opinion joined by Justice Harlan, said squarely that the state had shown no adequate justification for breaching the constitutional interest in free thought, speech, and association, especially at a university.

The Warren opinions in *Watkins* and *Sweezy* were of exceptional significance in his development and the Court's. They were bold attempts by the Court to protect individual liberty in the area where, at the time, it was under the most severe attack in the United States. No one could doubt the courage of the Chief Justice and his colleagues in taking on the legislative red-hunters and the forces supporting them; it is the craftsmanship and wisdom of the opinions that were and may still be questioned. They were opinions that talked too much. They were overbroad, surrounding a kernel of legal accomplishment with a large quantity of moralizing. The critics on the right were so outrageous, so willfully misleading, that they were entitled to no sympathy.[2] But it is also true that a dry, careful, brief opinion limited to the only point really decided in *Watkins*—the statutory necessity of demonstrating pertinence—would have been less provocative than what the Chief Justice wrote. And if his broad words unduly alarmed the right, they also promised too much to those on the other side. For the latter thought the Court had imposed comprehensive restraints on legislative inquiries, and they were wrong.

Two years later, in *Barenblatt* v. *United States,* 360 U.S. 109 (1959), the issue of compelled testimony before the House Committee on Un-American Activities was again before the Court. This time a five-man majority of Justices Frankfurter, Harlan, Clark, Whittaker, and Stewart affirmed the conviction of a one-time Vassar instructor for refusing to answer questions about Communist associations. Justice Harlan, for the majority, dismissed as superfluous wordage the passages in *Watkins* criticizing the breadth of the committee's charter and warning against exposure for exposure's sake. Chief Justice Warren and Justices Black, Douglas, and Brennan dissented. The substantial unity presented by the Court two years earlier was shattered; or, rather, it was shown to have been a façade. The division in *Barenblatt* reflected deep differences in approach, and of course the gap might always have been unbridgeable. But one wonders whether what was done in *Watkins* had not, in retrospect, worried the more cautious members of the Court, especially Justice Harlan, and led them to take an unduly permissive view of the legislative investigating power—whether, in sum, the pendulum had swung too far one way in 1957, and therefore had been pushed too much the other way in 1959. A more skillful disposition of the earlier cases might have held a substantial majority of the Court on a middle course, avoiding any large constitutional strictures against the investigators but limiting their effective power

---

2. David Lawrence, a newspaper columnist, wrote after Watkins: "The Supreme Court of the United States has crippled the effectiveness of Congressional investigations. By one sweeping decision, the Court has opened the way to Communists, traitors, disloyal citizens and crooks of all kinds . . . to refuse to answer any questions which the witness arbitrarily decides for himself are not 'pertinent' to a legislative purpose." *Washington Evening Star,* June 19, 1957, p. A27, col. 1.

by an insistence on procedural regularity. There undoubtedly were such grounds for reversal in *Barenblatt* if the majority had wanted to invoke them.

For some years the four dissenters in *Barenblatt*—Warren, Black, Douglas, Brennan—found themselves repeatedly outvoted in cases involving communism. The juice was drained from the *Sweezy* case in *Uphaus* v. *Wyman,* 364 U.S. 388 (1960), upholding a contempt conviction for refusing to answer the same New Hampshire attorney general's questions. The same five to four majority upheld the constitutionality of the Smith Act clause punishing mere membership in a party advocating the government's overthrow, at least when the defendant was an "active" member, *Scales* v. *United States,* 367 U.S. 203 (1961). And the same majority sustained against Fifth and First Amendment objections an order of the Subversive Activities Control Board requiring the Communist party to register as a Communist action group; *Communist Party* v. *S.A.C.B.,* 367 U.S. 1 (1961).

Then the membership of the Court changed. Justice Whittaker was replaced by Justice White. Most significantly, Justice Frankfurter retired; Justice Goldberg took his seat, giving way in turn in a few years to Justice Fortas. And in time the whole character of the Court's decisions in this controversial area (and in others) changed. In the mid-1960's there was a steady stream of cases upholding individual claims against the claims of national security. In *Aptheker* v. *Secretary of State,* 378 U.S. 500 (1964), the Court struck down a clause of the Subversive Activities Control Act of 1950 making it a crime for a member of an organization under a registration order to apply for or use a passport; a majority of six to three found a violation of the right to travel encompassed in the "liberty" protected by the Fifth Amendment against deprivation without due process of law. In *Albertson* v. *S.A.C.B.,* 382 U.S. 70 (1965), a unanimous Court held that individual members of the Communist party could invoke the Fifth Amendment privilege against compelled self-incrimination to avoid having to register under the 1950 act. In *Lamont* v. *Postmaster,* 381 U.S. 301 (1965), a statute requiring the Post Office to detain "Communist political propaganda" from abroad until the addressee requested its delivery was unanimously held a violation of the First Amendment—the first federal statute ever to fall under that great amendment.

Chief Justice Warren made two major contributions to this series of judgments. *United States* v. *Archie Brown,* 381 U.S. 437 (1965) held unconstitutional a 1959 statute making it a crime for a Communist party member to serve as a labor union officer. A Warren opinion for the Court termed the statute a bill of attainder, a legislative act inflicting punishment on an individual or distinctly defined group. Many found this ground historically unpersuasive, since similar federal statutes had not been regarded as imposing "punishment" and the Court had rejected many challenges under the Constitution's attainder clause in like circumstances. Justices White, Clark, Harlan, and Stewart dissented. Finally, in *United States* v. *Robel,* 389 U.S. 258 (1967), the Court struck down a provision of the Subversive Activities Control Act forbidding the employment in defense plants of any person belonging to an organization required to register under the act. The Chief Justice, writing for himself and four colleagues, found the provision in conflict with the First Amendment's protection of freedom of association because it overbroadly covered both active and passive Communist party members and both sensitive and non-sensitive positions in defense facilities.

It is a long way from *Barsky,* allowing small-minded state administrators to penalize for his associations a member of a profession unrelated to security, to *Robel,* frontally rejecting a congressional mandate for the security of defense facilities. The natural conclusion would be that Chief Justice Warren, as his views matured, came to a constitutional judgment that the values of free speech and association overwhelmingly outweighed the interest in social order asserted by government. But that was not always his judgment. As suggested earlier, he did care strongly about some societal interests. There were areas in which he put the values of individual liberty aside because he felt government had to govern.

The treatment of sex in the arts was one such area, an interesting one because the Chief Justice was ordinarily so committed to freedom of expression. Apart from the agitated cases involving communism, the Warren Court made one of its most enlightening and most permanent contributions in its development of fresh doctrine to buttress freedom of speech and of the press. The pathbreaking opinion was Justice Brennan's in *New York Times* v. *Sullivan,* 376 U.S. 254 (1964), holding that comment on the performance of public officials was constitutionally privileged, even when erroneous, unless made with knowledge of the error or in reckless disregard of the truth. The Chief Justice joined that opinion and wrote another, for a unanimous Court, in a case that extended *New York Times: Bond* v. *Floyd,* 385 U.S. 116 (1966), which barred the Georgia legislature from excluding a duly elected member because of his radical views. But those cases concerned expression on matters political, not sexual.

The Warren Court sometimes aroused hilarity by its confused grapplings with obscenity. (See, for example, Justice Stewart's opinion in *Jacobellis* v. *Ohio,* 378 U.S. 184 [1964].) But the net result of its activity in the field, however ill-explained, could not be in doubt. From a country with a tradition of blue-nosed Puritanism, the United States in a relatively short time became one of the most permissive in the world. The Chief Justice stood out from this trend—the one undoubted example of his resistance to a long-term judicial movement toward greater liberty. Not that he was insensitive to the demand for freedom of expression in books or films. One of his most impressive opinions was a dissent in *Times Film* v. *Chicago,* 365 U.S. 43 (1961), a decision upholding in the abstract (so abstract, in fact, that the Court should have refused to decide the issue) the requirement that a film be submitted to a local board of censors before public exhibition. But when obscenity was put more concretely to the Court as an issue, the Chief Justice was troubled. In the leading case *Roth* v. *United States,* 354 U.S. 476 (1957), he expressed alone the view that what should be at issue in an obscenity prosecution is "the conduct of the defendant . . . not the obscenity of a book or picture." The suggestion was that a professional peddler of smut might be punished for selling a particular book while a scholarly bookshop proprietor dealing in the same work would go free. No other Justice saw much in that view at the time, but in 1966 Justice Brennan adopted it without acknowledgment in *Ginzburg* v. *United States,* 383 U.S. 463. This extraordinary decision held that, although the works in question were assumed to be within the protection of the Constitution, one Ralph Ginzburg could be convicted and sent to a federal penitentiary for five years because he had promoted their sale in a coarse and pandering manner. (He had certainly been vulgar, among other things applying for a second-class mail permit from a place called Intercourse, Pa.; whether that particular thrust affected his rights under the First Amendment was not made clear.) The bewildering *Ginzburg* doctrine was much criticized at birth and thereafter showed no sign of ever being followed in another case, but its origin in the Chief Justice's view of the obscenity problem should be recalled. Another revealing case was *Jacobellis* v. *Ohio,* 378 U.S. 184 (1964), in which the town of Cleveland Heights, Ohio, had prosecuted a theatre manager for showing a French film, "Les Amants," that had been distributed all over the United States without objection. The conviction was reversed, Justice Brennan in the prevailing opinion taking the view that the constitutional standard of obscenity must be a national one and that, by that standard, the film was unobjectionable. The Chief Justice, dissenting, said that every local community should be allowed to set its own obscenity standard, reviewable constitutionally only by a threshold test of "sufficient evidence." This was a remarkable position to be taken by a judge who was prepared to make every local policeman in the country follow a Supreme Court code of practice for taking suspects' confessions. See *Miranda* v. *Arizona,* 384 U.S. 436 (1966).

The anomaly on censorship must have a straightforward explanation. Earl Warren looked at the problem as a man with three daughters. Although he might in general be mightily opposed to restrictions on free expression, here was a social danger that government simply had to be allowed to attack.

Another striking instance of deference to an asserted governmental interest came in a case testing the right to travel to Cuba. In *Zemel* v. *Rusk,* 381 U.S. 1 (1965), a six to three majority upheld the Secretary of State's power to refuse an applicant a passport valid for travel to Cuba. The Chief Justice's opinion had some positively Frankfurterian passages. "The requirements of due process," he wrote, "are a function not only of the extent of the governmental restriction imposed but also of the extent of the necessity for the restriction. Cuba is the only area in the Western Hemisphere controlled by a Communist government . . . That the restriction which is challenged in this case is supported by the weightiest considerations of national security is perhaps best pointed up by recalling that the Cuban missile crisis of October, 1962, preceded the filing of appellant's complaint by less than two months." But this weighty consideration of the government's interest in the challenged restriction was altogether at odds with the rationale of such cases as *Robel* and *Aptheker.* There the government asserted a need to prevent dangerous travel and infiltration of defense plants; the Court dismissed these assertions because the government had included in its restraint both harmless and dangerous activity—a fact equally true of the Cuban travel ban. The explanation of the Chief Justice's attitude in *Zemel* must, again, be a simple one: on the question of how to deal with a Communist foreign power, he believed the President and his advisers had to have the power to govern. Instead of focusing on the citizen's rights to exclusion of virtually all else, he looked at this problem as a responsible government official would—and a patriot. It was a matter of common sense to him, not of consistency in judicial philosophy.

A final case in which a personal feeling about the needs of society overcame the Chief Justice's usual approach to similar questions of individual rights was *Marchetti* v. *United States,* 390 U.S. 39 (1968). Over his lone dissent the Court overruled earlier decisions upholding the federal tax and registration requirements for gamblers and held that a gambler could successfully avoid prosecution for violation of the statutes by invoking the Fifth Amendment privilege against self-incrimination. The decision was no surprise; it seemed dictated by the 1965 decision in *Albertson* v. *Subversive Activities Control Board,* allowing Communist party members to avoid registration by invoking the privilege. The Chief Justice, however, found "a critical distinction" from that case. There the registration requirement "clashed head-on with protected First Amendment rights," while here gambling could "in no sense be called a protected activity." The suggested distinction is breathtaking in its ingenuity. If taken seriously, it would mean that anyone's Fifth Amendment freedom from self-incrimination would depend on whether he could also claim the protection of some other Constitutional provision. But of course the Fifth Amendment makes no distinction between the criminal charges one may face, giving speakers preferred status over gamblers; it extends the privilege to all. The Chief Justice, it must be concluded, was just reluctant to inhibit government control of gambling, no matter what he had agreed to in other cases.

The *Marchetti* dissent was revealing because it contrasted not only with the Chief Justice's specific position on the right of Communists to the protection of the Fifth Amendment but with the tone of his whole approach to the criminal law. For it took only a few years after his assent in *Irvine* in 1954 to establish him as a judge determined to prevent abuses in law enforcement by placing the most stringent restrictions on police and prosecutors and judges. Although he did not write the opinions himself, he presided over the accelerating application to the states of constitutional protections long confined to federal criminal cases: the Fourth Amendment's bar against unreasonable searches and seizures, *Mapp* v. *Ohio,* 367 U.S. 643 (1961), overruling *Wolf* v. *Colorado,* 338 U.S. 25 (1949); the Sixth Amendment guaranty of the right to counsel, *Gideon* v. *Wainwright,* 372 U.S. 335 (1963), overruling *Betts* v. *Brady,* 316 U.S. 455 (1942); the Fifth Amendment privilege against self-incrimination, *Griffin* v. *California,* 380 U.S. 609 (1965), overruling *Adamson* v. *California,* 332 U.S. 46 (1947); and other decisions. The willingness of a majority of the Warren Court to sweep away old lines between state and federal authority in order to vindicate constitutional rights was also notably displayed in *Fay* v. *Noia,* 372 U.S. 391 (1963), holding by a vote of five to four that the federal courts in *habeas corpus* proceedings may examine the constitutionality of a state prisoner's conviction even though he failed to pursue adequate appeal procedures provided by the state.

The Chief Justice's special contribution to the process of change in the criminal law was made on that most controversial subject—confessions. The Supreme Court, beginning in 1936 with *Brown* v. *Mississippi,* 297 U.S. 278 (1936), had long outlawed as denials of due process of law any state convictions based on "involuntary" confessions. A suspect's statement might be deemed not voluntary because he was physically tortured before he made it, as in *Brown.* Or the Court might rule out a confession because of psychological pressures or tricks by the police, such as a threat to take a woman suspect's children from her if she did not confess, *Lynumn* v. *Illinois,* 372 U.S. 528 (1963). A confession would be excluded if obtained by coercion even though other evidence supported its accuracy. Chief Justice Warren himself explained the reason in a characteristic confession case, *Spano* v. *New York,* 360 U.S. 315, 320 (1959): "The abhorrence of society to the use of involuntary confessions does not turn alone on their inherent untrustworthiness. It also turns on the deep-rooted feeling that the police must obey the law while enforcing the law; that in the end life and liberty can be as much endangered from illegal methods used to convict those thought to be criminals as from the actual criminals themselves."

The traditional confession case always turned, in the Supreme Court, on a judgment of long-stale happenings—how long a suspect had been questioned, what the police had done and said, and so forth. These rather elusive facts led again and again to particularistic judicial quarrels about whether a suspect's statement had been "voluntary." And so, over time, judges and legal commentators tried to develop standards that would be clearer and more self-executing. One proposition pushed especially hard by some libertarian reformers was that every suspect should be entitled to see a lawyer immediately after arrest; this would most effectively protect him from police coercion—just as did the rule, for federal cases only, excluding confessions obtained by the police after an "unnecessary delay" in bringing a prisoner before a magistrate; *McNabb*

v. *United States,* 318 U.S. 332 (1943). But the law enforcement
community was just as determined to prevent the intrusion of lawyers
into the process of police questioning, fearing with some reason that
lawyers' advice would usually be "Don't talk." And so the crucial
constitutional issue in the criminal law during the 1960's came to
be the right to counsel at the time of arrest. A special American
Law Institute study of pre-trial procedure in criminal cases took a
hard look at the counsel question as well as other ideas for assuring
the rights of suspects during questioning, such as filming the inter-
view; other legal groups undertook studies, and commentators de-
bated. But the Supreme Court did not wait.

As early as 1958 the Court had before it a claim that a confession made after the police had refused to let an arrested man
see his own retained lawyer should automatically be void. In
Crooker v. *California,* 357 U.S. 433, a five to four majority rejected
the claim, noting that this suspect had been advised by the police
of his right to remain silent and holding that the admissibility of
confessions must continue to be determined by "all the circumstances." The Chief Justice was one of the dissenters. In 1963, when
a similar case was decided, the replacement of Justice Frankfurter
by Justice Goldberg produced a different result: Justice Goldberg
wrote for a majority of five in *Escobedo* v. *Illinois,* 378 U.S. 478,
holding void a confession taken from a suspect who had not been
warned of his rights and who had been refused permission to see his
lawyer. When a police inquiry narrows its "focus" to one man with
the purpose of obtaining a confession, Justice Goldberg said, "under the circumstances here" he must be permitted to consult his
lawyer. No one was clear how far that elusive language went. The
obscurity was dispelled three years later in *Miranda* v. *Arizona,* 384
U.S. 436 (1966). In a massive opinion, the Chief Justice laid out a
new charter of protections for the criminal suspect immediately after
arrest: The police must warn him before any questioning that he
has a right to remain silent, that any statement he makes may be
used against him, and that he has a right to see a lawyer before or
during the interrogation. Moreover, if he cannot afford to retain
counsel, one must be provided for him. If the police omit any of these
requirements, no confession then obtained will be admissible.

Miranda was an earthquake in the world of law enforcement.
Since most criminal suspects are too poor to hire a lawyer themselves, the demand for appointed counsel was likely to have the most
sweeping impact. From Congress and the state courthouses there
flowed angry denunciations of the Supreme Court, and especially of

the Chief Justice. Undoubtedly the criticism was exaggerated; law enforcement did not come to a stop, and even when police meticulously applied the new rules, most accused men would probably waive their right to counsel. Undoubtedly also, many of the self-righteous critics really wanted to continue unfair police advantages over the often frightened, isolated, overborne suspect. But fairer critics had more weighty objections to *Miranda.* There was here no question of a moral vacuum that the Court had to fill, as in the racial area or in the persecution of persons with alleged Communist associations. Many groups in the community, inspired largely, it should be said, by the Court's own earlier decisions, were working actively to find solutions for the confession dilemma. There seemed no urgent reason for the Court to step in and cut off study and experimentation by declaring a constitutional absolute. Moreover, the Chief Justice's opinion did not summon up compelling reasons in logic or experience for taking the radical step. At points the opinion would have to be called disingenuous; it suggested, for example, that the English practice under the Judges Rules was to provide counsel for all suspects upon arrest, whereas the practice is precisely to the contrary. Finally, the technique used by the Chief Justice, of laying out an entire code of police procedure after arrest, struck many as more suitable for a legislature than a court. This sense of the decision having a legislative quality was heightened when, a week after deciding *Miranda,* the Court decided that it should not be applied retroactively. An opinion by the Chief Justice did not stop at saying that old cases, long since tried and appealed, were outside the new rules. It said they would apply only to cases in which the trials began after June 13, 1966, the day *Miranda* was announced. This excluded many defendants who were arrested at about the same time as Miranda, and in fact dozens whose petitions for review were held in the Supreme Court while *Miranda* and three companion cases were considered. The opinion did not point to any differences between these prisoners and *Miranda;* they were just unlucky. The decision thus seemed to reduce justice to whim. Or rather, some thought the Court, in its desire to lay down a broad new rule without worrying the public about emptying the jails, overlooked the particular individuals concerned. But that would be the very opposite of the judicial function. The *Miranda* case and its aftermath were undoubtedly motivated by a deep desire to purify the soiled standards of American criminal procedure, and history may show that they were effective. For many, that result would be an adequate answer to others' doubts about judges so openly playing a law-making role.

One word more must be said about Earl Warren's record in the field of criminal law. If a ghost of *Irvine* v. *California* remained, it vanished in 1967, when in *Katz* v. *United States* the Supreme Court held eavesdropping and wiretapping subject to the restraints of the Fourth Amendment.

So many myths bedevil the terrible American dilemma of race relations that to set straight even the Supreme Court's part in the drama would be utterly beyond the scope of an article on Chief Justice Warren[3]. But no summary of his record would be complete without some discussion of the cases that made him a beloved symbol to the world and a figure of controversy at home.

When he was appointed in 1953, a right-wing columnist, John O'Donnell of the *New York Daily News,* estimated that the Chief Justice's philosophy would "not collide head-on" with the Republican party's "desire to hold their new-won southern support, the votes of a Dixie that will not stomach . . . abolition of its traditional racial segregation." Perhaps O'Donnell remembered the Japanese relocation program. But there was never one moment of doubt about Earl Warren's attitude as a judge toward questions of race— there was no uncertain first step, no *Barsky* case, in this field. He unhesitatingly and consistently opposed racial discrimination in any form.

He took office with the legal movement against school segregation already well under way. For fifteen years the Supreme Court had been whittling quietly away at the misnamed separate but equal doctrine holding that segregated public facilities met the Fourteenth Amendment's demand for "the equal protection of the laws"—misnamed because, in fact, the schools and hospitals and other facilities provided for Negroes were almost never equal. In 1950 the Court had held that a state could not offer Negroes graduate education in a newly founded, inferior institution but had to admit them to the white university—and, once there, treat them the same as other students; *Sweatt* v. *Painter,* 339 U.S. 629 (1950); *McLaurin* v. *Oklahoma,* 339 U.S. 637 (1950). The trend of legal history was against segregation.

But to command an end to segregation in all public schools

---

3. For a description of the legal background of the segregation issue, see chapter 2 of Lewis, *Portrait of a Decade: The Second American Revolution* (1964).

would not be an easy next step for any court. In 1953, seventeen southern and border states, with forty per cent of the country's enrollment, required segregation in public schools; and here, unlike higher education, there was involved the compulsory association of children day after day. It was not surprising, therefore, that when Warren became Chief Justice, the Supreme Court had already gone to great lengths to delay resolution of the question. A first school case came to the Court in 1951; it was returned to the lower court for further findings. In 1952 that case was back on the docket, with others, and in 1953 the Court heard argument; but at the end of the term, in June, it ordered the cases reargued in the next term. No authoritative accounts of the thinking of the Justices at that stage have been published, but some surmises can be made: Chief Justice Vinson did not think it was right or timely for the Supreme Court to challenge the constitutionality of segregation itself; he would at most have favored a decision that the Negro schools in these cases were insufficiently "equal" to meet the old test. Vinson might well have carried at least one other Justice with him. And one or two others, fearing the reaction to a judicial desegregation order, were inclined to put the whole issue to Congress. There is reason to think that Justice Frankfurter, especially, was concerned about resistance if the Court ordered wholesale desegregation of schools in the South at once. On this point the Justice Department had made an important suggestion in a brief filed as a friend of the court: that the Court declare the unconstitutionality of school segregation but allow time to implement the principle because of the "practical difficulties."

That was the posture when the new Chief Justice took over. In December the cases were reargued. On May 17, 1954, in *Brown* v. *Board of Education,* 347 U.S. 483, the Chief Justice for a unanimous Court declared school segregation unlawful. The unanimity was a striking and, as subsequent history showed, an essential aspect of the decision. Without Earl Warren the Court could almost certainly not have achieved agreement; his national standing, his experience, and his freedom from old quarrels within the Court enabled the new Chief Justice to play a crucial part in bringing unanimity about. The actual formula, which followed the Justice Department suggestion of omitting a fixed decree, clearly owed much to other hands as well. When a year later Chief Justice Warren wrote the opinion on implementation, he called for desegregation to be carried out "with all deliberate speed"—a phrase much favored by Justice Frankfurter.

The *Brown* opinion, quite apart from the political attacks, was criticized on internal grounds by some lawyers North and South. The southerners made much of the opinion's Footnote 11, which cited some social scientists as "modern authority" for the proposition that segregating people gives them a feeling of inferiority and does psychological damage. But the footnote, if unfortunately pretentious, was superfluous. After the racist horrors of the mid-twentieth century no expert was needed to show that separating people on account of their race was intended to debase them. And the proposition was no more "sociology," an epithet used by southern commentators, than was the Supreme Court's original separate but equal thesis in *Plessy* v. *Ferguson,* 163 U.S. 537 (1896), that there was nothing invidious about segregation unless the Negroes chose "to put that construction upon it." Life had simply shown the falsity of the thesis.

In the North, some commentators sympathetic to the ideal of racial equality found the *Brown* opinion inadequate because it dealt so narrowly with the possible effects of school segregation on children's "hearts and minds." The suggestion was that the Chief Justice and the Court should instead have provided a general philosophical framework showing to what extent, if any, the law may make racial distinctions. This criticism became more pointed as the Court in the following years extended the desegregation principle to such areas as buses and parks in *per curiam* opinions that merely cited *Brown* without giving any further explanation. But imperfections in the opinion hardly prove that the Court should have followed some other course. Americans know now that the problem of race is more difficult than the Justices of the Supreme Court and most others imagined in 1954, but it would surely have been even more intractable if the Court at that point in history had put the imprimatur of the Constitution on racial segregation.

The South's political reaction to the school decision need not be elaborated. If the Chief Justice had hoped to carry his reputation as a consensus politician on to the Court, he was quickly disappointed. By September, 1954, his attendance at an academic celebration of the College of William and Mary in Williamsburg was enough to bring a boycott by Senator Harry F. Byrd and Governor Thomas B. Stanley. The poisonous attacks on the Chief Justice that poured out in the next decade—the obscene speeches by southern senators, the state legislative resolutions, the John Birch billboards—often fastened on other matters but had their origin in the racial issue.

The violence of the attacks upon him may, ironically, have

helped to liberate him from the habit of political compromise and make him even more determinedly independent as a judge. He was a proud man and a brave one. It is possible that he saw his role at first as one of moderation but that the political assaults stiffened his resolve to be himself as a judge. Certainly, on the racial issue itself, neither he nor the Court gave an inch. The test came when the Little Rock, Arkansas, school board sought to suspend a desegregation decree in 1958 because of the threat of violent resistance. The Supreme Court met in special session on August 28 to consider the case, and no one present at the argument was left in doubt about the feelings of the Chief Justice. When counsel for the school board mentioned the opposition of Arkansas Governor Orval Faubus to desegregation, suggesting that it was a ground for delay, the Chief Justice—outraged—said from the bench: "I have never heard such an argument made in a court of justice before, and I have tried many a case through many a year. I never heard a lawyer say that the statement of a governor as to what was legal or illegal should control the action of any court." An opinion signed by all nine members of the Court to emphasize their unanimity said the Negro children's constitutional rights in Little Rock were "not to be sacrificed or yielded to the violence and disorder which have followed upon the actions of the Governor and Legislature." *Cooper* v. *Aaron,* 358 U.S. 1 (1958).

A decade later the turbulence in American race relations had passed from the courts to other forums. Congress, under pressures in some part produced by the Supreme Court's decisions, at last enacted comprehensive civil rights legislation to assure Negroes equal access to the vote and public facilities and accommodations in the South. After much pain and struggle the blot of legal discrimination was disappearing from the United States. The issue was now an economic and social one; it was being fought in the streets of northern cities—and in the consciences of their white and black citizens. How far beyond the law the issue had moved was shown by the quiet reception given in 1967 to a Supreme Court decision that would once have caused tremors: The Chief Justice, for a unanimous Court, wrote in *Loving* v. *Virginia,* 388 U.S. 1, that state laws prohibiting racial intermarriage violated the Fourteenth Amendment.

As governor of California, Warren always defended that state's grotesque system of apportionment, which limited any county to one member of the state senate no matter what its population. As Chief

Justice he rather soon indicated that he would take a different view, although he did so in a case so obscure that hardly anyone noticed. In 1958 some liberal-minded citizens of Georgia decided to try a further constitutional attack on that state's device for discriminating against urban voters—the county unit system. There had been a succession of suits over the years, all of them impaled on the principle stated by Justice Frankfurter in 1946 in *Colegrove* v. *Green,* 328 U.S. 549, that courts must avoid the "political thicket" of disputes over legislative representation, leaving them to be resolved politically—which of course they could not be, since the rural interests holding power refused to give up their control. In 1958, the lawyers for the Georgia complainants tried the device of calling for a three-judge federal constitutional court and, when that was refused, going directly to the Supreme Court for a writ of *mandamus* ordering the convening of the special court. Their application to the Supreme Court was rejected in an unelaborated *per curiam* order, but there was this note: "The Chief Justice, Mr. Justice Black, Mr. Justice Douglas, and Mr. Justice Brennan think that a rule to show cause should issue," *Hartsfield* v. *Sloan,* 357 U.S. 916. The dissenters believed, if one understood correctly, that the state of Georgia should have to show why the unit system was so beyond constitutional attack that no special court should be summoned to hear the issue. No one could be sure how much that small dissent to a small order meant—until 1962. Then, in *Baker* v. *Carr,* 369 U.S. 186, the Court turned away from its hands-off doctrine and said that issues of fairness in legislative apportionment could be considered by the federal courts. The vote was six to two, with Justice Frankfurter writing in passionate dissent, his last great opinion before retiring. For the majority, Justice Brennan carefully avoided spelling out the ultimate meaning of what everyone knew could be a revolutionary decision. What standard would be applied to legislative districts? Would population alone be the test, or could a state weigh geography? Would the same standard apply to both houses of a legislature, or could one be based on population and the other on something else? The Court left all the questions to the future.

The answers were given by the Chief Justice on June 15, 1964. In the pillared courtroom that day some listeners, as he spoke, felt as if they were present at a second American Constitutional Convention. The Court held that every house of every state legislature must be apportioned on the basis of population alone, with the districts as nearly equal as practicable. That meant that nearly all the fifty states would have to redistrict their legislatures, that political patterns fixed for decades would be destroyed. There had been few cases in any court so significant to a nation's political system as *Reynolds* v. *Sims,* 377 U.S. 533. The question asked by the Chief Justice in his opinion really determined the answer. He did not ask whether the Constitution applied to the whole issue of apportionment, or if so what theories of representation ought to be considered. He began with the premise that the democratic norm was equal treatment of individual voters and then asked what departures from absolute population equality the Constitution would countenance. He considered the demand for representation of geographical areas and dismissed it with disarming simplicity: "Legislators represent people, not acres or trees. Legislators are elected by voters, not farms or cities or economic interests. . . . The weight of a citizen's vote cannot be made to depend on where he lives."

In these cases even more was in question than the character of American legislatures: The issue was the place of the Supreme Court in the American system of government. Justice Harlan made that plain in his dissent. "These decisions," he said, "give support to a current mistaken view of the Constitution and the constitutional function of this Court. This view, in a nutshell, is that every major social ill in this country can find its cure in some constitutional 'principle,' and that this Court should 'take the lead' in promoting reform when other branches of government fail to act. The Constitution is not a panacea for every blot upon the public welfare, nor should this Court, ordained as a judicial body, be thought of as a general haven for reform movements."

The issue of the Court's function could not be framed more starkly than it was in the Reapportionment Cases. On the one hand, the precedents ran uniformly against judicial intervention, and history suggested that the apportionment question bristled with political difficulties. On the other, it was a situation crying for reform in which the political branches were almost by definition unable to act; unless the Supreme Court intervened, corrosion of confidence in state government would continue unchecked. Seen in those terms, the issue for the Supreme Court was not a legal one in any ordinary sense of the term; it was an issue of statesmanship. That assuredly is the standard by which Earl Warren would want to be judged as Chief Justice of the United States.

REAPPORTIONMENT: SUCCESS STORY OF THE WARREN COURT

Robert B. McKay*

E ARL Warren became Chief Justice of the United States in October 1953. Shortly after the end of his fifteenth term in office, Chief Justice Warren indicated his wish to retire upon Senate confirmation of a successor. When President Johnson's nomination of Associate Justice Abe Fortas to be Chief Justice was passed over without action in the closing days of the ninetieth Congress, Warren resumed the center seat for the October 1968 term rather than let the position remain vacant. But in so doing the Chief Justice let it be known that he had not given up hope of retiring in the near future to permit work outside the Court for the more efficient administration of justice.

Whether Earl Warren continues as Chief Justice for a short time only or for several years, 1968 will almost certainly be regarded as a proper vantage point for reviewing the work of the Warren Court. As the Kennedy-Johnson period comes to a close, President Nixon will undoubtedly have several nominations to make to the Court; these nominations will probably bear a different stamp from those of the recent past, as indeed the problems of the next period will themselves be different from those that faced the Warren Court.

From the perspective of history, a decade and a half is not long. But in the history of the Supreme Court of the United States, the period from 1953 to 1968 was uniquely important. Even the first fifteen years of John Marshall's long tenure as Chief Justice did not produce decisions more noteworthy than those of the Warren Court. Of the opinions delivered between 1801 and 1816, the only ones that were inescapably marked with lasting significance for the constitutional process in the United States were *Marbury v. Madison*[1] and *Martin v. Hunter's Lessee*.[2] Although the vital principles of judicial review and federal supremacy in the judicial system were developed during the early years of the Marshall Court, these doctrines scarcely touched the social fabric of the day. Cases before the Warren Court, on the other hand, have more often than not involved social issues critically important to every level of American

---

* Dean and Professor of Law, New York University School of Law. B.S. 1940, University of Kansas; LL.B. 1947, Yale University.—Ed.

1. 5 U.S. (1 Cranch) 49 (1803).
2. 14 U.S. (1 Wheat.) 304 (1816).

society. Indeed, the fundamental concept of federalism itself has been re-examined in the context of problems that stirred the conscience and aroused the passions of contemporary society. To understand fully the impact of the Warren Court, one need only reflect upon four principal areas in which the Court has helped to reshape the nation's destiny.

First. The revolution in race relations might have come without Supreme Court participation; but there is no denying that it dates from *Brown v. Board of Education,*[3] an opinion written by Chief Justice Warren during his first term. It is true that the problems of school segregation and racial discrimination have not been resolved in the intervening fourteen years, but no one should have expected that any number of judicial statements could work that kind of magic even though the Warren Court's desegregation decisions so clearly spoke the conscience of the majority and so properly expressed the constitutional ideals of the nation. The Court has said and done most of what it can say and do. The balance is up to Congress and to the people, and there the matter now rests uneasily.

Second. The early years of the Warren Court coincided with the high tide of McCarthyism in the United States—a period of suspicion, incipient isolationism, and limitation of first amendment freedoms. The Warren Court reasserted the values of the open society for which the Constitution stands and rode out the storm of congressional and public criticism during the late 1950's. The first amendment decisions during that period and in the early 1960's provided significant encouragement to those who resisted the then-prevailing preference for conformity of opinion, expression, and conduct.

Third. Standards of fairness in the criminal justice system deserve the closest judicial scrutiny; any such examination presents problems that are difficult of rational solution at any time, but particularly so when the public's natural concern for "law and order" has been sloganized into a criticism of Supreme Court efforts to assure fairness in criminal procedure. The Warren Court has nonetheless staked out major guidelines for virtually every significant aspect of criminal justice. Unless the Warren Court's successor unexpectedly revises the principles that now control the right to counsel, search and seizure, self-incrimination, and the rest, we may anticipate that the natural process of adjustment will involve matters of detail rather than major overhaul.

Fourth. The only complete newcomer on the federal judicial

---

3. 347 U.S. 483 (1954).

scene during the decade and a half of the Warren Court is legislative
apportionment and congressional districting, the subject of the
present comments. The fascinating thing about this major engage-
ment of the Warren Court is that the principal decisions came to the
Court late—1962 and after. Although these decisions precipitated a
revolution in the concept and practice of legislative representation
at every level of government, they were implemented quickly and
with surprisingly little dislocation. The following remarks are intended to report the fact of that adjustment and to explain, to the
extent the phenomenon is now understandable, why the change was
so easily accomplished. When compared with the delay in public
acceptance of decisions in the other areas mentioned above, the
success of the reapportionment cases seems even more remarkable.
Others in this Symposium have commented on the other major areas
of Supreme Court action during the last fifteen years, building in
each case on what had gone before. My story is limited to the six
years between 1962 and 1968.

I. Malapportionment and Equal Protection of the Laws[4]

Until 1962, there was no recognized remedy in federal courts for
even the most extreme inequality of population among otherwise
comparable legislative representation districts. It made no difference
whether the disparity was among the congressional districts in a
state, election districts for a state legislature, or local government
districts of various types. Between 1872 and 1929 Congress had
required that members of the House of Representatives be elected
from districts "containing as nearly as practicable an equal number
of inhabitants."[5] However, this provision was never enforced, and it
was eliminated altogether in 1929.[6] Population differentials soared;
by 1964 the most populous district in each of six states had more
than three times the number of persons in the least populous, and
nearly all congressional districts were seriously out of balance.[7] In
addition, almost none of the state courts sought to correct the even
more severe malapportionment that existed in state legislatures[8] and

---

4. For further discussion of the matters commented on in the statement that fol-
lows, *see* R. DIXON, DEMOCRATIC REPRESENTATION: REAPPORTIONMENT IN LAW AND
POLITICS (1968); R. McKAY, REAPPORTIONMENT: THE LAW AND POLITICS OF EQUAL REPRE-
SENTATION (1964).

5. 17 Stat. 28 (1872).

6. 46 Stat. 21.

7. Wesberry v. Sanders, 376 U.S. 1, 49-50 (1964) (appendix to opinion of Justice
Harlan).

8. Ratios between the most populous and least populous district in a state were
not uncommonly more than 100 to 1.

local governmental bodies, despite the fact that some specific state constitutional provisions required substantial equality of population.

By 1960 malapportionment in the United States had attained such proportions that the integrity of representative government was in many instances endangered. Yet the extent of the disparity continued to grow, fortified as it was by four assumptions from the past that had become unreliable guides to the future in the 1960's.

First, until 1962 it was widely believed that federal courts would not review individual voter complaints about malapportionment, either because they lacked jurisdiction over such matters, or because the claims were not justiciable, or for both reasons. There was considerable basis for this belief, supported as it apparently was by *Colegrove v. Green,*[9] in which Justice Frankfurter had cautioned that "[c]ourts ought not to enter this political thicket."[10] Although a few commentators had warned that *Colegrove*—decided in 1946—should not be read as a denial of jurisdiction and/or justiciability, the issue was not squarely faced in the Supreme Court again until 1962, when the Court held in *Baker v. Carr*[11] that claims of population inequality among election districts are indeed within the jurisdiction of the federal courts; that the issues are justiciable; and that individual voters have standing to raise the issues. Thus fell the first assumption—the procedural gambit—leaving as the next line of defense assumption number two: the substantive claim that no provision of the Constitution requires substantial equality of population among election districts.

During the period when it was generally believed that the Court would not review claims of legislative malapportionment, there was no great need for defenders of the status quo to develop elaborate constitutional arguments in behalf of an issue they thought could not arise. With the decision in *Baker v. Carr*, however, all that was changed. Justices Frankfurter and Harlan, in basing their dissents to *Baker* mainly on the justiciability issue, previewed the more refined arguments Justice Harlan was later to make (sometimes joined by Justices Clark and Stewart) in *Reynolds v. Sims*[12] and the companion cases decided in 1964.[13] But assumption number two was laid to rest

9. 328 U.S. 549 (1946).
10. 328 U.S. at 556. *See also* MacDougall v. Green, 335 U.S. 281 (1948) and cases discussed, and distinguished, in Baker v. Carr, 369 U.S. 186, 208-37 (1962).
11. 369 U.S. 186 (1962).
12. 377 U.S. 533 (1964).
13. Justice Harlan's dissent for all the cases appears in Reynolds v. Sims, 377 U.S. 533, 589 (1964). The principal dissenting statement of Justice Stewart, joined by Justice Clark, appears in Lucas v. Colorado General Assembly, 377 U.S. 713, 744 (1964), applicable also to WMCA, Inc. v. Lomenzo, 377 U.S. 633 (1964).
Justice Harlan, who alone finds the fourteenth amendment totally inapplicable, has restated and refined his argument in subsequent apportionment cases,

in *Reynolds*,[14] which held with exquisite simplicity that "the Equal Protection Clause requires that a State make an honest and good faith effort to construct districts, in both Houses of its legislature, as nearly of equal population as is practicable."[15]

A third assumption was that even if the fourteenth amendment could be interpreted to require population equality in state legislative election districts, there was nothing in that amendment or elsewhere in the Constitution that would impose a similar limitation on the drawing of congressional district lines by state legislatures. However, when this question was presented to the Court in *Wesberry v. Sanders*[16] (before the decision in *Reynolds*), only Justice Clark thought the equal protection clause determinative;[17] and Justices Harlan and Stewart thought that no constitutional provision limited congressional districting. But six members of the Court found a command of substantial population equality in article I, section 2, of the Constitution, which provides that representatives be chosen "by the People of the Several States." In an extensive review of historical sources, Justice Black concluded for the majority that this clause "means that as nearly as practicable one man's vote in a congressional election is to be worth as much as another's."[18]

A fourth and final assumption, to which the Court put the lie in 1968 in *Avery v. Midland County*,[19] was the lingering belief, even after *Reynolds*, that the representative function in local governmental units was somehow different than in state legislative bodies. For a time there seemed to be some basis for this view, at least where the local governmental units had no obvious legislative functions.[20] But in *Avery* the Court held, as should have been expected from the beginning, that the Constitution permits no substantial variation from equal population in drawing districts for units of local government having general governmental powers over the entire geographic area served by the body.[21]

---

including Avery v. Midland County, 390 U.S. 474, 486 (1968).

Justices Harlan and Stewart have also objected to application of the equal protection clause of the fourteenth amendment in other political rights cases, including Katzenbach v. Morgan, 384 U.S. 641, 659 (1966), a dissent applicable also to Cardona v. Power, 384 U.S. 672 (1966).

14. 377 U.S. 533 (1964).
15. 377 U.S. at 568, 577.
16. 376 U.S. 1 (1964).
17. The majority did not find it necessary to consider the fourteenth amendment in view of its conclusion that art. I, § 2 requires equality among congressional districts, 376 U.S. at 8 n.10.
18. 376 U.S. at 7-8.
19. 390 U.S. 474 (1968).
20. *See* Sailors v. Board of Educ., 387 U.S. 105 (1967); Dusch v. Davis, 387 U.S. 112 (1967).
21. Avery v. Midland County, 390 U.S. 474, 485 (1968). For further discussion, *see*

II. The Impact of Reapportionment
A. *The Initial Response*

The Supreme Court decisions that applied the equal-population principle to all levels of government were thought by some to have saved representative government from self-destruction. Others, like Senator Barry Goldwater in his unsuccessful presidential campaign of 1964, viewed the decisions as an abuse of judicial power not justified by any provision of the Constitution. Friends and critics alike agreed on one proposition: Representative government in the United States would be significantly affected by implementation of the new requirement.

In 1968, just four years after *Reynolds*, and in the same year as *Avery*, the public outcry has faded to a whisper. Criticism of the Supreme Court, a noisy issue in the 1968 presidential campaign, did not emphasize the reapportionment decisions. The mood, even among politicians, is that the decisions are acceptable; the accommodations have largely been made.

In retrospect, this development is not hard to understand. The initial objections to the decisions came from two groups whose uneasy alliance should never have been expected to come to much. First, there were the intellectual critics who express alarm at each new judicial intervention in matters that they had not previously admitted to the charmed circle of federal judicial authority. These critics were more concerned with *Baker v. Carr*, which they regarded as a breach of their first canon, judicial restraint, than with the substance of the rules in *Wesberry*, *Reynolds*, and *Avery*. The second group of critics were the "practical" politicians, particularly those who saw in reapportionment a threat not only to their legislative power, but also sometimes to their very seats.

Perhaps sensing that this alliance of principle and self-interest could not long survive, opponents of reapportionment swiftly mounted an attack on the decisions—and on the Court itself—in Congress. At first, efforts were made to limit the jurisdiction of the federal courts so that most reapportionment cases could not be heard; but this was too frontal an attack even for many critics of the decisions and the Court. Next, amendment of the Constitution was sought in order to provide that the equal-population principle would apply to only one house of a bicameral state legislature. The final attack, and the most nearly successful, was the campaign for a constitutional convention under a never-used provision of article V

Symposium: One Man—One Vote and Local Government, 36 Geo. Wash. L. Rev. 689 (1968).

of the Constitution. Ultimately, all of these efforts were unsuccessful.[22]

Direct frontal attack on the decisions—by constitutional amendment or otherwise—was probably never destined to make much progress for the simple reason that the public did not oppose the decisions. This should not have been surprising since malapportionment had worked to the disadvantage of a majority of all the voters, including the politically sophisticated and highly vocal group in the cities and suburbs.

B. *Reapportionment Effected—The Success Story*

When *Wesberry* and *Reynolds* were decided in 1964, students of the political process believed that accommodation to the equal-population standard would be accomplished, if at all, only after extensive litigation that would take many years, perhaps decades. For once, the prophets of gloom were wrong; it is not easy to think of any other major Supreme Court decisions to which significant adjustment was so swiftly accomplished. While there was some foot-dragging, and judicial proceedings were often necessary, the astonishing fact is that by the spring of 1968, four years after the key decisions, the task of revision was essentially complete.

Within this period congressional district lines were redrawn in thirty-seven states. Of the remaining thirteen, five have a single representative each; two elect representatives at large; and several did not require redistricting. Although several states may need further change for reasons discussed in the final section of this Article, the fact remains that by April 1968 only nine states had any district with a population deviation in excess of ten per cent from the state average, while twenty-four states had no deviation as large as five per cent from the state norm.[23]

State legislatures responded with similar speed and integrity to the even more painful task of redrawing their own district lines; this often entailed the necessary consequence of making impossible the re-election of some of their own members. By the spring of 1968 every state had made some adjustment, and it seemed probable that more than thirty of the state legislatures satisfied any reasonable interpretation of the equal-population principle.

---

22. For a review of these campaigns, *see* Bonfield, *The Dirksen Amendment and the Article V Convention Process*, 66 MICH. L. REV. 949 (1968); McKay, *Court, Congress, and Reapportionment*, 63 MICH. L. REV. 255 (1964).

23. Bulletin of ILGWU [International Ladies' Garment Workers Union] Political Department (April 22, 1968).

C. *Substantive Impact—The Character of the Reapportioned Bodies*

Reapportionment and redistricting are still too new to permit definitive evaluation of their impact. Even before careful study is completed, however, some conclusions can be drawn. It was no surprise to those familiar with the pattern of malapportionment, for example, that the principal beneficiaries of reapportionment and redistricting were less the cities than the suburbs. In the decade between the 1950 and 1960 censuses eight of the largest cities in the United States lost population, while the suburbs gained population from urban and rural areas alike. One result of this population shift was that in some Southern states, particularly Florida and Tennessee, a genuine two-party system emerged as suburban voters began to pursue aggressively specific political goals. This was not, however, an exclusively Southern phenomenon according to Republican Party analysts, who concluded from study of the 1966 congressional races that Republicans might gain from ten to twenty-five seats in the House of Representatives in twenty-two states.[24]

Another predictable consequence of fair apportionment was the unseating of a number of legislators. Where prior malapportionment had been severe, the turnover was correspondingly large. For example, the first legislature after reapportionment in Maryland contained eighty per cent freshman legislators; in Connecticut more than half were new; and in California nearly half of the members of the legislature were there for the first time.

With the influx of so many inexperienced legislators there was sometimes a certain amount of confusion about goals and techniques. But the novice legislators frequently seized the reins of authority with surprising decisiveness, often with results that were applauded; seldom were they criticized for being less effective than their predecessors in the exercise of power. Moreover, the size of the legislature was dramatically reduced in several instances, a change approved by most students of government. The Connecticut house was reduced from 294 representatives to 177; the Vermont house from 246 to 150; and the Ohio legislature from 137 to 99.

Evaluation of legislative performance is in the eye of the beholder; thus, it is difficult to generalize about the success of legislative programs after reapportionment. However, there were observable trends in the form of increased aid for schools, greater home rule, increased consumer protection, stronger civil rights legislation,

---

24. *See* McKay, **Reapportionment** Reappraised 18-19 (Twentieth Century Fund pamphlet 1968).

curbs on air and water pollution, and reform of criminal justice. A reapportioned Missouri legislature was hailed by the *St. Louis Post Dispatch* as probably "the most creative session in the mid-term of a governor in the State's history."[25] And a study of the 1966 and 1968 biennial session of the Virginia general assembly concluded that "[b]oth sessions enacted outstanding legislative programs in response to strong gubernatorial leadership and growing public demands for more and better governmental services."[26]

The fears that reapportionment would lead to urban dominance did not materialize in such primarily rural states as Idaho, Kansas, Montana, and North Dakota. In New Mexico the Farm and Livestock Bureau, the state's largest agricultural organization, pronounced the reapportioned legislature "one of the finest"; and the reapportioned Vermont house drew "lavish praise from all quarters" for its 1966 session.[27]

The impact of reapportionment on local government is necessarily more speculative because of the almost infinite variety of local government structures—counties, cities, school boards, and other special purpose districts, to name only the most common.[28] But there is reason for cautious optimism that fairly based election districts will be as salutary for local government as for state legislatures.

III. Some Open Questions

As a matter of wise institutional policy, the Supreme Court of the United States ordinarily does not try to answer at first encounter every question that might arise in connection with a novel problem. The reapportionment decisions are almost unique in the comprehensiveness of the early rulings. There are of course some unanswered questions in the wake of these decisions, but the number is surprisingly small. The original decisions were sweeping, direct, and relatively clear. Qualifications were few, except for the fairly obvious reminder that in state legislative districting (or in drawing lines for congressional districts and local government units), "it is a practical impossibility to arrange legislative districts so that each one has an identical number of residents, or citizens, or voters. Mathematical exactness or precision is hardly a workable constitutional requirement."[29]

---

25. *Id.* at 17.

26. Wells, *A Pattern Emerges*, 57 Natl. Civ. Rev. 453 (1968).

27. McKay, *supra* note 24, at 17-18.

28. *See Symposium, supra* note 21.

29. Reynolds v. Sims, 377 U.S. 533, 577 (1964).

From this qualification more or less directly arise three important questions for which final answers have not been given—and perhaps should not yet be expected—because key elements in these decisions depend upon relatively indefinite factors of judgment. Nevertheless, guidance is available, both in the Court's original decisions and in its subsequent reaffirmations of the principles involved. The questions, to which brief answers are suggested below, are (1) What population deviations are consistent with the standard of substantial population equality? (2) To what extent, if any, is the gerrymander forbidden by the Constitution? (3) What agency should be given authority to draw election district lines?

A. *Substantial Population Equality*

The standard fixed by the Court for congressional districting, state legislative apportionment, and local government line-drawing was similar, if not precisely identical, in the three principal decisions. The operative language in *Avery* is typical of the Court's formulations in the other reapportionment cases: "We hold today only that the Constitution permits no substantial variation from equal population in drawing districts for units of local government having general governmental powers over the entire geographic area served by the body."[30]

Although the Court emphasized in *Reynolds, Wesberry*, and *Avery* that mathematical exactness is not required,[31] it has insisted that population is the only proper basis of apportionment. In *Reynolds* the Court stated that "neither history alone, nor economics or other sorts of group interests, are permissible factors in attempting to justify disparities from population-based representation."[32] And in *Avery* the Court restated *Reynolds* as a holding that "bases other than population [are] not acceptable grounds for distinguish-

---

30. Avery v. Midland County, 390 U.S. 474, 484-85 (1968). In Wesberry v. Sanders, 376 U.S. 1, 7-8, the Court said: "The command of Art. I, § 2, that Representatives be chosen 'by the People of the several states' means that as nearly as practicable, one man's vote in a congressional election is to be worth as much as another's." And in Reynolds v. Sims, 377 U.S. 533, 568 (1964) the standard was thus defined: "We hold that, as a basic constitutional standard, the Equal Protection Clause requires that the seats in both houses of a bicameral legislature must be apportioned on a population basis."

31. Wesberry v. Sanders, 376 U.S. 1, 18 (1964); Reynolds v. Sims, 377 U.S. 533, 577, 579 (1964); Avery v. Midland County, 390 U.S. 474, 484-85 (1968). In *Reynolds* the Court observed that "[s]omewhat more flexibility may be constitutionally permissible with respect to state legislative apportionment than in congressional districting." 377 U.S. at 578. This is because of the greater number of districts in state legislatures so that local political subdivision lines may be used more extensively in state legislative districting than in congressional districting.

32. 377 U.S. at 579-80.

ing among citizens when determining the size of districts used to elect members of state legislatures."[33]

From this proposition—that population is the only permissible standard for districting even though mathematical exactness is not required—another proposition logically follows: population deviations among districts must be justified by the state. This principle emerged clearly in *Swann v. Adams*,[34] where the variations were thirty per cent among senate districts and forty per cent among house districts. The Court said, "*De minimis* deviations are unavoidable, but . . . none of our cases suggest that differences of this magnitude will be approved without a satisfactory explanation grounded on acceptable state policy."[35] Deviations from equality require justification, and the burden is on the state to supply rational explanation for instances of inequality. Apparently, the only acceptable justification for population variances is the use of political subdivision lines or other logical division lines in order to structure coherent districts. Use of such pre-established boundary lines may prevent an otherwise destructive gerrymander, but where this factor is claimed as the reason for population inequality, it must be demonstrated. The New Jersey Supreme Court made the point specifically in *Jones v. Falcey*: "Where the deviation obviously exceeds that needed to permit the use of political subdivisions, the deviation spells out unconstitutionality, and a court must so hold unless the record affirmatively reveals a tenable basis for legislative action."[36]

Some have sought a judicial statement of percentage points of maximum permissible deviation; but such a holding is not likely. The standard remains population equality—quite strict in congressional districting cases and somewhat more flexible for state and local legislative bodies.

B. *The Forbidden Gerrymander*

The gerrymander is a practice-tested and time-dishonored device of American politics that has been used most often for partisan advantage, but sometimes has also served to break up (or to combine) racial, ethnic, or socioeconomic groups thought to have common interests. Malapportionment is itself a particular kind of gerrymander in which advantage or disadvantage is based upon population concentration or dispersion. In the United States the population gerrymander usually, but not always, has been used to prefer rural over urban and suburban groups. The reapportionment decisions

---

33. 390 U.S. at 484.
34. 385 U.S. 440 (1967).
35. 385 U.S. at 444.
36. 48 N.J. 25, 40, 222 A.2d 101, 109 (1966).

have ruled that the population gerrymander is constitutionally forbidden, but initially at least there was little direct guidance on racial and partisan gerrymandering.

Gomillion v. Lightfoot[37] is the only case before 1968 in which the Court reached the merits of a claimed racial gerrymander; the Court held that the redrawing of municipal lines to exclude Negro voters was a violation of the fifteenth amendment.[38] Other cases that sought to raise the racial gerrymander issue have not been successfully pressed to a decision on the merits. In *Wright v. Rockefeller*,[39] a majority of the Court accepted "the findings of the majority of the District Court that appellants failed to prove that the New York Legislature was either motivated by racial considerations or in fact drew the districts on racial lines."[40] There was, however, nothing in the majority opinion to suggest approval of racial gerrymandering. Both dissenting opinions, by Justices Douglas and Goldberg, specifically stated that racially motivated districting is unconstitutional,[41] a proposition to which the majority took no exception, and with which disagreement is scarcely possible.

Although gerrymandering for partisan advantage has also not been squarely presented to the Court for decision, there is reason to believe that this, too, would be struck down upon a sufficient showing of political motivation in apportionment formulas or districting practices. In *Fortson v. Dorsey*,[42] the Court, commenting on a multimember constituency apportionment scheme, worried about the possibility that this method might in some circumstances "operate to minimize or cancel out the voting strength of racial or political elements of the voting population."[43]

Three cases scheduled for argument before the Supreme Court in December 1968 raise the question of partisan gerrymandering,

---

37. 364 U.S. 339 (1960).

38. Only Justice Whittaker thought that the case presented a violation of fourteenth amendment equal protection rights. 364 U.S. at 349. Justice Frankfurter, writing for the majority, apparently felt that judicial review on fourteenth amendment grounds was barred by Colegrove v. Green, 328 U.S. 549 (1946), which he said "involved a claim only of a dilution of the strength of their votes as a result of legislative inaction over a course of many years." But *Gomillion*, he said, involved "affirmative legislative action [that] deprives them of their votes and the consequent advantages that the ballot affords." 364 U.S. at 346. He may also have been seeking to preserve the *Colegrove* principle of nonjusticiability against the attack mounted in *Baker v. Carr*, in which probable jurisdiction was noted one week after the decision in *Gomillion*. 364 U.S. 898 (1960).

39. 376 U.S. 52 (1964). *See also* Connor v. Johnson, 386 U.S. 483 (1967); Honeywood v. Rockefeller, 376 U.S. 222 (1964).

40. 376 U.S. at 56.

41. *See also* Sims v. Baggett, 247 F. Supp. 96 (S.D. Ala. 1965); Fortson v. Dorsey, 379 U.S. 433, 439 (1965); Burns v. Richardson, 384 U.S. 73, 88 (1966).

42. 379 U.S. 433 (1965).

43. 379 U.S. at 439.

and possibly of racial gerrymandering as well. Two of the cases, *Preisler v. Kirkpatrick*[44] and *Preisler v. Heinkel*,[45] arise out of a holding by a three-judge district court that the 1967 congressional redistricting in Missouri did not satisfy the constitutional standard of population equality as nearly as practicable. The third case, *Wells v. Rockefeller*,[46] is an appeal from the decision of a three-judge federal district court upholding the 1968 congressional redistricting in New York against a challenge of partisan gerrymandering and excessive population variances. Decision of these cases should provide guidance on the remaining questions about the propriety of gerrymandering.

C. *Redistricting: Who Will Bell the Cat?*

The habit of legislative redistricting for partisan advantage is so deeply ingrained in the American legislative and political structure that it will be rooted out only with difficulty. The effort must be made, for the stakes are high: the effective functioning of representative democracy. Unfortunately, the answers are not easy. Implementation of the equal-population principle is an essential ingredient of ultimate success, but it is by no means a self-contained solution. Within the framework of absolute equality it is entirely possible to pervert the electoral process; the contortions of the gerrymander remain within easy grasp. Even judicial willingness to forbid racial, partisan, and other gerrymandering can protect against only the most blatant abuses.

There is accordingly an imperative need in every state for some politically acceptable device to remove the district line-drawing function from the partisan process. By 1967 seventeen states had committed a portion of the apportionment or districting function to nonlegislative agencies.[47] These plans range from executive initiative after legislative inaction for a specified period of time to a constitutionally established board of apportionment consisting of the governor, secretary of state, and attorney general. But none of the present plans is sufficiently removed from the ongoing political process to prevent partisan influence from taking its due. The question that urgently requires thoughtful debate is whether American democracy is now sufficiently mature to agree upon a nonpolitical

---

44. 279 F. Supp. 952 (E.D. Mo. 1967), *prob. juris. noted*, 390 U.S. 939 (1968).
45. 279 F. Supp. 952 (E.D. Mo. 1967), *prob. juris. noted*, 390 U.S. 939 (1968).
46. 281 F. Supp. 821 (S.D.N.Y.), *prob. juris. noted*, 37 U.S.L.W. 3133 (Oct. 15, 1968).
47. *See* NATIONAL MUNICIPAL LEAGUE, LEGISLATIVE DISTRICTING BY NONLEGISLATIVE AGENCIES, appendix (1967).

means of resolving this vital question of representative government —finding the best method for structuring election districts.[48]

---

48. The following statement of principles deserves study as approved by the Citizens Union Committee on Constitutional Issues, Position Paper No. 1, April 1967 (quoted from pages 55-56 of Legislative Districting by Non-Legislative Agencies, *supra* note 47). The proposed plan relates to New York State.

Reapportionment Outside the Legislature

Recommendations:

The following recommendations are not stated in formal constitutional language, but easily could be converted into a concise provision on legislative apportionment.

Legislative Districts

For the purpose of electing members of the Legislature (each house if there are to be two houses) the state should be divided into as many districts as there are members to be elected. Each district should consist of compact and contiguous territory.

All state legislative districts should be so nearly equal in population that no district has over 10 per cent more or less population than the statewide average for all districts.

Among state legislative districts wholly contained within a single county, no district should be allowed to have over 5 per cent more or less population than the average district population in that county.

Among state legislative districts wholly or partly within a city or town (or, in New York City, within a borough) no district should be allowed to have over one per cent more or less population than the average population of districts in that city, town or borough.

As nearly as is possible under the requirements of population equality, no county, city, town or village boundary should be crossed in the formation of districts.

At no time should a block enclosed by streets or public ways be divided.

Apportionment and Districting Commission

Within thirty days after receipt of the final figures of the decennial United States census, the Governor, after inviting nominations from the presidents of the state's institutions of higher learning, civic, educational, professional, and other organizations, should be required to name a ten-member commission to reapportion and redistrict the state legislative districts.

No member or employee of the Legislature should be allowed to be a member of the commission.

No more than five members of the commission should be allowed to be enrolled in the same political party.

The Governor should list at least one source for the nomination of each member of the commission.

If by reason of resignation, death or disability, any member of the commission should be unable to perform his duties, a successor shall be appointed by the Governor in the same manner as an original member of the commission is appointed.

The Legislature should be required to provide sufficient funds for the operation of the commission.

All decisions of the commission should be required to have the approval of six or more members.

Within ninety days of its appointment, the commission should submit its redistricting plan to the Governor, who, within thirty days after receipt of the plan, should be allowed to recommend amendment to the commission.

Thirty days thereafter the commission should promulgate its plan, with or without amendments.

The commission's plan should be published in the manner provided for acts of the Legislature and should have the force of law upon such publication.

Upon the application of any qualified voter, the Court of Appeals, in the exercise of original, exclusive and final jurisdiction, should review the commission's redistricting plan and should have jurisdiction to make orders to amend the plan to comply with the requirements of this constitution or, if the commission has failed to promulgate a redistricting plan within the time provided, to make one or more orders establishing such a plan.

THE WARREN COURT AND DESEGREGATION

Robert L. Carter*

Robert L. Carter

I.

WHEN Chief Justice Warren assumed his post in October 1953, the underpinnings of the "separate but equal"[1] concept had become unmoored beyond restoration. Full-scale argument on the validity of apartheid in public education was only weeks away, and the portent of change in the constitutional doctrine governing American race relations was unmistakable. Although the groundwork had been carefully prepared[2] for the Chief Justice's announcement in *Brown v. Board of Education*[3] that fundamental principles forbade racial segregation in the nation's public schools, the decision, when it was delivered on May 17, 1954, was more than a break with the past. In interpreting the fourteenth amendment as guaranteeing and securing to Negroes equality in substance rather than in mere form, the *Brown* decision was a revolutionary statement of race relations law.

Brown was the culmination of a trend, evident as early as *Missouri ex rel. Gaines v. Canada*,[4] away from the arid and sophistical reading of the Civil War amendments marked by the legalisms of *Plessy v. Ferguson*.[5] Instead, the Supreme Court in the first half of this century had begun to address itself to the task of formulating a pragmatic and realistic interpretation of what those amendments demanded in respect to the Negro's civil and political status. "Sophisticated as well as simpleminded" modes of racial discrimination were understood to be within the Constitution's reach.[6] The fourteenth amendment's guaranty of equal educational opportunity was said to be open-ended; it insured material equality;[7] it encompassed intangibles not subject to objective measurement;[8] and it forbade restrictions impairing and inhibiting a

---

* Member of the New York Bar. Former General Counsel, National Association for the Advancement of Colored People. A.B. 1937, Lincoln University; LL.B. 1940, Howard University; LL.M. 1941, Columbia University.—Ed.
1. Plessy v. Ferguson, 163 U.S. 537 (1896).
2. P. FREUND, THE SUPREME COURT OF THE UNITED STATES 172-73 (1961). Actually, McLaurin v. Oklahoma State Regents, 339 U.S. 637 (1950), had forecast what the Court would decide in *Brown*.
3. 347 U.S. 483 (1954).
4. 305 U.S. 337 (1938).
5. 163 U.S. 537 (1896).
6. Lane v. Wilson, 307 U.S. 268, 275 (1939).
7. Plessy v. Ferguson, 163 U.S. 537 (1896).
8. Sweatt v. Painter, 339 U.S. 629 (1950).

black student's ability to study and exchange views with other students.[9]

With the decision in *Brown*, enforced racial segregation in education was put beyond the pale. More than that, the approach to which the Warren Court was fully committed required an examination and evaluation of any act, practice, or device which was undertaken with government sponsorship, in order to determine whether in purpose or effect black students were thereby denied their constitutional right to truly equal educational opportunity. Similarly, a like test seemed to be applicable in all other areas of governmental activity. *Brown* thus extended to its natural consequences could mean that the fetters binding the Negro were at last being struck, and that he would henceforth be able to stretch himself to his full potential.

Decision in the school desegregation cases began the Warren Court's long involvement in the development of race relations law. Subsequent opinions soon underscored the universality, permanence, and enduring nature of the newly announced constitutional doctrine. Segregation was struck down in public parks,[10] in intrastate[11] and interstate[12] commerce, at public golf courses[13] and other recreational facilities,[14] in airports[15] and interstate bus terminals,[16] in libraries,[17] and in the facilities of public buildings[18] and courtrooms.[19] Unlawful discrimination was found in the listing of candidates for public office by race on the ballot;[20] in the Southern custom of addressing black witnesses by their first name;[21] and in making marriage[22] and sexual relations[23] between blacks and whites a crime.

In its refusal to tolerate open attempts to evade[24] or frustrate[25]

---

9. McLaurin v. Oklahoma State Regents, 339 U.S. 637 (1950).

10. Watson v. Memphis, 373 U.S. 526 (1963); New Orleans City Park Improvement Assn. v. Detiege, 358 U.S. 54 (1958) (memorandum decision).

11. Gayle v. Browder, 352 U.S. 903 (1956) (memorandum decision).

12. Boynton v. Virginia, 364 U.S. 454 (1960) (application of Interstate Commerce Act).

13. Holmes v. City of Atlanta, 350 U.S. 879 (1955) (memorandum decision).

14. Watson v. Memphis, 373 U.S. 526 (1963); Mayor & City Council of Baltimore City v. Dawson, 350 U.S. 877 (1955) (memorandum decision).

15. Turner v. Memphis, 369 U.S. 762 (1962).

16. Thomas v. Mississippi, 380 U.S. 524 (1965); Boynton v. Virginia, 364 U.S. 903 (1956) (memorandum decision).

17. Brown v. Louisiana, 383 U.S. 131 (1966).

18. Burton v. Wilmington Parking Authority, 365 U.S. 715 (1961).

19. Johnson v. Virginia, 373 U.S. 61 (1963).

20. Anderson v. Martin, 375 U.S. 399 (1964).

21. Hamilton v. Alabama, 376 U.S. 650 (1964).

22. Loving v. Virginia, 388 U.S. 1 (1967).

23. McLaughlin v. Florida, 379 U.S. 184 (1964).

24. Cooper v. Aaron, 358 U.S. 1 (1958).

25. Griffin v. County School Bd. of Prince Edward County, 377 U.S. 218 (1964).

compliance with *Brown*, the Warren Court made clear that the new doctrine was a fixed and permanent aspect of its approach to constitutional adjudication in the race relations field. In addition, a broadened definition of state action, encompassing all situations in which the state was significantly involved in supporting or encouraging discrimination, extended the reach of the fourteenth amendment.[26] The Court ruled that a state is under no affirmative obligation to enact antidiscrimination legislation, and that when such laws are promulgated, they may be repealed; but the Court added the precautionary caveat that if in the process of repeal the state tips the political balance in favor of racial discrimination, it violates the fourteenth amendment.[27]

The Court also sought to strengthen and further the desegregation process by protecting and undergirding the peaceful self-help activities of those individuals and groups seeking to eliminate segregation. The rationale for extending the constitutional guarantees of freedom of association and expression to membership in civil rights groups and their sponsorship of test litigation reveals the Warren Court at its best in adapting the Constitution's safeguards to real-life situations. Until the Civil Rights Act of 1964[28] empowered the federal government to use its resources in furthering desegregation, the only method available to secure compliance with *Brown* in the face of resistance was affirmative action by individuals or groups. The Supreme Court was sensitive to this problem, and when Alabama sought to still concerted group agitation and activity for desegregation by requiring public identification of all NAACP members in the state, the Court realized that such enforced disclosure would expose the members to coercion, intimidation, reprisals, and harassment. Recognizing that this would impair, if not destroy, concerted civil rights activity, the Court concluded that the constitutional guaranty of freedom of association embraced and included privacy in one's associational relationships, absent a countervailing state interest of compelling dimensions.[29] Subsequently, in

---

26. Burton v. Wilmington Parking Authority, 365 U.S. 715 (1961).

27. Reitman v. Mulkey, 387 U.S. 369 (1967). A variation on the *Reitman* formula involving a referendum repealing an open housing ordinance and barring all such future legislation except on referendum of the electorate is now pending before the Supreme Court. Hunter v. Erickson, #63, Oct. Term 1968.

28. 42 U.S.C. §§ 2000 (1964).

29. NAACP v. Alabama, 357 U.S. 449 (1958); Louisiana v. NAACP, 366 U.S. 293 (1961); *accord,* Bates v. Little Rock, 361 U.S. 516 (1960). Shelton v. Tucker, 364 U.S. 479 (1960), dealt with a more difficult aspect of the question than forced disclosure of membership. An Arkansas statute, broadly requiring public school teachers to list all organizational connections over a stated period of time as a prerequisite to employment, was held to be too unselective and sweeping. In Gibson v. Florida Legis-

striking down state efforts to make group sponsorship of civil rights litigation unlawful, the Court correctly classified such court action as a protected form of political expression for the black community[30] —and indeed for many years it was the only effective method of political expression available.

On the other hand, the Court's concern for keeping peaceful protest activity alive and its pragmatic approach to decision-making led to a rather bizarre development in the sit-in cases. While the Court was determined to support the efforts of college students to break the pattern of racial segregation in the South by organized sit-in activities, it was not prepared to extend *Shelly v. Kraemer*[31] in order to prohibit state enforcement of private discrimination in places of public accommodation, or to break new ground by adopting some other approach to decision that would bar state use of its breach of the peace or trespass laws to defeat this kind of civil rights effort.[32] Instead, it held to an ad hoc method of adjudication, rendering decisions good for one case and one case only.[33] The Court came

---

lative Investigation Comm., 372 U.S. 539 (1963), Florida sought disclosure of the names of all members of the NAACP in Miami to determine the extent of the organization's infiltration by Communists. The Court held that enforced disclosure could be allowed only after a showing of a nexus between the organization about which the membership inquiry was being made and subversion. For a more detailed discussion of this development, *see* Carter, *Association: Civil Liberties and the Civil Rights Movement*, in LEGAL ASPECTS OF THE CIVIL RIGHTS MOVEMENT 181 (1965). In addition to aiding this form of self-help, the Court granted certiorari in NAACP v. Webb's City, 375 U.S. 939 (1963), to review the validity of a state injunction barring peaceful consumer picketing sponsored by a civil rights group to pressure store owners to abandon their policy of segregation. The question was not decided, however, because on respondent's suggestion of mootness, the judgment was vacated and remanded to effectuate respondent's representation that the injunction would be set aside. 376 U.S. 190 (1964).

30. NAACP v. Button, 371 U.S. 415 (1963).
31. 334 U.S. 1 (1948).
32. In Bell v. Maryland, 378 U.S. 226 (1964), the six members of the Court who were prepared to decide on a constitutional basis the validity of state trespass convictions of sit-in demonstrators for refusing to leave a restaurant on orders from the owner were evenly divided. The three other members of the Court were not prepared to face the issue, and thus the case was remanded to state court for reconsideration in light of the newly enacted law barring discrimination in places of public accommodations.
33. *See, e.g.*, Garner v. Louisiana, 368 U.S. 157 (1961) (no evidentiary basis for conviction for breach of peace, and conviction for criminal trespass could not be sustained since not charged); Peterson v. City of Greenville, 373 U.S. 244 (1963) (city ordinance held to require restaurant discrimination, hence exclusion of Negroes was unconstitutional state action requiring setting aside conviction for criminal trespass); Lombard v. Louisiana, 373 U.S. 267 (1963) (statements of mayor and chief of police construed as mandating continuation of the racial exclusion by restaurant owners and unconstitutional state action thus involved); Robinson v. Florida, 378 U.S. 153 (1964) (invalid state action embodying a state policy discouraging restaurant owners from serving the two groups without discrimination found in state regulations issued by the state board of health requiring restaurant owners with both white and black

out on the right side in supporting and sustaining this form of peaceful protest, but its reasoning was strained and tortured. Its decisions kept the sit-in movement viable until enactment of the Civil Rights Act of 1964, which reduced racial discrimination in places of public accommodation to an issue of minor significance.[34]

During the past fifteen years, the Supreme Court has undoubtedly concerned itself more with the affirmative development of substantive constitutional doctrine upholding equal rights than at any other time during its history. It has been criticized for its decisions and for its activism, but the criticism is misplaced. The Court in *Brown*, in requiring the elimination of enforced racial segregation as an essential prerequisite to equal education, did no more than the *Plessy v. Ferguson* Court had done in devising the separate-but-equal standard as an appropriate constitutional yardstick. Both Courts attempted to give what they saw as effective and meaningful import to the fourteenth amendment's guaranty of equal protection and, in so doing, both made national policy in the race relations field. *Plessy* paid homage to the equal rights verbiage of the fourteenth amendment while in fact legitimizing governmental subordination of blacks to whites. The rhetoric of *Brown*, on the other hand, sought to make the same grant of equality an ingredient of real life in the Negro community.

The problem is that while the Warren Court's rhetoric is broad and sweeping, its decisions have kept to a rather narrow path. It has in the main addressed itself solely to the task of outlawing formalized public discrimination—to the appearance rather than the substance of racism. The Court has not expanded or extended *Brown*. It has not dealt with the question of de facto school segregation—an issue which is as potentially explosive today as was formal segregation in 1954.[35] Therefore, we do not know what equal education

---

employees to provide separate lavatories for each race and each sex); Griffin v. Maryland, 378 U.S. 130 (1964) (special policeman employed by park was a deputy sheriff and arrested demonstrators in his role as state official, unlawful state action thus found). For full discussion of sit-in cases, *see* Paulson, *The Sit-In Cases of 1964: "But Answer Came There None,"* 1964 SUP. CT. REV. 137.

34. *See* Heart of Atlanta Motel v. United States, 379 U.S. 241 (1964). Katzenbach v. McClung, 379 U.S. 294 (1964), upheld the constitutionality of Title II of Civil Rights Act of 1964, 42 U.S.C. § 2000A (1964) (barring discrimination in public accommodations). In Hamm v. City of Rock Hill, 379 U.S. 306 (1964), the Court construed the federal civil rights law barring discrimination in places of public accommodation as requiring the abatement of all criminal prosecution under state law, both prior and subsequent to the passage of the Act, growing out of efforts to secure unsegregated access to public accommodation facilities.

35. *See* Bell v. School City of Gary, *Indiana* 213 F. Supp. 819 (N.D. Ind.), *aff'd*, 324 F.2d 209 (7th Cir. 1963), *cert. denied*, 377 U.S. 924 (1964) (holding that de facto school

means in the context of Northern-style school segregation.[36] Although the Court supported and protected the sit-in movement, it developed no cutting principles of law which would bar states from lending their weight, under the guise of enforcing criminal trespass laws, to the support of private discrimination practiced by restaurant or hotel owners.[37]

White supremacy, with or without formalized public discrimination, is the pervasive evil—the unyielding and persistent deterrent to fulfillment of the aims of the thirteenth, fourteenth, and fifteenth amendments. However, while the Warren Court did not go as far as it could have in the development of the substantive constitutional doctrine which *Brown* augured, what it did accomplish is of great significance. The broad rhetoric is there to build upon in the future. As stated earlier, the Court has attempted to deal forthrightly with one aspect of the race relations question—formalized public discrimination. And here, except for the troublesome problem of school segregation, it has done quite well. Moreover, the Court's perseverance has helped considerably in revealing the true dimensions of the race problem which confronts the nation today. What is now crystal clear is that solution of this problem will involve state and

---

segregation raised no constitutional question); Dowell v. School Bd., 244 F. Supp. 971 (W.D. Okla. 1965), aff'd, 375 F.2d 158 (10th Cir.), *cert. denied*, 387 U.S. 931 (1967), (avoidance of de facto segregation constitutionally required). Balaban v. Rubin, 40 Misc. 2d 249, 242 N.Y.S.2d 973 (Sup. Ct. 1963), aff'd, 14 N.Y.2d 193, 199 N.E.2d 375, 250 N.Y.S.2d 281, *cert. denied*, 379 U.S. 881 (1964) (local school board's deliberate effort to eliminate racial imbalance constitutionally permissible). *See also* Booker v. Board of Educ., 45 N.J. 161, 212 A.2d 1 (1965). An interesting phenomenon is Downs v. Board of Educ., 336 F.2d 988 (10th Cir. 1964), *cert. denied*, 380 U.S. 914 (1965), and Dowell v. School Bd., *supra*. These two cases involved similar situations and like principles. In both cases transition from pre-*Brown* segregation to a unitary school system which *Brown* required was said to be completed. In *Downs*, when the transition resulted in a de facto situation which confined the black children to virtually the same educational isolation that had existed before, the courts held that no constitutional question was involved. In *Dowell* the trial court ruled that the transition necessitated an avoidance of a substitution of de facto school segregation for pre-*Brown* school segregation. The Supreme Court refused to review either holding, clearly demonstrating that it is not yet prepared to face the question. *See generally* Carter, *De Facto School Segregation: An Examination of the Legal and Constitutional Questions Presented*, 16 W. Res. L. Rev. 502 (1965); Fiss, *Racial Imbalance in the Public Schools: The Constitutional Concepts*, 78 Harv. L. Rev. 564 (1965); Peck & Cohen, *The Social Context of School Segregation*, 16 W. Res. L. Rev. 475 (1965); Wright, *Public School Desegregation: Legal Remedies for De Facto School Segregation*, 40 N.Y.U. L. Rev. 285 (1965).

36. For a most comprehensive analysis of that question, *see* Hobson v. Hansen, 269 F. Supp. 401 (D.D.C. 1967). *See also* Rousselot, *Achieving Equal Educational Opportunity for Negroes of the North and West: The Emerging Role for Private Constitutional Litigation*, 35 Geo. Wash. L. Rev. 698 (1967).

37. The difficulty the ad hoc decision poses can be seen in comparing Edwards v. South Carolina, 372 U.S. 229 (1963), with Adderley v. Florida, 385 U.S. 39 (1966), where, on virtually the same set of facts, the Court reached opposite results.

federal efforts of the greatest magnitude. The elimination of formalized public discrimination will not suffice.

Lately, the Court has seemed to show signs of wanting the executive and legislative branches of government to take over responsibility for fulfilling the commitment which the nation made to the black community in the Civil War amendments. It has made clear that Congress, in implementing the objectives of the fourteenth amendment, has power to prohibit private discrimination as well as that supported by the state.[38] Last term, instead of waiting for the open housing provisions of the Civil Rights Act of 1968[39] to take effect on January 1, 1969,[40] the Court resurrected the Civil Rights Act of 1866[41] as a viable federal law applicable to discrimination in the public and private sale or rental of housing.[42] The Court noted that racial discrimination which "herds men into ghettos and makes their ability to buy property turn on the color of their skin . . . is a relic of slavery."[43]

II.

After declaring in *Brown I* that segregated education denied the constitutional guaranty of equal protection, a year later in *Brown II* the Warren Court addressed itself to the question of what remedy should be granted.[44] The formula adopted by the Court—requiring a "good faith" start in the transformation from a dual to a unitary school system, with compliance being accomplished with "all deliberate speed"—was a grave mistake. It has kept the Court mired in the vexing problems of progress in school desegregation for the past thirteen years. Although the Court denied that this formula was intended to do more than allow time for necessary administrative changes which transformation to a desegregated school system required, it is clear that what the formula required was movement toward compliance on terms that the white South could accept. Until *Brown II*, constitutional rights had been defined as personal and present. In the exercise of that ephemeral quality called judicial statesmanship, the Warren Court sacrificed individual and immediate vindication of the newly discovered right to desegregated education in favor of a mass solution. This was frequently reflected by the Court's tendency to avoid individual solutions in favor of ap-

---

38. United States v. Guest, 383 U.S. 745 (1966).
39. 82 Stat. 73, tit. VIII.
40. Tit. VIII, § 803(a)(2).
41. 42 U.S.C. §§ 1981-82 (1964).
42. Jones v. Mayer Co., 392 U.S. 409 (1968).
43. 392 U.S. at 442-43.
44. 349 U.S. 294 (1955).

proving long-range desegregation plans that would presumably benefit large groups of students in the future.[45]

The Court undoubtedly failed to realize the depth or nature of the problem. It undertook to oversee the pace of desegregation and apparently believed that its show of compassion and understanding of the problem facing the white South would help develop a willingness to comply. Instead, the "all deliberate speed" formula aroused the hope that resistance to the constitutional imperative would succeed. As indicated above, the Court did condemn open resistance with firm resolve; but since its concern was to secure "an initial break in the long established pattern of excluding Negro children from schools attended by white children, the principal focus was in obtaining for these Negro children courageous enough to break with tradition a place in the white school."[46]

In its anxiety to get the desegregation process moving at all costs, the Court condoned the application of procedural requirements and pupil placement laws which it knew were designed to delay or evade substantial compliance with the principles enunciated in *Brown I*. For eight years after its implementation decision, the Court refused to review any case in which questions were raised concerning the validity of pupil placement regulations or the appropriateness of applying the doctrine of exhaustion of administrative remedies to frustrate suits seeking to vindicate the right to a desegregated education.[47] Plans which called for the desegregation of only one grade per year were left standing.[48]

---

45. In Hawkins v. Board of Control of Florida, 350 U.S. 413 (1956), the Court made clear that its "all deliberate speed" formula was applicable only to grade and secondary school desegregation. The personal and present nature of the right to equal education remained unimpaired at all other educational levels and thus required immediate vindication. More recently, in Watson v. Memphis, 373 U.S. 526 (1963), involving segregation in a public park, it made the same point.

46. Green v. County School Bd., 391 U.S. 430, 435 (1968).

47. Covington v. Edwards, 264 F.2d 780 (4th Cir. 1959), *cert. denied*, 361 U.S. 840 (1959) (pupil placement law validated and procedures established required to be followed); Carson v. Warlick, 238 F.2d 724 (4th Cir. 1956), *cert. denied*, 353 U.S. 910 (1956) (exhaustion of administrative remedies); Hood v. Board of Trustees, 232 F.2d 626 (4th Cir. 1956), *cert. denied*, 352 U.S. 870 (1956) (exhaustion of administrative remedies required); Shuttlesworth v. Birmingham Bd. of Educ., 162 F. Supp. 372 (N.D. Ala. 1958), *aff'd* (on the limited ground on which the district court rested its decision), 358 U.S. 101 (1958); *accord*, Holt v. Raleigh City Bd. of Educ., 265 F.2d 95 (4th Cir.), *cert. denied*, 361 U.S. 818 (1959) (requirement that parent and child follow procedures established by pupil placement board sustained); DeFebio v. County Bd., 199 Va. 511, 100 S.E.2d 760 (1957), *appeal dismissed and cert. denied*, 357 U.S. 218 (1958).

48. Kelley v. Board of Educ., 270 F.2d 209 (6th Cir. 1959), *cert. denied*, 361 U.S. 924 (1959); Slade v. Board of Educ., 252 F.2d 291 (4th Cir. 1958), *cert. denied*, 357 U.S. 906 (1958) (a plan of desegregation spread over a shorter space of time). *But see* Ennis v. Evans, 281 F.2d 385 (3d Cir. 1960), *cert. denied*, 364 U.S. 933 (1961) (state plan calling for desegregation grade-by-grade over twelve-year span, disapproved and total integration ordered by fall 1961); Evans v. Buchanan, 256 F.2d 688 (3d Cir. 1958),

As time passed and no appreciable progress was made, the Warren Court began to manifest impatience. In 1962, it announced in *Bailey v. Patterson*[49] that no substantial question was involved as to the invalidity of state laws requiring segregation; the issue, the Court stated, had been resolved. The following year the Court ruled that the doctrine requiring exhaustion of administrative remedies before relief could be sought in federal court had no application to questions of school desegregation.[50] In *Griffin v. Prince Edward County Board of Education*, which was decided in 1964, the Court stated that the time for mere deliberate speed had run out.[51] And a year later, in *Bradley v. School Board of Richmond*,[52] it stated that "[d]elays in desegregating school systems are no longer tolerable."[53]

In spite of these belated efforts, the Warren Court's formula has actually accomplished very little school desegregation. By the 1963-1964 school year, for example, the eleven states of the old Confederacy had a mere 1.17 per cent of their black students attending schools with white students. In 1964-1965, the percentage had risen to 2.25 per cent because of the effect of the Civil Rights Act of 1964.[54] For the 1965-1966 school year—as a result of guidelines devised by the United States Department of Health, Education, and Welfare—the percentage reached 6.01 per cent.[55] Fear of losing federal funds had become a motivating factor inducing school authorities to effectuate some small measure of desegregation.[56]

The reason for the specific failure of the Court's formula is reasonably clear. The Warren Court had placed the primary responsibility for making the transition from the old standard to the new one upon local public school officials. These people were most prone to resent and resist the changes ordered by the Court, and to look upon the newly enunciated constitutional doctrine as a personal repudiation. Moreover, the lower federal courts were given the elusive standard of "good faith" by which to measure compliance. This led the courts to require a showing of subjective evil intent on the

---

cert. *denied*, 358 U.S. 836 (1958) (state superintendent and state board of education under orders to formulate a plan of desegregation for entire state).

49. 369 U.S. 31 (1962).
50. McNeese v. Board of Educ., 373 U.S. 668 (1963).
51. 377 U.S. 216, 234.
52. 382 U.S. 103 (1965).
53. 382 U.S. at 105.
54. *See* United States v. Jefferson County Bd. of Educ.. 372 F.2d 836, 903 (5th Cir. 1966); SOUTHERN EDUC. REP. SERV. STATISTICAL SUMMARY (15th ed. 1965). *See also* Kurland, *Equal Educational Opportunity: The Limits of Constitutional Jurisprudence Undefined*, 35 U. CHI. L. REV. 583, 594 (1968).
55. For discussion of effectiveness of the Department of Health, Education, and Welfare guidelines in increasing the pace of desegregation, *see* Dunn, *Title VI, The Guidelines in School Desegregation in the South*, 53 VA. L. REV. 42 (1967).
56. *See, e.g.*, Green v. County School Bd., 391 U.S. 430 (1968).

part of local officials as a prerequisite to granting relief from needless delay.

At present, stricter standards for compliance are in effect. In the 1965 decisions of *Bradley*[57] and *Rogers v. Paul*,[58] the Court apparently concluded that a new yardstick had to be devised to assess compliance efforts. This new approach is to evaluate the desegregation on the basis of its effectiveness—to determine whether the plans gave "meaningful assurance of a prompt and effective disestablishment"[59] of the biracial school system. Effective results in eliminating segregation root and branch are now required, and desegregation plans must hold out a realistic promise of success.

With the decision in *Brown I* the Court embarked upon a course designed in the short run to transform the Southern biracial school system into a unitary school system. In the long run, *Brown I* signalled the end of all public impediments, whatever their source, which denied black children their right to equal education. In deciding to oversee the pace of desegregation, which was what *Brown II* entailed, the Warren Court took upon itself an unnecessary responsibility for the South's failure to respond. It would have fared better in not departing from the usual standard—in ordering the immediate vindication of the rights that it had declared to exist in *Brown I*. Such a course probably would not have resulted in desegregation at a faster pace, but it would have kept the Court's image from being tarnished by first yielding fruitlessly to expediency.

III.

Brown v. Board of Education fathered a social upheaval the extent and consequences of which cannot even now be measured with certainty. It marks a divide in American life. The holding that the segregation of blacks in the nation's public schools is a denial of the Constitution's command implies that all racial segregation in American public life is invalid—that all racial discrimination sponsored, supported, or encouraged by government is unconstitutional. As a result of this seminal decision, blacks had the right to use the main, not the separate, waiting room; to choose any seat in the bus; to relax in the public parks on the same terms as any other member of the community. This and more became their birthright under the Constitution.

Equal rights legislation could no longer be regarded as a gift

---

57. 382 U.S. 103.
58. 382 U.S. 198.
59. Green v. County School Bd., 391 U.S. 430, 435 (1968).

benignly bestowed by an enlightened and liberal-minded electorate. Antidiscrimination laws were no longer great milestones; rather, they served merely as administrative machinery useful for accomplishing what the fundamental law required. While such machinery was, of course, vital and important, these statutes could now be critically assessed not in respect to the "good intentions" which led to their enactment, but rather in terms of the results achieved in alleviating the particular forms of discrimination they were supposed to regulate.

Thus, the psychological dimensions of America's race relations problem were completely recast. Blacks were no longer supplicants seeking, pleading, begging to be treated as full-fledged members of the human race; no longer were they appealing to morality, to conscience, to white America's better instincts. They were entitled to equal treatment as a right under the law; when such treatment was denied, they were being deprived—in fact robbed—of what was legally theirs. As a result, the Negro was propelled into a stance of insistent militancy. Now he was demanding—fighting to secure and possess what was rightfully his. The appeal to morality and to conscience still was valid, of course, but in a nation that was wont to describe itself as a society ruled by law, blacks had now perhaps the country's most formidable claim to fulfillment of their age-old dream of equal status—fulfillment of their desire to become full and equal participants in the mainstream of American life.

Brown's indirect consequences, therefore, have been awesome. It has completely altered the style, the spirit, and the stance of race relations. Yet the pre-existing pattern of white superiority and black subordination remains unchanged; indeed, it is now revealed as a national rather than a regional phenomenon. Thus, *Brown* has promised more than it could give, and therefore has contributed to black alienation and bitterness, to a loss of confidence in white institutions, and to the growing racial polarization of our society. This cannot in any true sense be said to be the responsibility of the Warren Court. Few in the country, black or white, understood in 1954 that racial segregation was merely a symptom, not the disease; that the real sickness is that our society in all of its manifestations is geared to the maintenance of white superiority.

Having opened this Pandora's Box, the Court was left for a long time to handle the problem alone. It is to its credit that the Warren Court did not falter in its resolve or turn away from its commitment to cut away all government support for discrimination.

While I have reservations about what the Court has done or failed to do, I am forced to recognize that even if the Court had functioned as I suggest it should have, we would probably be no nearer to the elimination of racism in this country than we are today. For, whatever the Court does, our society is composed of a series of insulated institutions and interests antithetical to the Negro's best interest. Effective regulation and control of these institutions and interests must come not from the Supreme Court but from the bodies politic.

THE WARREN COURT AND
CRIMINAL PROCEDURE

*A. Kenneth Pye**

* Dean, School of Law, Duke University. B.A. 1951, State University of New York at Buffalo; LL.B. 1953, LL.M., 1955, Georgetown University.—Ed.

O N October 5, 1953, Earl Warren became Chief Justice of the United States. During the fifteen years of his tenure as Chief Justice, fundamental changes in criminal procedure have resulted from decisions of what is popularly called "the Warren Court." There may be a legitimate difference of opinion whether these changes constitute a "criminal law revolution" or merely an orderly evolution toward the application of civilized standards to the trial of persons accused of crime. Whatever the characterization, however, there can be little doubt that the developments of the past fifteen years have unalterably changed the course of the administration of criminal justice in America.

In 1953, a state criminal trial in the United States differed little from its predecessor of fifty or even a hundred years. The accused in theory was cloaked with a panoply of constitutional rights. Most unsophisticated observers would have concluded from reading the Bill of Rights that a criminal defendant was protected against an unlawful arrest or an unlawful search and seizure by the fourth amendment; that he was assured the privilege against self-incrimination by the fifth amendment; and that rights to the assistance of counsel in his own defense, a prompt and speedy trial by common-law jury, compulsory process for witnesses, and the right to confront witnesses against him were guaranteed by the sixth amendment. Furthermore, the eighth amendment's prohibition of excessive bail seemed to reflect a policy against pretrial incarceration. In addition, the constitutional rights of an accused were complemented by other statutes and rules such as those which provided that after arrest a suspect should be brought promptly before a judicial officer.[1]

There were few outcries from the police that they were being

1. The most common type of statute requires that a person arrested without a warrant be brought before a magistrate "without unnecessary delay." *E.g.,* ARIZ. REV. STAT. ANN. § 13-1418 (1956); PA. RULES OF CRIM. PROC. § 116(a) (1965). Others use language such as "forthwith" [WYO. STAT. ANN. § 7-12 (1957)], or "without delay" [ORE. REV. STAT. § 133.550 (1963)]. Some have specific time limits. *E.g.,* MO. REV. STAT. § 544.170 (1959) ("20 hours"); GA. CODE ANN. § 27-212 (Supp. 1967) ("without delay" and not later than 48 hours). Fourteen states have no general provisions. The authorities dealing with the effect of a violation of a statute upon the admissibility of a statement are collected in Annot., *Admissibility of Confessions as Affected by Delay in Arraignment of Prisoner,* 19 A.L.R.2d 1331 (1951).

handcuffed, and our criminal courts were not afflicted by docket delay. A high percentage of defendants chose to confess, and an even greater number cooperated with the system by pleading guilty. In the eyes of most Americans, ours was a system of criminal justice unusually responsive to the individual rights of persons accused of crime. Indeed, as able a jurist as Learned Hand cautioned that our danger did not lie in too little tenderness to the accused, but in "watery sentiment that obstructs, delays, and defeats the prosecution of crime."[2]

A lawyer called upon to defend a person charged with crime might have viewed the situation a little differently. A typical robbery trial of fifteen years ago had the great advantage of brevity. The victim would testify that from a fleeting glance she could now identify the young Negro who had snatched her purse at night while she stood waiting for a bus. If defense counsel cross-examined her on the issue of identity, the prosecutor would be permitted to rehabilitate the witness by proof of a prior identification in a lineup, which might or might not have been staged. A police officer would then testify that the defendant voluntarily confessed to the offense when confronted with the identification and that this confession was obtained without using any unlawful threats, inducements, or third-degree methods.

Cross-examination might reveal that the defendant was a young unemployed Negro of limited education, who had been arrested without probable cause, had been detained in violation of a state statute which required prompt presentment before a magistrate, had not received the assistance of counsel at these preliminary stages, and had not been informed of his right to remain silent. If the accused chose to testify on the issue of voluntariness of the confession, there might be substantial conflicting testimony concerning the length of confinement before the statement was obtained and the course of events in the interrogation room. If the defendant denied that he made any inculpatory statement, the prosecutor would call other police officers who would corroborate each other's testimony. The defendant's testimony would then stand by itself, unless his counsel could develop inconsistencies in the police stories through cross-examination. A brief argument would ensue on the question of voluntariness, after which the judge would normally resolve the issue of credibility against the accused and admit the confession; on

2. United States v. Garsson, 291 F. 646, 649 (S.D.N.Y. 1923).

occasion, he might submit it to the jury for its determination of voluntariness.[3]

In some cases, the state might be able to offer evidence that an item belonging to the victim was found on the defendant's person after he was arrested. Proof by the defendant that the arrest which preceded the search was unlawful would be deemed irrelevant in many states.[4] Even in a jurisdiction that would exclude evidence obtained as a result of an unlawful search, the defendant might have to play Russian roulette by admitting possession in order to have the necessary standing to move to suppress.[5] It was of no crucial legal significance that the defendant had not received counsel until the eve of the trial; that he had been incarcerated for a considerable period before trial because bail had been set at a figure well beyond his financial capacity to meet, despite the unlikelihood that he would flee the jurisdiction; or that he had been denied access to prior statements of the crucial government witnesses against him. Indeed, our mythical defendant would be considered fortunate to have a lawyer to represent him at trial, a privilege not guaranteed to defendants in over one quarter of the states.[6]

When the prosecution rested, the defendant could testify in his own defense, except in Georgia.[7] If he did, he could anticipate cross-examination based on prior convictions; in many states such cross-examination was not restricted to convictions having anything to do with credibility.[8] If the defendant declined to testify, in some states he would have to expect the prosecutor to comment on this fact.[9] If he chose to admit character evidence, he might find that the prosecutor would bring before the jury specific instances of his prior bad acts, or even arrests for which he had not been tried, through adroit cross-examination.[10] The defendant would usually be forced to rely upon friends or close members of his family for corroboration of his testimony, since disinterested third parties might well have dis-

---

3. *E.g.*, Stein v. New York, 346 U.S. 156 (1963).

4. The authorities are collected in the appendix to the opinion of the Court in Elkins v. United States, 364 U.S. 206, 224-32 (1960).

5. The standing cases are discussed in Jones v. United States, 362 U.S. 257 (1960).

6. Before *Gideon*, five states refused to provide counsel even when it was requested by the defendant. Eight other states provided counsel only when requested. Van Alstyne, *In Gideon's Wake: Harsher Penalties and the "Successful" Criminal Appellant*, 74 Yale L.J. 606 (1965).

7. Ferguson v. Georgia, 365 U.S. 570 (1961).

8. C. McCormick, Evidence §§ 42, 43, 158 (1954); 3 J. Wigmore, Evidence § 988 (3d ed. 1940).

9. Adamson v. California, 332 U.S. 46 (1947); 8 J. Wigmore, Evidence § 2272 (3d ed. 1940).

10. Michelson v. United States, 335 U.S. 469 (1948).

appeared during the period of incarceration between arrest and the time after indictment when counsel was appointed.[11] Rarely would the assertion of an alibi defense by a sister or mother be given much credence by a jury. If a defendant wished to appeal, he might find that his inability to pay the costs barred his path to review,[12] or that, if review were permitted, no adequate provisions existed to furnish him with a lawyer to brief and argue his case.[13] Superimposed over the whole system was the principle of "differential leniency"; a defendant who pleaded guilty and saved the state the cost of a trial could reasonably anticipate a much lighter sentence than a defendant who chose to assert his constitutional right to an adjudication of his guilt or innocence before a jury.[14]

The broad theoretical framework of criminal justice under the Bill of Rights made it relatively easy to assert that our system is based on the premise that it is better to let one hundred guilty men go free than to convict one innocent man. Few innocent men were in fact convicted, but it is doubtful whether this was primarily because of the protections provided to an accused, or whether it was the result of the efficient screening of cases before trial by prosecutors and the peculiarly American institution of prosecutorial discretion. Indeed, the effectiveness of the criminal process, if judged in terms of conviction rates, was apt to be misleading unless modified by the realization that a high percentage of crimes were not reported; that a high percentage of reported crimes were not solved; that prosecution was declined or charges were reduced in a high percentage of solved crimes; that a substantial percentage of those convicted would be placed on probation without adequate supervision; and that a substantial percentage of those sentenced to

---

11. The disadvantages resulting from the late appointment of counsel are discussed in Jones v. United States, 342 F.2d 863, 870-71 (D.C. Cir. 1964).

12. Even when a statute permitted an indigent to appeal *in forma pauperis*, he might be met with a standard of frivolity quite different from that used in prepaid appeals. A classic case is Kemp v. United States, 311 F.2d 774 (D.C. Cir. 1962), where an indigent was required to go to the Supreme Court in order to obtain leave to appeal [369 U.S. 661 (1962)] and then obtained a *per curiam* reversal of his conviction on the grounds of insufficiency of the evidence when his case was heard on the merits by the court of appeals, which had denied him leave to appeal.

13. The effects of not having counsel are described in Douglas v. California, 372 U.S. 353 (1963).

14. In a recent project of the American Bar Association concerning pleas of guilty, it was assumed that "conviction without trial will and should continue to be a most frequent means for the disposition of criminal cases," and that the existing plea-bargaining system which produces a high percentage of guilty pleas "cannot operate effectively unless trial judges in fact grant charge and sentence concessions to most defendants who enter a plea of guilty or *nolo contendere*." AMERICAN BAR ASSOCIATION, AMERICAN BAR ASSOCIATION PROJECT ON MINIMAL STANDARDS OF CRIMINAL JUSTICE: STANDARDS RELATING TO PLEAS OF GUILTY 2, 38 (1967).

imprisonment would be released before expiration of their full term without having had the benefit of any effective program of rehabilitation.

Perhaps more important was the disparity between the reality of the criminal process and the ideals of civilized conduct to which we as a nation had sworn allegiance. Despite the preferred values reflected in the Bill of Rights, the criminal trial was viewed solely as a truth-seeking process in which no other social values were deemed more significant than the determination of whether or not a particular defendant had committed the crime for which he was charged.[15] Protection of the rights of citizens who were not before the court was not deemed to be a function of the criminal process. Few would have suggested that it was consistent with the American ideal for police to engage routinely in "investigative arrests" without probable cause,[16] to search without warrants, or to engage in prolonged incommunicado interrogations in violation of prompt presentment statutes. Even fewer thought it was fair to try a defendant for a felony without a lawyer or deny him an appeal if he was poor. However, these were thought to be matters of local concern for which redress should be sought by civil suits, by better internal controls within police departments, or by appeals to state legislatures and state courts. The fact that the problems were most serious where the antagonism to change was the greatest was thought to be part of the cost we were required to pay for federalism.

In 1953, it would not have been unreasonable for a citizen to have asked himself: "Which of my rights are really important? To what extent does the Constitution limit the police in doing what they want to do in their efforts to solve crime? How would I be treated differently if the Bill of Rights were repealed?"

After fifteen years of decisions of the Warren Court, we can

---

15. *See, e.g.,* the argument against using the rules of evidence to deter police misconduct that was advanced by Justice Traynor in People v. Cahan, 44 Cal. 2d 434, 442-43, 282 P.2d 905, 910 (1955):

> The rules of evidence are designed to enable courts to reach the truth and, in criminal cases, to secure a fair trial to those accused of crime. Evidence obtained by an illegal search and seizure is ordinarily just as true and reliable as evidence lawfully obtained. The court needs all reliable evidence material to the issue before it, the guilt or innocence of the accused, and how such evidence is obtained is immaterial to that issue. It should not be excluded unless strong considerations of public policy demand it. There are no such considerations.

16. The widespread use of the practice in Washington, D.C., was documented in the HORSKY REPORT [REPORT AND RECOMMENDATIONS OF THE COMMISSIONERS' COMMITTEE ON POLICE ARRESTS FOR INVESTIGATION (1962)]. *See* Kamisar, Book Review, 76 HARV. L. REV. 1502 (1963). *See also* Foote, *Safeguards in the Law of Arrest,* 52 NW. U. L. REV. 16 (1957); LaFave, *Detention for Investigation by the Police: An Analysis of Current Practices,* 1962 WASH. U. L.Q. 331.

answer these questions with some confidence and considerable pride. The gulf between the illusion and reality of constitutional protection has been narrowed. The quality of justice meted out to the poor more closely approximates that available to the rich. In many areas we are beginning to implement rights to which we have paid lip service for decades. We have begun to remove much of the hypocrisy which characterized our criminal process. While perhaps not totally effective,[17] court decisions do restrain police from some unlawful practices which were previously regarded as routine. A defendant is assured most of the basic procedural rights whether he is tried in a state or a federal court. There has been a renaissance of interest in the administration of criminal justice in legislative chambers; this interest is reflected in such legislation as the Criminal Justice Act of 1964,[18] the Bail Reform Act of 1966,[19] and state statutes designed to implement the constitutional mandate of court decisions. Even the law schools now recognize that criminal procedure is a subject worthy of being taught.

The judicial philosophy expressed in these attempts to make the rich and the poor substantially equal before our criminal courts, to provide roughly equivalent basic rights in state and federal courts, and to supply the necessary implementation of constitutional rights which had previously existed only on paper did not spring from the head of Zeus one morning. There had been significant beginnings before Earl Warren became Chief Justice.

The federal courts had enforced an exclusionary rule in search and seizure cases for almost forty years;[20] they had also barred the admission of evidence obtained as a result of illegal wiretapping[21] and confessions obtained during a period of unnecessary delay between arrest and presentment before a commissioner.[22] The Supreme Court had developed a substantial body of precedent in the field of search and seizure during the preceding thirty years.[23] It had already

---

17. *See* LaFave & Remington, *Controlling the Police: The Judge's Role in Making and Reviewing Law Enforcement Decisions*, 63 MICH. L. REV. 987 (1965).

18. 18 U.S.C. § 3006a (1964). *See* Kutak, *The Criminal Justice Act of 1964*, 44 NEB. L. REV. 703 (1965).

19. 18 U.S.C. § 3146 (Supp. II, 1966); *see* Wald & Freed, *The Bail Reform Act of 1966: A Practitioner's Primer*, 52 A.B.A.J. 940 (1966).

20. Weeks v. United States, 232 U.S. 383 (1914).

21. Nardone v. United States, 302 U.S. 379 (1937).

22. McNabb v. United States, 318 U.S. 332 (1943).

23. Consent searches: Amos v. United States, 255 U.S. 313 (1921). Scope of search incident to an arrest: United States v. Rabinowitz, 339 U.S. 56 (1950); Harris v. United States, 331 U.S. 145 (1947); United States v. Lefkowitz, 285 U.S. 452 (1932); Go-Bart Importing Co. v. United States, 282 U.S. 344 (1931); Agnello v. United States, 269 U.S. 20 (1925); Gouled v. United States, 255 U.S. 298 (1921). Items subject to seizure: United States v. Lefkowitz, *supra*; Marron v. United States, 275 U.S. 192 (1927); Gouled v.

determined that the fourth amendment's prohibition against unreasonable searches—but not the federal exclusionary rule—applied
to the states through incorporation in the due process clause of the
fourteenth amendment.[24] Lawyers had routinely been provided to
indigent defendants in the federal courts since 1937.[25] The Court
had for almost twenty years reviewed state criminal convictions involving the voluntariness of confessions.[26] In the year before the
appointment of Chief Justice Warren, the Court had reversed a
state conviction on the grounds that the conduct of police officers
"shocked its conscience," "offended its sense of justice," and "ran
counter to the decency of civilized conduct."[27]

Justice Black had for some time urged that the Bill of Rights
should be applied to the states *in toto* through incorporation within
the due process clause of the fourteenth amendment.[28] But the arguments for blanket incorporation were not accepted by the Court,
and the protections of the fifth and sixth amendments had not thus
far been accepted as fit subjects for selective incorporation. In general, the Court concerned itself primarily with federal criminal
cases; review of state criminal judgments was limited to a small
group of cases each year, the most important of which frequently
involved the admission of confessions[29] or the question of whether a
defendant had been seriously disadvantaged by denial of counsel.[30]
In every year but one, the number of federal criminal cases greatly
exceeded the number of cases reviewed from state courts,[31] and this
situation was not reversed until 1961.[32]

It may be forcefully argued that the increased concern of the

---

United States, *supra*. Premises protected and abandonment: Hester v. United States,
265 U.S. 57 (1924). Search of moving automobiles: Brinegar v. United States, 338 U.S.
160 (1949); Carroll v. United States, 267 U.S. 132 (1925). Probable cause to arrest
without a warrant: Brinegar v. United States, *supra*; McDonald v. United States, 335
U.S. 451 (1948); Johnson v. United States, 333 U.S. 10 (1948). Fruit of the poison tree:
Silverthorne Lumber Co. v. United States, 251 U.S. 385 (1920).

24. Johnson v. Zerbst, 304 U.S. 458 (1937).
25. Brown v. Mississippi, 297 U.S. 278 (1936).
26. Wolf v. Colorado, 338 U.S. 25 (1948).
27. Rochin v. California, 342 U.S. 165 (1952).
28. Adamson v. California, 332 U.S. 46, 68-92 (1947) (dissenting opinion).
29. *E.g.*, Leyra v. Denno, 347 U.S. 556 (1954); Stein v. New York, 346 U.S. 156 (1953);
Watts v. Indiana, 338 U.S. 49 (1949); Haley v. Ohio, 332 U.S. 596 (1948); Ashcraft v.
Tennessee, 327 U.S. 274 (1946); Lisenba v. California, 314 U.S. 219 (1941); Chambers v.
Florida, 309 U.S. 227 (1940).
30. *E.g.*, Quicksall v. Michigan, 339 U.S. 660 (1950); Gryger v. Burke, 334 U.S. 728
(1948); Bute v. Illinois, 333 U.S. 640 (1948); Foster v. Illinois, 332 U.S. 134 (1947); Betts
v. Brady, 316 U.S. 455 (1942).
31. The cases reviewed are cataloged in the tables contained in the annual reviews
of the work of the Supreme Court in the *Harvard Law Review*.
32. *Id.*

Supreme Court in matters of criminal justice was almost inevitable. A Court which had divested itself of the function of czar in the field of economic regulation on the eve of World War II predictably would in the postwar era assume a greater role in protecting individual rights of minority group members, political dissidents, and persons accused of crime.[33] The vacuum created by abdication of a function which had occupied much of the Court's time for several decades called for a new sense of direction, and few areas were of greater national significance than the eradication of the social and political inequalities which seemed to be the hallmarks of the real American dilemma.

The Court's concern with criminal procedure can be understood only in the context of the struggle for civil rights. Professor McCloskey has observed that the Warren Court's "espousal of civil rights was less a matter of deliberate choice than of a predictable response to the wave of history."[34] Concern with civil rights almost inevitably required attention to the rights of defendants in criminal cases. It is hard to conceive of a Court that would accept the challenge of guaranteeing the rights of Negroes and other disadvantaged groups to equality before the law and at the same time do nothing to ameliorate the invidious discrimination between rich and poor which existed in the criminal process. It would have been equally anomalous for such a Court to ignore the clear evidence that members of disadvantaged groups generally bore the brunt of most unlawful police activity.

If the Court's espousal of equality before the law was to be credible, it required not only that the poor Negro be permitted to vote and to attend a school with whites, but also that he and other disadvantaged individuals be able to exercise, as well as possess, the same rights as the affluent white when suspected of crime. It required that the values expressed in the Bill of Rights have meaning to the vast majority of our citizens whose contact with the criminal process is limited to local police and local judges, and for whom protections in a federal criminal trial are only slightly more relevant than the criminal procedure of Afghanistan. The principles of the Bill of Rights had to be applied to modern police, prosecutorial, and judicial practices if they were to retain their vitality in a modern age.

The issue posed to the Warren Court was not whether it would

---

33. R. McCloskey, The American Supreme Court 181 (1960); Mason, *Understanding the Warren Court: Judicial Review and Judicial Self-Restraint*, 81 Pol. Sci. Q. 523, 549-50 (1966).

34. R. McCloskey, *supra* note 33, at 226.

deal with the problems of inequality, illusory rights, and disparity in basic protections, but how far it would go in requiring changes and what priorities it would give to reform of the criminal process in the hierarchy of social and political problems which faced the nation. It could not be unmindful that any significant changes would trigger one or more of a traditional set of adjurations which assert that devotion to the principles of federalism requires that the states should have the widest latitude in the administration of their own systems of criminal justice; that the Court should not legislate (at least in matters of personal rights) but should interpret the Constitution to mean exactly what the Founding Fathers intended, regardless of changes in the social, political, or economic life of the nation; that it should be careful not to take any action that might impair the capacity of law enforcement agencies to deal with the problem of increasing crime which threatens the law-abiding citizens of the country; and that it should not seek to lead or educate the people concerning basic values of the American civilization, for these are the tasks entrusted to other branches of government. Perhaps, most important, the Court could not ignore the teaching of history that its prestige and independence is placed in jeopardy when it goes too far, too fast, for the mainstream of the public or its representatives in Congress.[35]

But the temper of the times provided strong reasons for the Supreme Court of the sixties to foresake the passivity advocated by Justice Frankfurter in favor of a more activist course. The danger of surging too far ahead of public or congressional opinion had to be balanced against the danger that too much restraint might make the legal process irrelevant to the pressing social needs of the day. If we are to persuade dissidents to stay within the system and out of the streets, we must have courts which are responsive to changing social values and which have the capacity to provide redress for basic grievances. It is to the credit of the Supreme Court that it recognized that the nation was in the midst of a social revolution before this became apparent to most of the elected representatives of the people, and that it sought to eliminate the basic defects in our system for the administration of criminal justice within our present structure. The result of this perceptive approach has been to immunize the Court from much of the alienation expressed against other institutions of our society not only by the disadvantaged, but also by large

---

35. *Id.* at 227; *see* A. MASON, THE SUPREME COURT FROM TAFT TO WARREN 282 (2d ed. 1968).

numbers of our youth,[36] upon whom the future of the nation depends.

Despite persuasive arguments urging different action,[37] the principles of federalism have yielded to the desire of the Court to provide equal justice to the rich and the poor in state and federal criminal proceedings. The notion of a national concept of basic justice does not seem too radical for America a century after the Civil War. It is not surprising that the majority of the Court has accepted the argument that the genius of federalism does not require that states be permitted to experiment with the fundamental rights of defendants in criminal cases any more than it permts experimentation with first amendment freedoms. The mere status of being in America should confer protection broad enough to protect any man from the vagaries of a state which by inertia or design fails to keep pace with a national consensus concerning the fundamental rights of the individual in our society.[38]

The greatest strides forward have been in the implementation of constitutional rights which have existed only in theory in the past. The decisions with the greatest significance are clearly the right-to-counsel cases.[39] With a lawyer present in criminal proceedings there is substantial assurance of justice; without one most other procedural rights are meaningless. The game is quite different when each side has a goalie. The sixth amendment has real vitality when an indigent who is unable to retain counsel is provided a lawyer to plead his case. The fourth amendment's protection against unreasonable searches and seizures means something when it is reinforced by the exclusionary rule.[40] The fifth amendment has content when it provides protection in a police station[41] and prevents a prosecutor from urging that a jury draw inferences of guilt from the defen-

---

36. W. BEANEY, THE SUPREME COURT: THE PERSPECTIVE OF POLITICAL SCIENCE 33-49 (1967).

37. Eloquent opposition to the Court's approach to federalism and the Bill of Rights has been expressed by Judge Friendly, *The Bill of Rights as a Code of Criminal Procedure*, 53 CALIF. L. REV. 929 (1965), and by Justice Harlan in his dissenting opinions and several speeches. *E.g.*, Harlan, Address at American Bar Center, Aug. 13, 1963; Harlan, The Bill of Rights and the Constitution, Aug. 9, 1964, quoted in A. MASON, *supra* note 35, at 258.

38. A. NORTH, THE SUPREME COURT: JUDICIAL PROCESS AND JUDICIAL POLITICS 179 (1966).

39. Douglas v. California, 372 U.S. 353 (1963); Gideon v. Wainwright, 372 U.S. 335 (1963). *See* Kamisar & Choper, *The Right to Counsel in Minnesota: Some Field Findings and Legal-Policy Observations*, 48 MINN. L. REV. 1 (1963). *See also* Mempa v. Rhay, 389 U.S. 128 (1967); Anders v. California, 386 U.S. 738 (1967).

40. Mapp v. Ohio, 367 U.S. 643 (1961).

41. Miranda v. Arizona, 384 U.S. 436 (1966).

dant's silence in the courtroom.[42] Observance of procedural safe-guards in trial courts is rendered more likely when the rights to appeal[43] and counsel[44] are available to the poor. The probability that constitutional rights will be respected in unsympathetic state courts becomes more likely when collateral attack on state court judgments is permitted within the federal judicial system.[45]

The results of the decisions of the Warren Court can be seen by examining the differences in the way our hypothetical yoke robbery case would be conducted today. The Court's prohibition against a lineup in the absence of counsel (or adequate safeguards sufficient to render the lineup "a less-than-critical" stage of the proceedings) might be violated by the police. But, violation of the defendant's right to counsel at this stage would render the in-court identification of the defendant inadmissible if the identification was tainted by the lineup. At the very least, it would mean the loss of the testimony concerning the alleged victim's prior identification at the lineup.[46] The confession obtained without informing the witness of his rights or permitting him an opportunity to exercise them would be inadmissible,[47] although disputes over whether a warning was given, and, if so, whether there had been a valid waiver still require the resolution of credibility conflicts between the police and the accused. The evidence obtained from the person of the accused following his unlawful arrest would be inadmissible.[48] It is doubtful that he would be required to admit possession as a prerequisite to a motion to suppress.[49] In many states the defendant will be able to obtain appointed counsel at a preliminary hearing,[50] and in a number of juris-

---

42. Griffin v. California, 380 U.S. 609 (1965).

43. Coppedge v. United States, 369 U.S. 438 (1962); Griffin v. Illinois, 351 U.S. 12 (1956).

44. Anders v. California, 386 U.S. 738 (1967); Hardy v. United States, 375 U.S. 294 (1964); Douglas v. California, 372 U.S. 353 (1963).

45. Fay v. Noia, 372 U.S. 391 (1963); Townsend v. Sain, 372 U.S. 293 (1963). *See* Meador, *The Impact of Federal Habeas Corpus on State Trial Procedures*, 52 VA. L. REV. 286 (1966).

46. Gilbert v. California, 388 U.S. 263 (1967); United States v. Wade, 388 U.S. 218 (1967).

47. Miranda v. Arizona, 384 U.S. 436 (1966).

48. Beck v. Ohio, 379 U.S. 89 (1964); Mapp v. Ohio, 367 U.S. 643 (1961).

49. *See* Jones v. United States, 362 U.S. 257 (1960); People v. Martin, 45 Cal. 2d 755, 290 P.2d 855 (1955); Weeks, *Standing To Object in the Field of Search and Seizure*, 6 ARIZ. L. REV. 65 (1964); Note, *Standing To Object to an Unreasonable Search and Seizure*, 34 U. CHI. L. REV. 342 (1967); Comment, *Standing To Object to an Unlawful Search and Seizure*, 1965 WASH. U. L.Q. 488.

50. "At least sixteen states usually appoint counsel at or before the preliminary hearing." AMERICAN BAR ASSOCIATION, ADVISORY COMMITTEE ON PROSECUTION AND DEFENSE FUNCTIONS, AMERICAN BAR ASSOCIATION PROJECT ON MINIMUM STANDARDS FOR CRIMINAL JUSTICE: STANDARDS RELATING TO PROVIDING DEFENSE SERVICES 45 (1967).

dictions there are now bail reform acts enabling an impecunious defendant to obtain his pretrial liberty.[51]

Criminal discovery before trial is still quite narrow,[52] and the defendant's right to obtain prior inconsistent statements of a government witness who testifies at the trial is not generally recognized.[53] However, the suppression of evidence favorable to an accused by the prosecutor is subject to constitutional attack.[54] In some jurisdictions, substantial limitations have been placed upon cross-examination of character witnesses[55] and the use of prior convictions to impeach.[56] The prosecutor may no longer comment on the accused's failure to take the stand.[57] A poor man convicted of a crime may appeal in any case where an appeal is permissible for the more affluent defendant,[58] and counsel will be provided for him at least in a first appeal.[59] Strict adherence to constitutional principles is being enforced through the federal writ of habeas corpus as well as by direct review by the Supreme Court.[60]

The results of these changes are being felt in more and longer trials. Although there appears to have been no drastic change in the percentage of acquittals, there are undoubtedly acquittals or decisions not to prosecute in some cases which would have resulted in convictions in 1953. There may be some cases where compliance with the standards of conduct required of the police have resulted in unsolved cases which could have been solved by an illegal search or

---

51. *See* BAIL AND SUMMONS, 1965 PROCEEDINGS: INSTITUTE ON THE OPERATION OF PRETRIAL RELEASE PROJECTS; AMERICAN BAR ASSOCIATION ADVISORY COMMITTEE ON PRETRIAL PROCEEDINGS, AMERICAN BAR ASSOCIATION PROJECT ON MINIMUM STANDARDS FOR CRIMINAL JUSTICE, STANDARDS RELATING TO PRETRIAL RELEASE 4 (1968).

52. Everett, *Discovery in Criminal Cases—In Search of a Standard,* 1964 DUKE L.J. 477 (1964); Goldstein, *The State and the Accused: Balance of Advantage in Criminal Procedure,* 69 YALE L.J. 1149 (1960); Rezneck, *The New Federal Rules of Criminal Procedure,* 54 GEO. L.J. 1276 (1966); Traynor, *Ground Lost and Found in Criminal Discovery,* 39 N.Y.U. L. REV. 228 (1964); *Bibliography: Criminal Discovery,* 5 TULSA L.J. 207 (1968).

53. Jencks v. United States, 353 U.S. 657 (1957); 18 U.S.C. § 3500 (1964); Note, *The Jencks Right: Judicial and Legislative Modifications, the States and the Future,* 50 VA. L. REV. 535 (1964).

54. Giles v. Maryland, 386 U.S. 66 (1967); Miller v. Pate, 386 U.S. 1 (1967); Brady v. Maryland, 373 U.S. 83 (1963).

55. *See, e.g.,* Luck v. United States, 348 F.2d 763 (D.C. Cir. 1965). The subsequent history of *Luck* is discussed in Circuit Note, *Criminal Law and Procedure,* 56 GEO. L.J. 58, 116-28 (1967).

56. Awkard v. United States, 352 F.2d 641 (D.C. Cir. 1965); Shimon v. United States, 352 F.2d 449 (D.C. Cir. 1965).

57. Griffin v. California, 380 U.S. 609 (1965).

58. Coppedge v. United States, 369 U.S. 438 (1962); Griffin v. Illinois, 351 U.S. 12 (1956).

59. Anders v. California, 386 U.S. 738 (1967); Hardy v. United States, 375 U.S. 294 (1964); Douglas v. California, 372 U.S. 353 (1963).

60. Fay v. Noia, 372 U.S. 391 (1963); Townsend v. Sain, 372 U.S. 293 (1963).

a compelled waiver of the privilege against self-incrimination. We really do not know how much effect the Court decisions have had. The one certainty is that the quality of our system of justice is much improved.

This rapid transition to a real adversary system in the criminal trial has occasioned widespread opposition. Few people continue to assert that the Court decisions have caused crime, but there is a vocal lobby which asserts that the decisions have unreasonably limited the police in their effort to apprehend criminals and solve crimes.

The first general outcry was occasioned by the *Mallory*[61] decision in 1957, in which the Court, speaking through Justice Frankfurter, did little more than reiterate the position which it had taken fourteen years earlier in *McNabb*:[62] that in a federal prosecution a statement obtained during a period of unnecessary delay between arrest and presentment before a commissioner was inadmissible. The opinion triggered a legislative furor in Congress, but the bill which would have overruled the holding in the case failed to pass.[63] No other bill obtained the requisite support until 1967 when the Congress modified the *Mallory* rule in the District of Columbia by the passage of the so-called Three-Hour Bill.[64] Last summer, both the legislation enacted the previous year for the District of Columbia and the stricter *Mallory* rule still applicable to federal courts outside of the District were modified by the provisions of the Omnibus Crime Control and Safe Streets Act which provided that no statement should be inadmissible "solely because of delay . . . if such confession is found by the trial judge to have been made voluntarily and if the weight to be given the confession is left to the jury and if such confession was made or given by such person within six hours immediately following his arrest . . . ."[65]

---

61. Mallory v. United States, 354 U.S. 449 (1957).

62. McNabb v. United States, 318 U.S. 332 (1943).

63. The history of the congressional fight over *Mallory* in the 85th Congress is detailed in Hogan & Snee, *The McNabb-Mallory Rule: Its Rise, Rationale and Rescue,* 47 Geo. L.J. 1 (1958).

64. Title III of Public Law 90-226, 81 Stat. 734, (1967) provides:

Sec. 301(a) Any person arrested in the District of Columbia may be questioned with respect to any matter for a period not to exceed three hours immediately following his arrest. Such person shall be advised of and accorded his rights under applicable law respecting any such interrogation. In the case of any such arrested person who is released without being charged with a crime, his detention shall not be recorded as an arrest in any official record.

(b) Any statement, admission, or confession made by an arrested person within three hours immediately following his arrest shall not be excluded from evidence in the courts of the District of Columbia solely because of delay in presentment.

65. 18 U.S.C. § 3501(c) (Supp. IV, 1968). The statute also provides that the time limitation contained in the statute should not apply to cases where a longer period of delay is reasonable in view of the means of available transportation and the distance required to be travelled.

The second major outcry resulted from the *Mapp* case in 1961,[66] in which the exclusionary rule was applied to evidence obtained in violation of the fourth amendment by state law enforcement officers. The police opposition to *Mapp* was in sharp contrast to the reception of its predecessor, *Wolf v. Colorado*,[67] which had applied the fourth amendment to the states fourteen years earlier. It seems quite clear that many police departments deliberately ignored the requirements of the fourth amendment during the period between *Wolf* and *Mapp*. Several post-*Mapp* cases applying the fourth amendment to arrests without a warrant[68] and to the adequacy of an affidavit submitted in support of a warrant[69] followed, but these cases were accompanied by other decisions which dealt sympathetically with bona fide attempts at compliance[70] and which declined to apply all of the rigors of the federal rules of search and seizure to the states.[71] It appears that most police forces are learning to live with the results.

The case which seemed to galvanize opposition into a potent political force was the *Miranda* decision[72] in 1966. The Chief Justice, speaking for a divided Court, laid down the basic requirements which must be met before an admissible confession can be obtained from a defendant.[73] With little empirical data to back up their contentions, critics asserted that many crimes could not be solved without confessions, and that warnings of rights or provision of counsel would preclude most defendants from confessing. The limited empirical research which has been done since the opinion casts substantial doubt upon these conclusions,[74] but confessions had

---

66. Mapp v. Ohio, 367 U.S. 643.

67. Wolf v. Colorado, 338 U.S. 25 (1949).

68. *E.g.*, Beck v. Ohio, 379 U.S. 89 (1964).

69. *E.g.*, Riggan v. Virginia, 384 U.S. 152 (1966); Aguilar v. Texas, 378 U.S. 108 (1964).

70. *E.g.*, United States v. Ventresca, 380 U.S. 102 (1965).

71. Ker v. California, 374 U.S. 23 (1963).

72. Miranda v. Arizona, 384 U.S. 436. Escobedo v. Illinois, 378 U.S. 478 (1964), engendered vigorous criticism, but it was tempered by the hope of some critics that the case would be limited to its facts and not extended as the Court ultimately chose to do in *Miranda*. *See* Herman, *The Supreme Court and Restrictions on Police Interrogation*, 25 Ohio St. L.J. 449 (1964); Enker & Elsen, *Counsel for the Suspect: Massiah v. United States and Escobedo v. Illinois*, 49 Minn. L. Rev. 47 (1964).

73. To comply with the opinion, the police are required to inform a suspect in a custodial interrogation that he has a right to remain silent, that anything that he says can and will be used against him, that he has the right to the advice and presence of a lawyer, and that a lawyer will be provided for him if he is unable to afford one. 384 U.S. at 467-73. *See* Kamisar, *A Dissent from the Miranda Dissents: Some Comments on the "New" Fifth Amendment and the Old "Voluntariness" Test*, 65 Mich. L. Rev. 59 (1966); *Symposium, Interrogation of Criminal Defendants—Some Views on Miranda v. Arizona*, 35 Fordham L. Rev. 169 (1966).

74. Medalie, Zeitz, & Alexander, *Custodial Interrogation in Our Nation's Capital: The Attempt To Implement Miranda*, 66 Mich. L. Rev. 1347 (1968); Robinson, *Police and Prosecutor Practices and Attitudes Relating to Interrogation as Revealed*

so long been a vital tool of police investigative technique that asser-tions of reduced efficiency accompanied by a rise in the crime rate were apparently enough to persuade many people that the Court had gone too far in protecting individual rights.[75] Most critics of the opinion did not deny that the inherent coerciveness of a police sta-tion was in reality a compulsion exercised against a defendant's right to remain silent. Yet it was argued that the need for confes-sions was so great that this coerciveness should be overlooked as long as it did not go too far in the direction of forcing a statement from unwilling lips.[76] In addition, the legitimacy of the decision was ques-tioned with contentions that the fifth amendment had never been intended to apply in a police station.[77]

---

by Pre- and Post-Miranda Questionnaires: A Construct of Police Capacity To Comply, 1968 DUKE L.J. 425; Seeburger & Wettick, *Miranda in Pittsburgh—A Statistical Study,* 29 U. PITT. L. REV. 1 (1967); Note, *Interrogations in New Haven: The Impact of Miranda,* 76 YALE L.J. 1519 (1967).

75. The Report of the Senate Judiciary Committee states the argument forcefully:
   The Committee is of the view that it simply makes no sense to exclude from a jury what has traditionally been considered the very highest type of evidence, and the most convincing evidence of guilt, that is, a voluntary confession or incriminating statement by the accused. This view is borne out by common ex-perience and general acceptance, and by almost 200 years of precedent in the courts of this country.
   The Committee also feels that the majority opinion not only runs counter to practically all the precedent in the State and Federal courts, but that it misconstrues the Constitution. The Committee alines itself wholeheartedly with the view expressed by the dissenting Justices and with what it feels are the views of the vast majority of judges, lawyers and plain citizens of our country who are so obviously aroused at the unrealistic opinions such as the Miranda decision which are having the effect of daily releasing upon the public vicious criminals who have voluntarily confessed their guilt.
S. REP. NO. 1097, 90th Cong., 2d Sess. (1968), 1968 U.S. CODE CONG. & AD. N. 1634, 1658-59.

76. *See* the dissent of Justice Harlan in Miranda v. Arizona, 384 U.S. 436, 515 (1966):
   Without at all subscribing to the generally black picture of police conduct painted by the Court, I think it must be frankly recognized at the outset that police questioning allowable under due process precedents may inherently entail some pressure on the suspect and may seek advantage in his ignorance or weak-nesses. The atmosphere and questioning techniques, proper and fair though they be, can in themselves exert a tug on the suspect to confess, and in this light "[t]o speak of any confessions of crime made after arrest as being 'voluntary' or 'uncoerced' is somewhat inaccurate, although traditional. . . ." . . . Until today the role of the Constitution has been only to sift out *undue* pressure, not to assure spontaneous confessions.
See also Bator & Vorenberg, *Arrest, Detention, Interrogation and the Right to Counsel: Basic Problems and Possible Legislative Solutions,* 66 COLUM. L. REV. 62 (1966).

77. The Report of the Senate Judiciary Committee called the decision "an ab-rupt departure from precedent extending back at least to the earliest days of the Republic." S. REP. NO. 1097, 90th Cong., 2d Sess. (1968), 1968 U.S. CODE CONG. & AD. N. 1634, 1656. Justice White, while agreeing that the application of the fifth amendment to the police station was novel, and disagreeing with its wisdom, did not question the validity of the process by which the decision was reached:
   That the Court's holding today is neither compelled nor even strongly sug-gested by the language of the Fifth Amendment, is at odds with American and English legal history, and involves a departure from a long line of precedent does not prove either that the Court has exceeded its powers or that the Court

Shortly thereafter, the Supreme Court held that a police lineup is normally such a critical stage in a criminal proceeding that the defendant, absent waiver, must be represented by counsel—at least if the police department did not take steps which would "eliminate the risk of abuse and unintentional suggestion at lineup proceedings and the impediments to meaningful confrontation at trial . . . ."[78] The possibility of excluding eyewitness testimony again sounded the clarion for opponents of the Court's reform movement in criminal procedure. Their views gained ascendancy in the Omnibus Crime Control and Safe Streets Act of 1968 which provides that a confession shall be admissible in a federal court if it is voluntarily given. In this regard, the Act specifically states that the failure to advise a defendant that he was not required to make any statement or that he had a right to the assistance of counsel "need not be conclusive on the issue of the voluntariness of the confession."[79] In addition, the Act provides that the testimony of eyewitnesses "shall be admissible in evidence,"[80] presumably intending that such testimony shall be admissible even if it results from a lineup held in violation of the mandate of the *Wade* opinion.

The provisions of the new Act, of course, do not apply to state prosecutions where the *Miranda* and *Wade* cases remain in full effect. But the assertion of the power to overrule the Supreme Court on the admissibility of evidence obtained in violation of the fifth and sixth amendments raises a potential conflict between the branches of the government which is yet to be resolved.[81] It is difficult to see

---

is wrong or unwise in its present reinterpretation of the Fifth Amendment. It does, however, underscore the obvious—that the Court has not discovered or found the law in making today's decision, nor has it derived it from some irrefutable sources: what it has done is to make new law and new public policy in much the same way that it has done in the course of interpreting other great clauses of the Constitution. This is what the Court historically has done. Indeed, it is what it must do and will continue to do until and unless there is some fundamental change in the constitutional distribution of governmental powers. 384 U.S. at 531.

78. United States v. Wade, 388 U.S. 218, 239 (1967). *See* Comment, *Right to Counsel at Police Identification Proceedings: A Problem in Effective Implementation of an Expanding Constitution,* 29 U. PITT. L. REV. 65 (1967); Comment, *Lawyers and Lineups,* 77 YALE L.J. 390 (1967).

79. 18 U.S.C. § 3501(a)-(b) (Supp. IV, 1968).

80. 18 U.S.C. § 3502 (Supp. IV, 1968).

81. One possibility of avoiding the conflict would be the acceptance of the Senate Judiciary Committee's argument that the provisions of the new Act simply constitute an acceptance of the invitation to Congress contained in the Court's opinion wherein it encouraged Congress and the states to "exercise their creative rule-making capacities" to develop "effective ways of protecting the rights of the individual while promoting efficient enforcement of our criminal laws" [Miranda v. Arizona, 384 U.S. 436, 467 (1964)]. S. REP. No. 1097, 90th Cong., 2d Sess. 50 (1968), 1968 U.S. CODE CONG. & AD. N. 1634, 1659. The short answer to the argument is that the report as a whole makes it clear that the Senate Committee was attempting to overrule the

how the provisions of the new Act which in substance overrule *Miranda* and *Wade* in the federal courts can be upheld, unless the Court chooses to retreat from its holdings or finds some technique of statutory construction which would permit it to avoid the apparent conflict.

Perhaps more significant than what Congress did is what some Senators proposed that it should do. As reported from the Senate Judiciary Committee, the crime control bill would have denied lower federal courts jurisdiction to entertain collateral attacks on state court criminal judgments even if a defendant's constitutional rights had been abridged. The bill would also have deprived both the lower federal courts and the Supreme Court of the power to review the voluntariness of a confession admitted in a state criminal trial if the highest court of the state had found the confession voluntary.[82] Fortunately, these provisions attempting to limit the power of the federal judiciary to require compliance with the Constitution were deleted from the bill before its passage. However, the threat of impairing judicial independence through the limitation of jurisdiction still remains, and the Senate Judiciary Committee's report leaves little doubt that the threat of such jurisdictional restrictions was intended to be a gloved fist designed to keep the Supreme Court in line.[83]

Rarely do the opponents of the Warren Court give credit to the Court for changes which have helped law enforcement agents in their attempts to solve crime and apprehend criminals. The Court overturned a long line of precedents to permit the seizure of non-testimonial evidentiary material;[84] rejected contentions that the police should not be able to use informers;[85] and has generally allowed the police to conceal the identity of informers before trial.[86] More recently, it has permitted a stop and frisk where a police officer "observes unusual conduct which leads him reasonably to conclude in light of his experience that criminal activity may be afoot and that the persons with whom he is dealing may be armed and presently dangerous . . . ."[87] Cases holding that the fourth amendment applies

decision, not implement it. Furthermore, the statute does not provide alternative ways of protecting the privilege against self-incrimination.

82. S. 917, 90th Cong., 1st Sess. (1967).
83. *See* S. REP. No. 1097, 90th Cong., 2d Sess. (1968), 1968 U.S. CODE CONG. & AD. N. 1634, 1660-75.
84. Warden v. Hayden, 387 U.S. 294 (1967).
85. Hoffa v. United States, 387 U.S. 231 (1967); Lewis v. United States, 385 U.S. 206 (1966).
86. McCray v. Illinois, 386 U.S. 300 (1967).
87. Terry v. Ohio, 392 U.S. 1 (1968).

to electronic eavesdropping also make it clear that a statute with appropriate safeguards would meet constitutional muster.[88] The same realism that the Court has demonstrated in cases involving the implementation of defendants' rights has been evident in the Court's attitude toward effective law enforcement needs.

The most important question is whether the Court will continue along the paths which it has chosen to follow during recent years; whether it will engage in a holding operation until experience and education develop the necessary public and congressional climate for acceptance of further reforms; or whether the Court, influenced by the rising crime rate and the more general disrespect for law reflected in university and urban disturbances, will retreat from the positions advanced in its most controversial decisions. It is possible to speculate about the future, but the list of imponderables cautions against predictions. Some would argue that the Court's justifiable concern over judicial independence and supremacy requires self-restraint when the public reaction to the Court's decisions reveals that it is either too far behind or too far ahead of a national consensus. In this modern era, some even suggest that discretion requires the Court to follow the polls as well as the election returns.[89] Such analyses suggest the wisdom of a period of comparative passivity in which to accommodate law enforcement officials to the new rules with the aid of newly available federal financing. During such a period the Court would seek to interpret and enforce compliance with its existing decisions. For instance, it could provide additional guidance concerning what constitutes "custodial interrogation" or "waiver" within the meaning of *Miranda* and elaborate on the constitutional requirements for permissible electronic surveillance. However, the Court might refrain from deciding such volatile questions as what constitutes the outer limit of the "fruit of the poisonous tree" doctrine; whether counsel must be provided in misdemeanor cases and at preliminary hearings; whether most of our vagrancy and disorderly conduct statutes are constitutional; whether the denial of bail can be predicated upon dangerousness; whether the police have the right to stop and interrogate a person thought to be a suspect but known to be unarmed where there is no immediate danger of a crime being committed; whether the fourth, fifth, and eighth amend-

---

88. Katz v. United States, 389 U.S. 347 (1967); Berger v. New York, 388 U.S. 41 (1967). *See* Dash, *Katz—Variations on a Theme by Berger*, 17 CATHOLIC U. L. REV. 296 (1968); Blakey & Hancock, *A Proposed Electronic Surveillance Control Act*, 43 NOTRE DAME LAW. 657 (1968).

89. N.Y. Times, July 10, 1968, at 19, col. 1.

ments have the same meaning in urban riot situations as in routine criminal investigations and prosecutions; whether our system of plea bargaining with its built-in "differential leniency" is consistent with due process; and whether basic fairness requires a change in the scope of discovery in criminal cases. To some, such a period of passivity would indicate prudence. To others, valor is the better part of discretion, and they would contend that such an approach of "ducking the hard ones" would be an abdication of judicial responsibility.

The outlook of the man who replaces Earl Warren will be a significant element in the judicial equation. But history teaches us to avoid inferences of probable judicial performance on the Supreme Court from past experience in other capacities. It may be appropriate to remember that fifteen years ago one respected periodical suggested that Earl Warren was antilabor and questioned whether he harbored biased racial views;[90] another commentator predicted that he was a middle-of-the-roader who would "hold his helm to the center";[91] a third doubted his ability to provide strong leadership for the Court.[92] Proponents of the status quo must have gained heart by the Chief Justice's vote in *Irvine*[93] in the 1953 term, had doubts by the time he dissented in *Grunewald*,[94] *Groban*,[95] and *Briethaupt*[96] in the 1956 term, and seen the handwriting on the wall when the "gathering storm"[97] of the 1958 term produced the dissents in *Cicenia*,[98] *Crooker*,[99] *Palermo*,[100] *Pittsburgh Plate Glass*,[101] *Abbate*,[102] and *Bartkus*.[103]

It seems doubtful that any substantial long-term retreats will be taken from positions already assumed by the Court. Fortunately, the history of civil liberties in this country has been one of growth; there

---

90. 177 NATION 282-84 (1953).

91. Frank, *Affirmative Opinion on Justice Warren*, N.Y. Times Mag., Oct. 3, 1954, at 17.

92. Gressman, *The Coming Trials of Justice Warren*, 129 NEW REPUBLIC 8-10 (1953); *What's Ahead for the Supreme Court*, 35 U.S. NEWS & WORLD REPORT 36-38 (1953).

93. Irvine v. California, 347 U.S. 128 (1954).

94. Grunewald v. United States, 353 U.S. 391 (1957).

95. *In re* Groban, 352 U.S. 330 (1957).

96. Breithaupt v. Abram, 352 U.S. 432 (1957).

97. The phrase is that of Professor Kamisar. Kamisar, *Equal Justice in the Gatehouses and Mansions of American Criminal Procedure*, in CRIMINAL JUSTICE IN OUR TIME 38 (1965).

98. Cicenia v. Lagay, 357 U.S. 504 (1958).

99. Crooker v. California, 357 U.S. 433 (1958).

100. Palermo v. United States, 360 U.S. 343 (1959).

101. Pittsburgh Plate Glass Co. v. United States, 360 U.S. 395 (1959).

102. Abbate v. United States, 359 U.S. 187 (1959).

103. Bartkus v. Illinois, 359 U.S. 121 (1959).

have been temporary interruptions, but progress has been general. Experience has shown that law enforcement agencies can accommodate themselves to new rules by changing their techniques. They are learning to solve crimes without physical torture or psychological coercion. They will learn to solve them without violating the fourth or fifth amendments. Their task will be made easier by the belated recognition that federal funds are needed to help provide better selection procedures, training, organization, and equipment. The states survived federal judicial protection of freedom of religion and freedom of speech. They will survive federal protection of the rights of defendants in criminal cases.

With the passage of time and the constantly increasing influence of the post-World War II generation, a broader understanding will develop of what the Court has been trying to accomplish. A hundred years from now lawyers will not be amazed by the changes wrought by the Warren Court. They will wonder how it could have been otherwise in the America of the sixties.

THE WARREN COURT: RELIGIOUS LIBERTY AND CHURCH-STATE RELATIONS

Paul G. Kauper*

I. Background to the Warren Era

THE Warren Court will be remembered for a number of reasons, but for many Americans it is distinctively and immediately identified as the tribunal which put an end to prayer and Bible-reading exercises in the public schools. These cases were among the Court's most highly publicized decisions; they probably generated as much discussion, controversy, and criticism of the Court as the school desegregation, legislative reapportionment, and police interrogation decisions. The prayer and Bible-reading cases stood out among a relatively small but significant body of decisions in which the Warren Court was called upon to interpret the twin clauses in the opening language of the first amendment: "Congress shall make no law respecting an establishment of religion, or prohibiting the free exercise thereof . . . ." The purpose of this Article is to analyze the holdings of the Warren Court under these two clauses in an attempt to assess their significance by reference both to earlier interpretations and to the direction they may give to future development.

Some propositions had been well established before the era of the Warren Court. Fundamental to any consideration of the Supreme Court's treatment of religious liberty was the determination that the fourteenth amendment made the first amendment applicable to the states. Whatever the theory—whether a fundamental rights interpretation or an incorporation theory—the Court in the pre-Warren period had made clear that the free exercise principle explicitly stated in the first amendment as a restriction on Congress was equally applicable to the states under the fourteenth amendment.[1] The Court also left no doubt that the establishment limitation served as a restriction on the states.[2]

The dimensions of religious liberty, as epitomized in the free

---

* Henry M. Butzel Professor of Law, University of Michigan. A.B. 1929, Earlham College; J.D. 1932, University of Michigan.—Ed.

1. Murdock v. Pennsylvania, 319 U.S. 105, 108 (1943); Cantwell v. Connecticut, 310 U.S. 296, 303 (1940).
2. Everson v. Board of Educ., 330 U.S. 1 (1947).

exercise guarantee, had been well explored by the Supreme Court before Chief Justice Warren's tenure began. In a notable series of cases primarily involving claims asserted by Jehovah's Witnesses, the Court—whether resting its decisions on free speech and free press, on a concept of intellectual liberty distilled from the first amendment, or distinctively on religious liberty itself—had opened up a wide area for the expression and propagation of religious ideas.[3] Moreover, the cases had established that restrictions on religious liberty would not be lightly countenanced and would not be permitted except in cases presenting a clear and present danger to important public interests.[4] These cases suggested that religious liberty stood at the apex of the first amendment and was, indeed, a "preferred freedom."

By contrast, the interpretation of the establishment limitation had given rise to a limited amount of litigation before the Court prior to the Warren era. Three important cases had turned on the interpretation of this limitation. In *Everson v. Board of Education*,[5] the Court held that a state could reimburse parents for the cost of transporting their children by bus to a parochial school. In reaching this result and in stating its interpretation of the establishment limitation, the Court, speaking through Justice Black, enunciated the famous doctrine that the establishment clause does more than prohibit an established church or preferential treatment for one or more religions. According to him, this limitation prohibited government from giving any aid to religion, including public spending "to support any religious activities, or institutions whatever they may be called, or whatever form they may adopt to teach or practice religion."[6] Quoting Thomas Jefferson, Justice Black said that the establishment clause was intended to erect "a wall of separation between church and State."[7] In short, the first amendment embodies the separation principle. However, New Jersey had not breached the wall in the *Everson* case, since its purpose was not to aid religious education but to promote the valid public welfare purpose of providing safe transportation for children attending parochial schools. Thus the Court laid the foundation for the "secular purpose" doc-

---

3. *See* P. KAUPER, FRONTIERS OF CONSTITUTIONAL LIBERTY 107-12 (1956).
4. *See* Cantwell v. Connecticut, 310 U.S. 296 (1940).
5. 330 U.S. 1 (1947).
6. 330 U.S. at 16.
7. 330 U.S. at 16.

trine in the interpretation of the establishment limitation: government may advance lawful secular purposes with its spending programs even though this may result in some incidental benefit to a
religious group or activity.

The *Everson* dictum was translated into a concrete holding in
the *McCollum*[8] decision; the Court held unconstitutional a program
whereby public school children were "released" one hour a week
for religious instruction given on the school premises during the
regular school day by teachers supplied by the religious communities. According to the Court, the state was using its public school
program as a means of recruiting children for religious instruction
and subjecting them to pressure to attend these classes.

Shortly thereafter, the Court in *Zorach v. Clauson*[9] sharply limited *McCollum* by holding that a state could promote a plan of
released time for religious instruction where the instruction did not
take place on the school premises, even though in other respects the
plan resembled the one invalidated in *McCollum*. As the dissenters
pointed out,[10] the decision could hardly be reconciled with the basic
rationale of *McCollum*; moreover, the emphasis of Justice Douglas'
majority opinion was a striking departure from Justice Black's opinions in *Everson* and *McCollum*. Observing that "[w]e are a religious
people whose institutions presuppose a Supreme Being,"[11] Justice
Douglas said that the state may properly respect the religious nature
of our people and accommodate the public service to their spiritual
needs. Thus, in *Zorach* the Court laid the foundation for the
"accommodation theory": a state may, consistent with the establishment limitation, act in a positive way to accommodate its institutions and programs in order to provide the opportunity for its citizens to cultivate religious interests. While the decision in no sense
suggests that parents could demand as a matter of constitutional
right a program of released time, its basic reasoning was indicative
of the problems awaiting the Court in reconciling possible conflicts
between the free exercise guarantee and the establishment proscrip-
tion. Both the holding and the tenor of the opinion led some to
believe that the Court was retreating substantially from the hard
line of separation which characterized *Everson* and *McCollum*. Thus

---

8. McCollum v. Board of Educ., 333 U.S. 203 (1948).
9. 343 U.S. 306 (1952).
10. 343 U.S. at 316 (Justice Black), 322-23 (Justice Frankfurter), 325 (Justice Jackson).
11. 343 U.S. at 313.

after *Zorach* was decided in 1952, it was possible to speculate that the Court was moving to a softer position which would permit state programs supportive of religion as long as there was no preferential treatment of any religious group and no coercion of dissenters.

II. THE WARREN COURT AND THE FREE EXERCISE CLAUSE

Five cases decided by the Warren Court fall into the general category of free exercise of religion. In *Kreshik v. St. Nicholas Cathedral of the Russian Orthodox Church,*[12] the Court held that it was an impairment of religious liberty for the New York courts to transfer control over St. Nicholas Cathedral in New York City from the central governing authority of the Russian Orthodox Church to a group which had established an independent Russian Church of America. Soon thereafter, the Court in *Torcaso v. Watkins*[13] declared unconstitutional a provision of the Maryland Constitution requiring a justice of the peace to take an oath that he believed in God as a condition of taking office. In *Braunfeld v. Brown*[14] the Court held that a Sunday closing law did not violate the religious liberty of sabbatarians. But in the later case of *Sherbert v. Verner,*[15] the Court distinguished *Braunfeld* and held invalid a feature of the South Carolina unemployment compensation law which, as interpreted by the state supreme court, required denial of unemployment compensation benefits to a person who refused a job requiring Saturday employment because of sabbatarian convictions. And for reasons pointed out below, *United States v. Seeger*[16] should also be included among the Warren Court's free exercise decisions even though it did not rest on constitutional grounds. The Court there held that a person could qualify for a statutory exemption as a conscientious objector under the selective service laws on the basis of religious training and belief—defined by statute as "belief in relation to a Supreme Being"[17]—despite the fact that he did not profess belief in God in the orthodox sense.

---

12. 363 U.S. 190 (1960).
13. 367 U.S. 488 (1961).
14. 366 U.S. 599 (1961).
15. 374 U.S. 398 (1963).
16. United States v. Seeger, also the companion cases, United States v. Jakobson, Peter v. United States, 380 U.S. 163 (1965).
17. 50 U.S.C. app. § 456(j) (1964). This definition was eliminated in the 1967 amendments to the selective service statute. 50 U.S.C. app. § 456(j) (Supp. III), *amending* 50 U.S.C. app. § 456(j) (1964).

The decision in *Kreshik*, which dealt with the freedom of churches as corporate bodies,[18] may be contrasted with the remaining free exercise cases during the Warren era, which bore distinctively on the religious liberty of the individual; attention in the discussion below will be centered on the latter cases. By invalidating the Maryland oath requirement as a condition of public office, *Torcaso* in effect incorporated into the free exercise clause as a limitation on the states the express limitation in the body of the Constitution that no religious test shall be required as a qualification for any office under the United States.[19] The case may be viewed as resting on the simple proposition that no person may be discriminated against on religious grounds in the enjoyment of public office or privilege. While this appears elementary, several curious aspects of the opinion give it a special significance. Justice Black, in his review of the precedents, repeated passages from *Everson* and *McCollum*, thereby indicating that the Court was not retreating from the interpretation previously given to the establishment limitation. But strangely the Court did not explicitly rest its decision on the establishment clause, as it might well have done since freedom from coercion to accept an officially prescribed religious belief seems clearly to be a central value served by that provision. Moreover, Justice Black's observation that the effect of the oath was to favor those who profess a particular kind of religion—namely those who preferred a belief in God as against persons professing non-theistic religious beliefs[20]—points again to what readily appears as an argument under the establishment limitation as interpreted in *Everson*. Yet the Court formally grounded its decision on the free exercise limitation.[21] This suggests that both the free exercise and establishment clauses protect against discrimination on religious grounds in the enjoyment of public privilege; it also indicates that the free exercise clause protects both belief and nonbelief. Moreover, the famous footnote in Justice Black's opinion, documenting his

18. *Kreshik* was significant in that it extended to judicial action the previous holding in Kedroff v. St. Nicholas Cathedral of the Russian Orthodox Church in N. America, 344 U.S. 94 (1952), which had invalidated legislative interference with ecclesiastical affairs. The Court thereby converted the old federal common-law doctrine of Watson v. Jones, 80 U.S. (13 Wall.) 679 (1872), into a constitutional rule. *See* Casad, *The Establishment Clause and the Ecumenical Movement*, 62 MICH. L. REV. 419 (1964).

19. U.S. CONST. art. VI, para. 3.

20. 367 U.S. at 490.

21. 367 U.S. at 496.

point that the oath requirements gave a preference to a particular kind of religious belief, suggests a definition of religion which encompasses secular and humanistic beliefs and ideologies in addition to the traditional types of theistic belief.[22]

Seeger and its companion cases should be considered at this point for their bearing on *Torcaso*. The distinctive thing about *Seeger* is that the Court by *tour de force* interpreted "belief in relation to a Supreme Being"—required by statute as an element of the showing of religious belief and training necessary to sustain a claim of conscientious objector status[23]—to include any ethical belief which parallels the conventional belief in God as a source of moral duty. While *Seeger* rested on statutory grounds, it clearly had constitutional overtones, since a construction which limited exemption as a conscientious objector to persons resting their moral convictions on conventional theistic grounds would have been subject to attack under *Torcaso* as a discrimination against persons holding nontheistic ethical beliefs. Taken together, the *Torcaso* and *Seeger* opinions point to the conclusion that at least for purposes of the free exercise clause, the term "religion" embraces a wide variety of ethical beliefs, whether founded on theistic concepts or not; that a broad freedom of conscience comes within the protection of the free exercise clause; and that by virtue of the first amendment no preference may be granted or discrimination practiced by reference to a particular kind of religious belief as sanctioned by law.

Braunfeld and *Sherbert* are probably the most interesting cases of the Warren period on the issue of religious liberty. They deal basically with the same problem: whether or not the free exercise clause protects a person against the indirect restraint on his religious liberty which results when the application of a generally valid law places him at a special disadvantage because of his adherence to religious duty. Since this problem does not involve governmental acts which directly restrict religious acts or discriminate explicitly on religious grounds, it falls outside the range of the familiar types of restrictions on religious liberty. The issue in *Braunfeld* was whether orthodox Jews and others who because of religious conviction observe a day of rest other than Sunday must be exempted from

---

22. "Among religions in this country which do not teach what would generally be considered a belief in the existence of God are Buddhism, Taoism, Ethical Culture, Secular Humanism and others." 367 U.S. at 495 n.11.

23. *See* note 17 *supra*.

the coverage of a Sunday closing law. If such an exemption is denied, sabbatarians who observe both secular and religious law would be subjected to an economic disadvantage since they would be required to close their businesses two days per week. In *Braunfeld* the Court refused to go along with this economic discrimination argument; it chose to recognize the secular purpose served by Sunday closing laws and the importance of having a single day of rest prescribed by law. The Court emphasized that the restraint on religious liberty was an indirect one and asserted that substantial policy considerations militated against creating an exemption in favor of those who for religious reasons observe another day of rest.[24] Pointing to the administrative problems of policing a Sunday closing law with a recognized exemption based on religious obligation, the majority held the state was not constitutionally required to grant such an exemption.[25] Justice Brennan's strong dissent, supported by Justice Stewart, registered the view that this was a burden on the free exercise of religion which could not be justified by any compelling state interest.[26]

Braunfeld was sharply restricted, if not devitalized, by the later holding in *Sherbert* that South Carolina had violated the free exercise clause in the administration of its unemployment compensation law by cutting off unemployment compensation payments to a Seventh Day Adventist who had refused a job requiring Saturday work. According to the Court, the law forced the sabbatarian to make a choice between adhering to her religion and enjoying a public benefit; thus, the effect of the law was to discriminate against persons with religious objections to Saturday work.[27] The Court emphasized that only a compelling state interest warrants a restriction on religious liberty,[28] and the case makes clear that this standard is equally applicable to so-called indirect restraints on religious freedom. Justice Brennan, who wrote the majority opinion, attempted to distinguish the *Braunfeld* case on the ground that the same public

---

24. 366 U.S. at 606-09.

25. 366 U.S. at 608-09.

26. 366 U.S. at 610, 616. Justice Douglas dissented on the grounds both that the Sunday closing laws were laws establishing religion and that in so far as they compelled observance by sabbatarians they violated the free exercise clause.

27. The South Carolina law did recognize the position of a person who objected to working on Sundays on religious grounds, and the Court in support of its conclusion could, therefore, use the further argument that the law thereby discriminated against persons whose religion required a different day of rest.

28. 374 U.S. at 406.

policy considerations that justified a state in not exempting sabbatarians from a Sunday closing law were not present here.[29] Justices Douglas[30] and Stewart[31] in their concurring opinions, and Justice Harlan in his dissent,[32] indicated that they were not persuaded by this effort. Indeed, as Justice Harlan observed, the economic burden placed on the sabbatarian who complies with a Sunday closing law is greater than that suffered by an individual who is denied unemployment benefits for a restricted period of time.[33]

Perhaps it is only a matter of time before the Court reconsiders *Braunfeld*; in any event, the *Sherbert* case stands out as probably the landmark case during the Warren period on the question of religious liberty. The result of the Court's decision is to protect discrete minorities against laws which, while serving valid public purposes, have the effect of putting these groups at a special disadvantage. Equally important is the general proposition formulated in *Sherbert* that only compelling state interests warrant measures which substantially infringe upon the free exercise of religion. The impact of this formulation is evident in later cases decided by other courts.[34] Indeed, in view of its strong stand in *Sherbert*, it is surprising that the Court refused to review the Kansas Supreme Court's decision in *Kansas v. Garber*,[35] the Amish school case, thus passing up the opportunity to deal with the important issues of religious liberty raised therein.

III. THE WARREN COURT AND THE ESTABLISHMENT CLAUSE

Three important cases distinctively turning on the interpretation of the establishment clause were decided during the period under

29. 374 U.S. at 408-09.
30. 374 U.S. at 411-12.
31. 374 U.S. at 417-18.
32. 374 U.S. at 421.
33. 374 U.S. at 421.
34. *See*, e.g., People v. Woody, 394 P.2d 813, 40 Cal. Rptr. 69 (1964) (A state narcotics law could not constitutionally be applied to penalize the use by a California Indian tribe of peyote as part of a religious ceremony.); *In re* Jenison, 267 Minn. 136, 125 N.W.2d 588 (1963) (A Jehovah's Witness could not be required to serve on a jury where this ran counter to religious conviction). *See also* Galanter, *Religious Freedoms in the United States: A Turning Point?*, 1966 WIS. L. REV. 217; Gianella, *Religious Liberty, Nonestablishment, and Doctrinal Development, Part I, The Religious Liberty Guarantee*, 80 HARV. L. REV. 1381 (1967).
35. 197 Kansas 567, 419 P.2d 896 (1966), *appeal dismissed and cert. denied*, 389 U.S. 51 (1967). Chief Justice Warren and Justices Douglas and Fortas were of the opinion that probable jurisdiction should have been noted.
The Kansas Supreme Court held that the right of the Amish parents founded on religious considerations to direct the education of their children after reaching high school age was subordinate to the state's power to insure what it regarded as proper minimum education for all children in the state.

review. In *Engel v. Vitale*[36] and *Schempp v. School District of Abington Township*,[37] prayer and Bible-reading exercises in the public schools were condemned as a form of establishment.[38] Supplying textbooks free of charge to parochial school children was upheld in *Board of Education v. Allen*.[39] In addition, the Court upheld the validity of Sunday closing laws.[40] To these decisions must be added the recent holding in *Flast v. Cohen*[41] that a federal taxpayer has standing to challenge the constitutionality of federal spending alleged to violate the establishment limitation. To complete the picture, it should be noted that the Court passed up opportunities to review state court cases dealing with the validity of governmental grants to church-related colleges[42] and the validity of tax exemptions for property used for religious purposes.[43]

The cases dealing with religious exercises in public schools and state-financed distribution of textbooks to parochial school children have perhaps the greatest impact and long-run significance in terms of the substantive interpretation of the establishment clause. As previously observed, the prayer and Bible-reading cases, declaring invalid practices which had long been sanctioned in a number of states, attracted great attention and provoked widespread public controversy. These decisions generated charges that the Warren Court was godless and hostile to religion and led to a substantial, but in the end unsuccessful, movement in support of a constitutional amend-

---

36. 370 U.S. 421 (1962).

37. 374 U.S. 203 (1963). *See also* the companion case, Murray v. Curlett, 374 U.S. 203 (1963).

38. In *Engel* the Court held that the daily use in New York schools of the so-called Regents' Prayer violated the establishment clause. At the next term in the *Schempp* and *Murray* cases the Court broadened the *Engel* holding to include Bible-reading and the recitation of the Lord's Prayer. Justice Stewart wrote dissenting opinions in these cases.

39. 392 U.S. 236 (1968).

40. McGowan v. Maryland, 366 U.S. 420 (1961).

41. 392 U.S. 83 (1968).

42. The Maryland Court of Appeals held that capital grants by the legislature to church-related colleges which the Court found to be "sectarian" institutions, violated the establishment clause of the first amendment. Horace Mann League of the United States v. Board of Public Works, 242 Md. 645, 220 A.2d 51 (1966), *cert. denied*, 385 U.S. 97 (1966). Justices Harlan and Stewart were of the opinion that certiorari should have been granted.

43. The California, Rhode Island, and Maryland courts held that such exemptions did not violate the establishment clause. Lundberg v. County of Alameda, 46 Cal. 2d 644, 298 P.2d 1, *appeal dismissed sub nom.* Heisey v. County of Alameda, 352 U.S. 921 (1956) (Justices Black and Frankfurter dissenting); General Fin. Corp. v. Archetto, 176 A.2d 73 (R.I. 1961), *appeal dismissed*, 369 U.S. 423 (1962) (Justice Black dissenting); Murray v. Comptroller of Treasury, 241 Md. 383, 216 A.2d 897, *cert. denied*, Murray v. Goldstein, 385 U.S. 816 (1966).

ment to validate the practices held unconstitutional by the Court.[44] These cases definitely established the secular character of the public schools as a constitutional requirement; they also suggested questions about the validity of all religious observances in public life. Equally important, however, was that in *Schempp* the Court made clear that the objective study of religion and of the Bible in its literary and historical aspects is properly a part of public education. This recognition gave a special positive significance to these cases.

The *Allen* case, which upheld the public lending of secular textbooks free of charge to children in parochial schools, is significant not only because it affirms and extends the secular-purpose doctrine of *Everson*, but also because it suggests openings for other types of federal and state programs designed to provide benefits to church-related institutions or students attending church-related schools. The decision has great relevance for federal spending programs already underway and for similar state programs already adopted or under consideration.[45]

In the long run, the *Flast* case may turn out to be the Warren Court's most important decision on church-state problems. The issue was whether a federal taxpayer has standing to challenge a federal appropriation on the ground that it violates the establishment clause. In *Frothingham v. Mellon*,[46] decided in 1923, the Court had held that a federal taxpayer did not have the requisite interest to challenge spending for a purpose allegedly beyond the legislative competence of Congress. It has been commonly assumed since *Frothingham* that the case stood as a bar to any suit by a federal taxpayer to challenge federal spending on constitutional or statutory grounds. But in *Flast* the Court limited *Frothingham* by holding that a federal taxpayer does have standing to challenge federal spending

---

44. On various proposals to amend the Constitution to permit prayer and Bible-reading exercises in the public schools, *see Proposed Amendments to the Constitution Relating to School Prayers, Bible Reading, etc., A Staff Study for the House Comm. on the Judiciary*, 88th Cong., 2d Sess. (Committee Print 1964); *Hearings on Proposed Amendments to the Constitution Relating to Prayers and Bible Reading in the Public Schools Before the House Comm. on the Judiciary*, 88th Cong., 2d Sess. (1964). *See also* Note, *School Prayer and the Becker Amendments*, 53 GEO. L.J. 192 (1964).

45. Pennsylvania recently enacted legislation authorizing grants to private schools as a contribution to the cost of providing secular educational services. Act. No. 109, 24 P.S. §§ 5601-09 Reg. Sess. (1968), 3 PURDON'S PENNSYLVANIA LEGISLATIVE SERVICE 232 (1968). A proposal to authorize limited tuition grants to parents sending children to private schools was introduced at the recent session of the Michigan legislature. S.B. 1124 Reg. Sess. (1968).

46. 262 U.S. 447.

allegedly violative of the establishment clause, since this clause is a specific limitation on Congress and impliedly creates a right in federal taxpayers to be free from spending which amounts to an establishment of religion. By finding such a right in the taxpayer, the Court actually built on a substantive interpretation in order to meet the remedial problem.[47] The specific holding in *Flast* is particularly significant since, until this decision, the *Frothingham* doctrine had barred litigation instituted by taxpayers challenging the use of federal funds, under authority of statutes directed to general welfare purposes, to aid church-related activities or institutions. We may now expect a spate of federal cases challenging such uses of funds. Perhaps decisive answers will soon be forthcoming to questions which have been the subject of prolonged controversy but which have gone unresolved for lack of a proper party to present the issue. An incidental effect of the decision may be to put an end to proposals for legislation which would expressly vest federal courts with jurisdiction to hear taxpayers' suits challenging federal appropriations on first amendment grounds.[48]

What contributions, if any, did the Warren Court make to the doctrinal development of the establishment clause? One thing is quite clear: the notion which developed after the *Zorach* case that the Court was about to engage in a general retreat from ideas expressed in *Everson* and *McCollum* proved to be ill-founded. At least the Warren Court has taken occasion in its opinions to reaffirm general ideas expressed in earlier decisions indicating a hard line on separation. Whether the Court means what it says, and whether everything it says can be reconciled with its holdings is another matter. The Court's tendency to cite and quote from prior decisions in cases raising the establishment issue obscures the doctrinal development. For instance, in the *Torcaso* case, which appeared formally to rest on the free exercise clause, Justice Black reviewed his prior

---

47. Dilution of the standing requirement in establishment cases was evident already in the prayer and Bible-reading cases where the Court held that it was not necessary to prove an invasion of personal freedom in order to challenge a school practice on establishment grounds. Parents objecting to these religious practices brought the suits in these cases. Justice Black in *Engel* did not even discuss standing, Justice Clark and Justice Brennan mentioned the standing problems in footnotes in their opinions in *Schempp* (374 U.S. at 224 n.9, 266 n.30).

48. Senator Ervin proposed such legislation in 1966. *See Hearings on S. 2097 Before the Subcomm. on Constitutional Rights of the Senate Comm. on the Judiciary*, 89th Cong., 2d Sess. (1966). For discussion of the proposed legislation, *see* Editorial Note, *The Insular Status of the Religion Clauses: The Dilemma of Standing*, 36 GEO. WASH. L. REV. 648 (1968).

opinions in *Everson* and *McCollum* and found in them support for the idea that the state cannot involve itself in religious matters by prescribing a religious test for public office. And, in stating its position on the establishment clause in the Sunday closing cases, the Court reviewed at length the earlier cases from *Everson* through *Zorach*, again suggesting that it was not rejecting the prior learning. In the end, of course, the Court found the Sunday closing laws valid on the basis of the exception to the separation principle suggested in the *Everson* case itself: that laws directed toward secular ends are valid even though they result in incidental benefits for religious purposes. In this sense the Sunday closing cases added no new doctrinal development and simply affirmed the basic rationale of the *Everson* holding. It should be noted, however, that both Chief Justice Warren in his majority opinion[49] and Justice Frankfurter in his extended concurring opinion[50] did suggest the further consideration that even a law which incidentally aids religion while furthering a secular purpose may be invalid if alternatives are open to the state for achieving the same result without conferring this incidental benefit. Justice Brennan also referred to this test in his extended concurring opinion in the *Schempp* case,[51] discussed below. The alternative-means approach has important implications as a limitation on the secular-purpose doctrine, but it remains to be determined whether this test has assumed a definitive significance in the interpretation of the establishment clause. If it has attained such a significance, it is still unclear how the test is to be applied in a variety of situations.

The school prayer and Bible-reading cases offer the greatest insight into the Court's current thinking about the establishment clause. In the first case, *Engel v. Vitale*,[52] the Court dealt rather simply with the New York Regents' prayer by saying that a statute which prescribed a prayer for daily use in the public schools violated a fundamental purpose of the establishment clause, which was designed to prohibit governmental sanction for any kind of religious belief or practice. Justice Black's opinion was notable because, except for one brief reference to the *Everson* case in a footnote, it completely lacked documentation. This suggested that while speak-

---

49. 366 U.S. at 450-52.
50. 366 U.S. at 466-67.
51. 374 U.S. at 294-95.
52. 370 U.S. 421 (1962).

ing for the majority of the Court in writing an opinion designed to secure as much support as possible, he was not disposed to give interpretations of prior cases which might alienate such support. Obviously any reliance on *McCollum*, which some felt would have justified the result, would have required an attempt to distinguish *Zorach*. But Justice Black did make the important point that it was not necessary for the petitioners, who were parents, to show that there was an invasion of religious liberty; since the establishment clause is an independent ground for decision, a showing that the challenged practice also violates the free exercise clause is not required.[53]

The *Schempp* case,[54] which followed in quick succession and which dealt with the issue of both prayer and Bible-reading in the public schools, was far more revealing in terms of the Court's interpretation of the establishment clause. Justice Clark, writing for the majority, reviewed all the prior cases and did not suggest any basic incompatibility between *McCollum* and *Zorach*. While reaffirming the holding in *Engel* that the establishment clause prohibits ritualistic exercises in the public schools, even though attendance is voluntary, he went on at great length to justify the Court's conclusions in the case before it and to allay fears that the Court was intent on an antireligious course with respect to the public schools. He affirmed the view that for the purpose of raising an establishment clause question it was not necessary to prove a violation of religious liberty. The really critical part of his establishment interpretation, however, appeared in that part of the opinion stating that what the first amendment requires is neutrality.[55] This marks the first time that neutrality as a central canon of interpretation appeared in the cases. Justice Black had already mentioned neutrality in *Everson*; he said that if the state elected to be neutral as between children attending public and parochial schools in the matter of providing bus transportation the Court could not say that this was unconstitutional.[56] The Court would not force the state, in administering a program aimed at the safe transportation of school children, to discriminate against children going to parochial schools. And Justice Douglas in *Zorach* stated that government must be neutral on the issue of com-

---

53. 370 U.S. at 430.
54. School Dist. of Abington Township v. Schempp, also Murray v. Curlett, 374 U.S. 203 (1963).
55. 374 U.S. at 215, 222-27.
56. 330 U.S. at 17-18.

petition between sects.[57] But it was in *Schempp* that neutrality, as opposed to separation, assumed a position of primary importance in the interpretation of the establishment clause.

This was a significant development, in part because neutrality had been proposed by several writers as the authoritative guide to interpretation. Professor Katz had stated that the underlying purpose of both religion clauses is to promote religious liberty; that separation is a subordinate instrumental concept to achieve this purpose; and that while the establishment clause requires government to be neutral as between religion and nonreligion, this neutrality must be interpreted in the light of the free exercise clause. Thus, neutrality cannot be used as a basis for denying the free exercise of religion or for discriminating on a religious basis in the dispensation of public benefits.[58] Professor Kurland, in his instructive study of the Supreme Court's decisions, propounded the theory that what the first amendment forbids is a classification which results in either preference or discrimination based on the religious factor.[59] This theory, too, results in a neutralistic interpretation in the sense that laws and practices must be general in application and must not be designed to favor or discriminate against religion.

In implementing the neutrality idea in *Schempp*, Justice Clark said that the decisive test was whether either the purpose or the primary effect of the enactment was the advancement or inhibition of religion: "That is to say that to withstand the strictures of the Establishment Clause there must be a secular legislative purpose and a primary effect that neither advances nor inhibits religion."[60] This test fits in well with the neutrality idea—neutrality is identified with secularity of both ends and means. The difficulty with *Schempp* is that there is no indication in Justice Clark's opinion that the Court was rejecting the *Zorach* case, where there was clearly a breach of the neutrality idea in that the Court sanctioned a state program which was deliberately designed to further the religious interests of parents and children. Moreover, the emphasis in Justice Clark's opinion on the compulsive aspects of the Bible-reading and prayer exercises somewhat weakens the conclusion that these exercises were invalid simply because they reflected a positive interest of the state

---

57. 343 U.S. at 314.
58. Katz, *Freedom of Religion and State Neutrality*, 20 U. Chi. L. Rev. 426 (1953).
59. P. Kurland, Religion and the Law (1962).
60. 374 U.S. at 222.

in religious matters. Instead, the opinion suggests that their invalidity turned on the element of coercion implicit in the school situation. This ambiguity is reflected also in the separate opinion of Justice Goldberg, joined by Justice Harlan. While agreeing that the state must be neutral toward religion, nevertheless they warned that an untutored devotion to neutrality could lead to results which partake of "a brooding and pervasive devotion to the secular and a passive, or even active, hostility to the religious"—results which are not only not compelled by the Constitution, but are prohibited by it.[61] Justice Brennan, in a long concurring opinion expressing his adherence to neutrality and the results reached in *Engel* and *Schempp*, listed a whole series of cases where he thought the state could accommodate these programs to serve religious interests.[62] But there can be no reconciliation between strict neutrality and the neutrality which permits or requires an accommodation to religious interests.[63] This difference is suggested by Justice Clark's opinion in *Schempp*, where he spoke both of "strict neutrality, neither aiding nor opposing religion,"[64] and of "wholesome neutrality."[65]

So while the *Schempp* case spoke much of neutrality, the various opinions are ambiguous on this question. It is evident that not all members of the Court are ready to accept the Kurland idea that the state can do nothing which in any way uses the religious factor as the basis for preferential classification. It seems clear that prayer and Bible-reading practices have been held invalid not simply because they violate the neutrality principle but because this particular breach of neutrality has involved the states so deeply in religious matters as to have a coercive effect on the liberty of dissenters and nonconformists.[66] *Schempp* can thus be viewed as a case protecting the freedom of the minority.

On the same day the Court decided the *Schempp* case, it held in

---

61. 374 U.S. at 306.

62. 374 U.S. at 294-304.

63. For analysis of the neutrality emphasis in the *Schempp* opinion, *see* Kauper, *Schempp and Sherbert, Studies in Neutrality and Accommodation*, 1963 RELIGION AND THE PUBLIC ORDER 3, 10-23. *See also* Gianella, *Religious Liberty, Nonestablishment, and Doctrinal Development, Part II, The Nonestablishment Principle*, 81 HARV. L. REV. 513 (1968).

64. 374 U.S. at 225.

65. 374 U.S. at 222.

66. *See, e.g.,* the statement in Justice Goldberg's concurring opinion that the "pervasive religiosity and direct governmental involvement inhering in the prayer and Bible-reading practices" could not be characterized simply as accommodation by the state in the interests of religious liberty. 374 U.S. at 307.

Sherbert[67] that as a matter of constitutional right a Seventh Day Adventist, *because of her religion,* was entitled to special treatment under the South Carolina unemployment compensation law. Here the Court approached the problem from the vantage point of the free exercise clause. The deliberate legislative policy of giving aid to religious groups through exemptions in tax and regulatory laws, evident in both federal and state statutes, cannot be reconciled with neutrality. Yet the Court in *Sherbert* went beyond saying that a legislature *may* grant a preferential exclusion on religious grounds and held that it *must* do so. The free exercise clause as interpreted in *Sherbert* thus negates neutrality. At the same time, the constitutionally required accommodation to religious liberty does not in this case violate the establishment clause—even though it departs from neutrality—since here the state's involvement in religion is minimal and the positive assistance given to one citizen's religious beliefs poses no threat to others' theistic or nontheistic beliefs.[68] *Schempp* and *Sherbert* can be reconciled, not on the basis of an abstract conception of neutrality, but on the basis that both serve to protect important facets of the basic liberty that gives unity to the religion clauses of the first amendment. Given this explanation, *Schempp* was a significant contribution to the meaning of religious liberty in our pluralistic society.

The decision in *Allen,*[69] holding that it does not violate the establishment clause for a state to lend secular textbooks free of charge to children in parochial schools, has important implications— even though on the surface it adds nothing new to the interpretation of the establishment limitation. Obviously the result fits the neutrality theory, since the state here elected to pursue a policy of not discriminating against parochial school children in the disbursement of funds for educational purposes. On the other hand, it is quite clear that *Allen* is not consistent with a strict separation theory, at least in terms of the doctrinaire no-assistance idea expressed in *Everson.* Yet it can be reconciled with the actual holding in *Everson* on the ground that, even under a strict separation theory, the state is not precluded from pursuing secular purpose programs which give incidental aid to religion. This is precisely the theory on which the

67. Sherbert v. Verner, 374 U.S. 398 (1963).
68. 374 U.S. at 409. *See Schwarz, No Imposition of Religion: The Establishment Clause Value,* 77 YALE L.J. 692 (1968).
69. 392 U.S. 236 (1968).

Allen case rests. Following the decision in the prayer and Bible-
reading cases, the question had arisen whether *Everson* was still good
law. *Everson* had been decided by a five-to-four vote, and Justice
Douglas, who voted with the majority, subsequently indicated that
he thought *Everson* had been wrongly decided.[70] A very substantial
change has occurred in the Court's personnel in the meantime. Of
the nine Justices who participated in *Everson*, only Justices Black
and Douglas are now on the bench. Both dissented in *Allen* along
with Justice Fortas. This means that the majority in the *Allen* case
consisted of six Justices who did not take part in *Everson*. Justice
White, who delivered the majority opinion which received the support of five other Justices, rested the case squarely on the authority
of *Everson* and its secular-purpose theory.[71] In this connection, he
also made a revealing use of the primary purpose-primary effect test
enunciated by Justice Clark in *Schempp*.

Allen does more than merely affirm *Everson*. It rejects the notion
that the *Everson* holding is limited to forms of aid for parochial
school children, such as transportation, school lunches, and health
programs which, unlike books, are not directly involved in the teaching and learning processes. Perhaps what is really important about
Allen is its affirmation of the role of private education in the American educational system, the recognition that parochial schools serve
a secular purpose in addition to their sectarian function, and the
clear acceptance of the idea that the establishment clause is no bar
to state assistance in furthering this secular function.[72]

Allen opens up new vistas for application of the secular purpose
theory. It should be pointed out, however, that the Court has never
dealt with the question whether government may make direct grants
to church-related educational institutions on a theory of assisting

---

70. *See* his concurring opinion in Engel v. Vitale, 370 U.S. 421, 443 (1962).
71. 392 U.S. at 242-44.
72. 392 U.S. at 247-48 (footnotes omitted):
   Underlying these cases, and underlying also the legislative judgments that have
preceded the court decisions, has been a recognition that private education has
played and is playing a significant and valuable role in raising national levels
of knowledge, competence, and experience. Americans care about the quality of
the secular education available to their children. They have considered high quality
education to be an indispensable ingredient for achieving the kind of nation,
and the kind of citizenry, that they have desired to create. Considering this attitude, the continued willingness to rely on private school systems, including
parochial systems, strongly suggests that a wide segment of informed opinion,
legislative and otherwise, has found that those schools do an acceptable job of
providing secular education to their students. This judgment is further evidence
that parochial schools are performing, in addition to their sectarian function,
the task of secular education.

them in the performance of secular functions. In *Everson* the school board reimbursed the parents for the cost of students' transportation. In *Allen* the state supplied textbooks which had to be approved by the state department of education although the parochial school authorities made the initial choice (a point emphasized in the dissenting opinions).[73] Reserved for future decision is the question of to what extent the concept of secular purpose or of neutrality, invoked to support various forms of governmental aid for parochial school education, is limited by the manner in which the benefit is conferred, the extent of state involvement in religious affairs, and the retention of public administrative control.[74]

The cases interpreting the establishment clause have done little to resolve the conceptual ambiguities bequeathed by the pre-Warren decisions. On the one hand, the Court, while continuing to pay verbal respect to the strict separation theory first enunciated in *Everson*, has used the opening provided by that case for the secular purpose doctrine. It followed this theory in the Sunday closing cases and in the school textbook cases. On the other hand, in *Schempp* the Court formulated a neutrality theory as the central canon in the construction of the establishment limitation. Yet we may wonder what kind of neutrality the Court was talking about. Indeed, Justice Harlan has recently observed that "[n]eutrality is a coat of many colors."[75] Because of the degree of state involvement, neutrality obviously suited the *Schempp* case as a theory for decision. But the Court did not disavow *Zorach*, which rested on accommodation; and on the very same day that it decided *Schempp*, it limited neutrality by holding in *Sherbert* that a state was required in the name of free exercise to grant a religious exemption from a law which served a valid public purpose. Moreover, in *Allen*, where the Court could have used neutrality as an adequate basis for decision, it chose instead to pursue the secular purpose theory. In following and expanding upon this theory, the Court said nothing about the alternative-

---

73. 392 U.S. at 254-55, 269-70.

74. Answering the argument that all teaching in a sectarian school is religious or that the processes of secular and religious training are so intertwined that secular textbooks furnished to students by the public are in fact instrumental in the teaching of religion, the Court said in the *Allen* case that nothing in the record supported the proposition that all textbooks are used by the parochial schools to teach religion. "We are unable to hold, based solely on judicial notice, that this statute results in unconstitutional involvement of the State with religious instruction." 392 U.S. at 248.

See Choper, *The Establishment Clause and Aid to Parochial Schools*, 56 CALIF. L. REV. 260 (1968).

75. Board of Educ. v. Allen, 392 U.S. 236, 249 (1968).

means test which it had intimated in the Sunday closing cases was a limitation on the application of the secular-purpose concept.[76]

IV. CONCLUSION

On the whole there can be no serious quarrel with the results reached by the Warren Court in the cases arising under the religion clauses of the first amendment. The Court, distinguished generally for its emphasis on libertarian values, has been sensitive and hospitable to claims made in the name of religious liberty—which encompasses a wide variety of values served by both the free exercise and establishment clauses. The free exercise clause has been employed effectively to protect discrete minorities, dissenters, and nonbelievers. The "compelling considerations of public policy" test has taken its place along with the "clear and present danger" test as a judicial vehicle for invalidating both direct and indirect restraints which operate in a substantial way to burden the free exercise of religion. Whatever other criticisms may be directed against the Warren Court, a fair reading of these opinions should dispel the notion that it has been hostile to religion.

A common thread running through the decisions under both of the religion clauses is an awareness of and sensitivity to the demands both for equality of treatment in a religiously pluralistic society and for special protection of minority groups against the claims and assumptions of the majority. The prayer and Bible-reading cases must ultimately rest on the consideration that religious exercises in public schools, though sanctioned by the majority, constitute a substantial threat to the liberty of nonconforming groups. Similarly, the Court's decision in *Allen* reflects a judicial appreciation of the pluralistic character of our educational system and the freedom of choice implicit within it.

Leaving aside the results, one may venture criticism of the way in which the Court handled some of the cases. *Braunfeld* seems clearly out of line with *Sherbert*, and it may be asked why the Court did not overrule it in the latter decision instead of distinguishing it on

---

76. *See* note 48 *supra* and accompanying text.

It may be argued abstractly that it is unnecessary for the state to help further the secular education of children attending parochial schools since they are free to attend the public schools in order to obtain a secular education. Omission of any consideration of the alternative means test in *Allen* may suggest that this test has no relevancy if the alternative means for achieving the intended public benefit requires the sacrifice of important constitutional freedoms.

grounds that are hardly persuasive. A large part of the public furor aroused by Justice Black's blunt opinion in *Engel* might well have been avoided if the Court had given thought to the public impact of the decision and dealt more discreetly with the issue—as Justice Clark did in the later *Schempp* opinion. And, in turn, both decisions would have been strengthened had the Court bottomed the holdings on the psychologically coercive aspects of religious practices in the classroom.

The earlier analysis of the Court's interpretation of the establishment clause points up the continued failure to resolve the ambiguities, if not inconsistencies, bequeathed by the opinions of the pre-Warren era. Although neutrality appears to have emerged as the dominant theme, the cases reveal no clear perception of what is meant by neutrality. How is it reconciled with the separation principle stressed in the language of *Everson?* Does neutrality yield to a superior demand of religious liberty? Is there a difference between "secular purpose" and "neutrality"? And is the Court prepared to push the "alternative means" test as a limitation on secular purpose? The resolution of these questions depends upon a systematic analysis and ordering of the values implicit in the religion clauses of the first amendment. This is a task the Warren Court will pass on to its successor. Ironically, by opening up the floodgates to litigation in the *Flast* decision, the Warren Court has made certain that the post-Warren Court will have the opportunity to undertake this task.

"UNINHIBITED, ROBUST, AND WIDE-OPEN"—
A NOTE ON FREE SPEECH AND
THE WARREN COURT

*Harry Kalven, Jr.**

THERE are several ways to give at the outset, in quick summary, an over-all impression of the Warren Court in the area of the first amendment. The quotation in the title can for many reasons be taken as its trademark. The quotation comes, of course, from a statement about public debate made in the Court's pre-eminent decision, *New York Times v. Sullivan,*[1] and it carries echoes of Alexander Meiklejohn.[2] We have, according to Justice Brennan, "a profound national commitment to the principle that debate on public issues should be uninhibited, robust, and wide-open . . . ."[3] What catches the eye is the daring, unconventional selection of adjectives. These words capture the special quality of the Court's stance toward first amendment issues. They express the gusto and enthusiasm with which the Court has tackled such issues. They indicate an awareness that heresy is robust; that counterstatement on public issues, if it is to be vital and perform its function, may not always be polite. And, most significantly, they express a desire to make a fresh statement about the principles of free speech rather than simply repeat the classic phrases of Holmes in *Abrams*[4] and Brandeis in *Whitney.*[5] The Court is interested enough to be minting contemporary epigrams—to be making it its own.

For a further impression of the Court's work in the first amendment field, we might turn to the 1959 case involving *Lady Chatterly's Lover* in movie form, *Kingsley Pictures Corp. v. Regents.*[6] Chiefly because of an inability to agree on precisely how the court below had disposed of the case, the Supreme Court, although unanimous in reversing, found it necessary to produce six separate opinions.[7] Of particular interest for the moment is Justice Stewart's opinion: he

---

* Professor of Law, University of Chicago. A.B. 1935, J.D. 1938, University of Chicago.—Ed.

1. 376 U.S. 254 (1964).

2. Meiklejohn, *Free Speech in Relation to Self-Government,* republished in A. MEIKLEJOHN, POLITICAL FREEDOM (1960); *cf.* Kalven, *The New York Times Case: A Note on the Central Meaning of the First Amendment,* 1964 SUP. CT. REV. 191, 221; Brennan, *The Supreme Court and the Meiklejohn Interpretation of the First Amendment,* 79 HARV. L. REV. 1 (1965).

3. 376 U.S. 254, 270 (1964).

4. Abrams v. United States, 250 U.S. 616 (1919).

5. Whitney v. California, 274 U.S. 357 (1927).

6. 360 U.S. 684 (1959).

7. *See* Kalven, *The Metaphysics of the Law of Obscenity,* 1960 SUP. CT. REV. 1, 28-34.

read the court below as banning the movie because it had dealt too sympathetically with adultery. In meeting this objection he was moved to restate the basic principle with notable freshness:

> It is contended that the State's action was justified because the motion picture attractively portrays a relationship which is contrary to the moral standards, the religious precepts, and the legal code of its citizenry. This argument misconceives what it is that the Constitution protects. Its guarantee is not confined to the expression of ideas that are conventional or shared by a majority. It protects advocacy of the opinion that adultery may sometimes be proper no less than advocacy of socialism or the single tax. And in the realm of ideas it protects expression which is eloquent no less than that which is unconvincing.[8]

Again what strikes the special note is not just the firm grasp of the basic principle but the gallantry, if you will, of its restatement. It is easier to champion freedom for the thought we hate than for the thought that embarrasses.

Yet another way of reducing to quick summary the special quality of this Court with regard to first amendment issues is to compare the opinions in *Curtis Publishing Company v. Butts*,[9] decided in 1967, with the opinion in *Debs v. United States*.[10] The *Debs* case was decided March 10, 1919, exactly one week after *Schenck*[11] had launched the clear-and-present-danger formula. In an opinion by Justice Holmes, the Court affirmed Debs' conviction (carrying a ten-year prison sentence) for attempting to incite insubordination, disloyalty, mutiny, and refusal of duty in the armed forces and for attempting to obstruct the recruiting and enlistment service of the United States in violation of the Espionage Act of 1917. The overt conduct of Debs consisted solely in making a public speech to a general adult audience in Canton, Ohio. At the time he was a major national political figure, and in 1920 he was to run as the Socialist candidate for President from prison and receive over 900,000 votes.[12]

The speech itself, which is summarized in Justice Holmes' opinion, involved a criticism of war in general and World War I in particular from a Socialist point of view. It asserted, for example, that "the master class has always declared the war and the subject class has always fought the battles . . . ."[13] It expressed sympathy for several others already convicted for their opposition to the war, say-

---

8. 360 U.S. at 688-89.
9. 388 U.S. 130 (1967).
10. 249 U.S. 211 (1919).
11. Schenck v. United States, 249 U.S. 47 (1919).
12. There is a discussion of the case and its background in Z. CHAFEE, FREE SPEECH IN THE UNITED STATES 84-86 (1941).
13. 249 U.S. 211, 213 (1919).

ing that "if they were guilty so was he."[14] It appears that most of the speech was devoted to Socialist themes apart from the war, and it concluded with the exhortation: "Don't worry about the charge of treason to your masters; but be concerned about the treason that involves yourselves."[15] During the trial Debs addressed the jury himself and stated: "I have been accused of obstructing the war. I admit it. Gentlemen, I abhor war. I would oppose the war if I stood alone."[16]

The Court disposed of the case in a perfunctory two-page opinion, treating as the chief question whether a jury could find that "one purpose of the speech, whether incidental or not does not matter, was to oppose not only war in general but this war, and that the opposition was so expressed that its natural and intended effect would be to obstruct recruiting."[17] The first amendment defense exacted only the following sentence from Justice Holmes: "The chief defenses upon which the defendant seemed willing to rely were the denial that we have dealt with and that based upon the First Amendment to the Constitution, disposed of in *Schenck v. United States* . . . ."[18] The decision was unanimous and without any comment from Justice Brandeis.[19]

Let us now jump a half century to *Butts*. At issue there was a judgment under state law in a libel action brought by a noted football coach against a national magazine for an article which in effect accused him of "fixing" a college football game by giving his team's secrets in advance of the game to the opposing coach. The case produced an elaborate outpouring of opinions and an intricate pattern of votes in the five-to-four decision affirming the judgment. All Justices agreed that since Butts was a public figure, the reporting of his activities was in the public domain and therefore the state libel law was subject to the discipline of the first amendment. The Justices divided over what level of privilege the defendant publisher must be given to satisfy the constitutional concern with freedom of

---

14. 249 U.S. at 214.

15. 249 U.S. at 214.

16. 249 U.S. at 214.

17. 249 U.S. at 215.

18. 249 U.S. at 215. Holmes' reaction makes it evident that the clear-and-present-danger dictum did not in his mind become a constitutional test until sometime after *Schenck*. Professor Chafee has suggested Holmes was waiting for *Abrams*: "Looking backward, however, we see that Justice Holmes was biding his time until the Court should have before it a conviction so clearly wrong as to let him speak out his deepest thoughts about the First Amendment." Z. CHAFEE, FREE SPEECH IN THE UNITED STATES 86 (1941). It would be a worthwhile task to explore what it meant about Justice Holmes that he could see *Abrams* but not *Debs* as the "clearly wrong" case.

19. It did, however, evoke an eloquent shocked dissent from Professor Ernst Freund of The University of Chicago Law School. See Freund, *The Debs Case and Freedom of Speech*, NEW REPUBLIC, May 3, 1919, at 13.

speech. Three separate positions were expressed: Justices Black and Douglas would have granted an absolute or unqualified privilege not defeasible by any showing of malice. At the other extreme, Justice Harlan, joined by Justices Clark, Fortas, and Stewart, held the privilege defeated by a showing of "highly unreasonable conduct constituting an extreme departure from the standards of investigation and reporting ordinarily adhered to by responsible journalists." The middle ground was occupied by Justices Brennan, White, and the Chief Justice, who would have adhered to the standards set forth in *New York Times* and thus would have held the privilege defeasible by actual malice—defined as "knowing falsehood or reckless disregard for truth." Out of this unpromising and apparently trivial factual context came deeply felt essays on freedom of speech by Justices Harlan, Black, and the Chief Justice.[20] In wondering about all this on another occasion, I observed:

> This is perhaps the fitting moment to pause to marvel at the pattern of the Court's argument on this issue. The Court was divided 5 to 4 on whether the constitutional standard for the conditional privilege of those who libel public figures is that it be defeasible only upon a showing of reckless disregard for truth or merely on a showing of an extreme departure from professional newspaper standards! Further it was understood that the chief significance of the standard relates simply to how jury instructions will be worded. Yet this nuance triggered a major debate in the court on the theory of free speech.[21]

And in speculating on why these issues held such extraordinary power to move the Supreme Court—after noting that in the sequence of cases following *New York Times* the Court had located a novel and difficult issue involving "public speech interlaced with comments on individuals"—I could only add: "Second, it shows once again—and it is a splendid thing—that all members of this Court care deeply about free speech values and their proper handling by law. Only a concerned Court would have worked so hard on such a problem."[22]

The difference between *Debs* and *Butts* is a measure of how much the Court's approach to free speech has changed over the years since World War I. And it is a difference, it will be noted, in result, in theory, in style, and, above all, in concern.[23]

---

20. The details on the judicial patterns are analyzed in Kalven, *The Reasonable Man and the First Amendment: Hill, Butts and Walker*, 1967 SUP. CT. REV. 267.

21. *Id.* at 307.

22. *Id.* at 308.

23. Of course, by no means is all of this difference to be attributed to the Warren Court, *but see* text part II *infra*. Two other recent decisions clamor for comparison with the *Debs* case: Bond v. Floyd, 385 U.S. 116 (1966), where the Court enjoined the

But even as one acknowledges the deep concern of this Court for the first amendment, there is need to pause at the outset for a perplexity and an irony. The perplexity is one that must have troubled all the contributors to this Symposium: What exactly is one referring to when he speaks of the Warren Court?[24] Are we simply using the Chief Justiceship as a device to mark off a span of years? Would it have been any more arbitrary to talk of the work of the Court from, say, 1958 to 1964? If we find some distinctive traits in that work, as both friends and critics of the Court are so readily prone to do in the first amendment area, to whom are we ascribing them? To some durable *team* of Justices? To the special influence of the Chief? The Court's roster during the Warren years has included some seventeen Justices, and the "Warren Court" has for varying periods of time numbered among its members Justices Minton, Burton, Clark, Whittaker, Reed, Jackson, Goldberg, and Frankfurter.[25] Perhaps we should adapt the old Greek conundrum and ask if we can comment on the same Court twice.

I would hesitate to adopt the alternative and say that what unifies the topic is the distinctive influence of the Chief Justice on the Court's response to the first amendment. This would require not only that we find a distinctive pattern of decisions, but that we connect it up somehow to the chairmanship of the Chief—which seems to me to attribute excessive power to that office.

But perhaps I am being too solemn about it all. There has indeed been a kind of first amendment team: Black and Douglas have been on the Court during the entire tenure of the Chief Justice. Brennan and Harlan were appointed in 1956, and Stewart in 1958. And it is the analysis and response of these six Justices to the first amendment that I have chiefly in mind in considering the Warren

---

Georgia legislature from refusing to seat Julian Bond for making a speech expressing "sympathy and support for the men in this country who are unwilling to respond to a military draft"; and United States v. O'Brien, 391 U.S. 367 (1968) where the Court upheld against a first amendment challenge the federal statute making it a felony knowingly to destroy or mutilate a draft card. In some respects the *O'Brien* case is reminiscent of the Court's response in *Debs* and perhaps indicates that no Supreme Court has yet acted with much independence about speech during wartime. In any event, one careful commentator has found the treatment of the first amendment issues in the *O'Brien* case "astonishingly cavalier." Alfange, *Free Speech and Symbolic Conduct: The Draft Card Burning Case*, 1968 SUP. CT. REV. 1.

24. It should be acknowledged that Professor Cox in his lively and lucid review of the Court's work was able to proceed effectively without any prefatory worries over the unity of the topic. A. COX, THE WARREN COURT (1968). The book begins: "The appointment of Earl Warren as Chief Justice of the United States in 1953 marked the opening of a new period in our constitutional development."

25. *See* the convenient chart of the Justices in W. LOCKHART, Y. KAMISAR, & J. CHOPER, CONSTITUTIONAL RIGHTS AND LIBERTIES, app. A (2d ed. 1967).

Court's reaction to free speech issues.[26] At least we match here the rough unity of topic provided, say, by talk of the greatness of the New York Yankees in the middle 1920's.[27]

The irony, of course, is that it is still the Warren Court—at least temporarily. Due to the vagaries of everyone's politics, the October term has opened with Earl Warren back in his customary center seat. The wretched controversy over the Fortas appointment was interpreted widely as an attack more on the Court as a whole than on Justice Fortas. The Senate was presumably providing its own commentary on the work of the Warren Court. And for our immediate purposes, it is striking how much of the Senate's concern was with the work of the Court in the first amendment area. There is a temptation to brood over the gap which appears to have been created between the first amendment values the Court has championed and those the public, or a considerable segment of the public, will tolerate. Is there, then, a *political* limit on the meaning of the first amendment? Two offsetting considerations should, in any event, be noted. The Senate's free-speech grievances related almost exclusively, so far as I could tell, to the decisions on obscenity and did not put in issue the striking work of the Court in other areas of first amendment concern.[28] Further, such a gap between public and judicial attitudes may be a healthy sign. The tradition has never been that freedom of speech was a value to be left to majority vote; indeed, that may be the whole point of the first amendment and of judicial review under it.

I.

At the Museum of Science and Industry in Chicago there is a chart which occupies a long wall and which graphs over time the changes in human technology. The time span is some 50,000 years, and the introduction of each technological advance—from the first crude stone used as a tool for digging to today's latest electronic or space age wonders—is entered on the graph. The result is a stunning visual impression of the acceleration of cultural inheritance. Man has made more major technical advances in the past 100 years than in the previous 49,900!

---

26. It is arguable that the core of the Warren Court, at least for first amendment cases, has really been just the four: Justice Brennan, Justice Stewart, the Chief Justice, and Justice Harlan. While Justices Black and Douglas have joined in the decisions, they have often stood somewhat apart in matters of doctrine as in obscenity, libel, and congressional committee sequences.

27. You know—Ruth, Gehrig, Meusel, Lazzeri, Combs, Hoyt, et al.

28. However, The Chicago Tribune, Oct. 13, 1968, carried an editorial on the Court entitled, "Will the Supreme Court Mend Its Ways?" which listed and expressed displeasure over some eleven decisions inhibiting the control of subversive activities.

There is a general analogy here to the making of law. Invention seems to breed invention, and precedent breeds more precedent. But I cite the Museum wall to make a specific point about the Warren Court. If one were to imagine a comparable scheme charting the incidence of first amendment cases from 1791 to date, the parallel would be striking indeed; we would get a proper sense of the accelerated accumulation of first amendment precedents in the past fifteen years. The point is, I think, a neutral one. It goes for the moment not to the quality of the Court's answers but to its willingness to confront first amendment questions at an unprecedented rate. The result is that a great part of the law, and a greater part of what is of interest today to the teacher or commentator, is the work of the Warren Court.

Even the quickest survey makes the point. All of the constitutional decisions on obscenity have come from this Court, starting with *Roth*[29] in 1957; if one is interested in law and obscenity he will perforce find himself studying essentially the work of the Warren Court.[30] Similarly, the constitutional law on libel has—with the exception of *Beauharnais*[31] in 1952—come from this Court, starting with *New York Times*[32] in 1964. And, moving to areas where there was some prior precedent, the impression is not much changed. Think what *Watkins*,[33] *Barenblatt*,[34] *Sweezy*,[35] *Uphaus*,[36] *Braden*,[37] *Wilkinson*,[38] *Yellin*,[39] *Gibson*,[40] and *DeGregory*[41] have added to the law on congressional investigating committees; the precedents previously consisted of little more than *Kilbourn v. Thompson*[42] in 1881, *McGrain v. Daugherty*[43] in 1927, and *Rumely v. United States*[44] in 1953. Or, to take one final ready example, think of the law on use of the public forum: the major stimulus to the development of this body of law provided by the Jehovah's Witnesses in the 1930's and

---

29. 354 U.S. 476 (1957).

30. *See* Kalven, *supra* note 7; Magrath, *The Obscenity Cases: Grapes of Roth*, 1966 Sup. Ct. Rev. 7.

31. Beauharnais v. Illinois, 343 U.S. 250 (1952).

32. 376 U.S. 254.

33. Watkins v. United States, 354 U.S. 178 (1957).

34. Barenblatt v. United States, 360 U.S. 109 (1959).

35. Sweezy v. New Hampshire, 354 U.S. 234 (1957).

36. Uphaus v. Wyman, 360 U.S. 72 (1959).

37. Braden v. United States, 365 U.S. 431 (1961).

38. Wilkinson v. United States, 365 U.S. 399 (1961).

39. Yellin v. United States, 374 U.S. 109 (1963).

40. Gibson v. Florida Legislative Investigation Comm., 372 U.S. 539 (1963).

41. DeGregory v. Attorney General of New Hampshire, 383 U.S. 825 (1966).

42. 103 U.S. 168.

43. 273 U.S. 135.

44. 345 U.S. 41.

early 1940's[45] has been overshadowed by the notable contributions of the Warren Court in *Garner v. Louisiana,*[46] *Edwards v. South Carolina,*[47] *Cox v. Louisiana,*[48] *Brown v. Louisiana,*[49] and *Adderley v. Florida.*[50]

Let me approach the matter a little less impressionistically. Taking Lockhart, Kamisar, and Choper's casebook, *Constitutional Rights and Liberties,* we can make the point in rough quantitative terms. The book is intensely concerned with first amendment issues, and the latest edition[51] devotes some 340 pages to them. The editors rate eighty-nine cases worthy of special study; of these, a total of fifty-five, or over 60 per cent, have been decided by the Warren Court.

There is perhaps one other way of putting into perspective how much the Warren Court has enriched the constitutional doctrine of freedom of speech, press, and assembly. It is to compare the classic book in the field, Chafee's *Free Speech in the United States,* first published in 1920 and republished in elaborated form in 1941, with the current corpus of law. A book today performing the function of Chafee's volume would look notably different, deal to a considerable degree with different principles, and confront to a considerable extent different problems. If the analytic density of the Chafee book were to be maintained, the contemporary treatment would surely require two volumes; and the second volume would be devoted to the work of the Warren Court.

II.

It is not feasible within the compass of this Article to attempt a systematic review of the results the Court has achieved in the various areas of first amendment law. I should prefer, therefore, to check off briefly some of the new *ideas* the Court has introduced into the field.

New York Times may have effected a major alteration in official thinking about free speech. To begin with, the Court introduced the attractive notion that the first amendment has a "central meaning" and thus suggested the possibility of a "core" theory of free speech. The central meaning suggested in *Times* appears to be the notion that seditious libel is not actionable.

It must be admitted that the promise of radical rethinking of the

---

45. *See* Kalven, *The Concept of the Public Forum: Cox v. Louisiana,* 1965 Sup. Ct. Rev. 1.

46. Garner v. Louisiana, 368 U.S. 157 (1961).

47. 372 U.S. 229 (1963).

48. 379 U.S. 536 (1965).

49. 383 U.S. 131 (1966).

50. 385 U.S. 39 (1966).

51. 1967.

theory and rationale of the first amendment which this invites has not as yet been judicially pursued.[52] The Court has been careful, however, to preserve the status of *New York Times* as a key precedent.[53] The Court has also made visible a new kind of problem in *Times* and its sequelae: the question of whether falsity in fact as contrasted with falsity in doctrine is entitled to any protection. This problem arises when discussion of issues in the public domain is interlaced with statements of fact about particular individuals. The issue is whether in protecting the individual's interest in reputation or privacy we will give him a veto power over the general discussion. This was the problem in *Times* itself and again in *Time Inc. v. Hill, Butts,* and *Associated Press v. Walker*; it looms as a large issue since much public discussion appears to have this mixed quality.[54] The dilemma is a difficult one, but the Court has confronted it and, to my mind, has made real progress toward a satisfactory solution.

Perhaps equally important is the abrogation of outmoded ideas by the Court; the most significant step here, I suggest, has been the great reduction in the status and prestige of the clear-and-present-danger test. Immediately prior to the advent of the Warren Court, this test had a considerable claim as *the* criterion of the constitutionality of an exercise of governmental authority over communication. In limited areas the test may still be alive, but it has been conspicuous by its absence from opinions in the last decade. Since the test—whatever sense it may have made in the limited context in which it originated—is clumsy and artificial when expanded into a general criterion of permissible speech, the decline in its fortunes under the Warren Court seems to be an intellectual gain.

Another major conceptual contribution of the Warren Court has been development of the idea of self-censorship. A regulation of communication may run afoul of the Constitution not because it is aimed directly at free speech, but because in operation it may trigger a set of behavioral consequences which amount in effect to people censoring themselves in order to avoid trouble with the law. The idea has appeared in several cases, and, while the Court has not yet addressed a major opinion to it, it has all the earmarks of a seminal concept. The cases have varied in context from *Speiser v.*

---

52. See note 2 *supra.*

53. Kalven, *The Reasonable Man and the First Amendment: Hills, Butts and Walker,* 1967 Sup. Ct. Rev. 267, 308.

54. This appears to be an instance of a general problem. Compare Judge Hand's comment on another instance of utterances with "a double aspect." United States v. Dennis, 183 F.2d 201 (2d Cir. 1950). *See also* Kalven, *supra* note 7, at 11-12.

Randall,[55] to *Smith v. California,*[56] to *Time Inc. v. Hill.*[57] In *Speiser* the Court invalidated a state statute requiring affidavits of non-Communist affiliation as a condition for a tax exemption. The vice was a subtle one: as the Court understood the state procedure, the affidavit was not conclusive; thus the burden of proof of nonsubversion was left on the applicant. The Court stated:

> The vice of the present procedure is that, where the particular speech falls close to the line separating the lawful and the unlawful, the possibility of mistaken factfinding—inherent in all litigation—will create the danger that the legitimate utterance will be penalized. The man who knows that he must bring forth proof and persuade another of the lawfulness of his conduct necessarily must steer far wider of the unlawful zone than if the State must bear these burdens.[58]

In *Smith* the Court confronted an ordinance imposing strict criminal liability on the sellers of obscene books. Again, the Court found the vice in the chain of consequences such regulation might engender:

> By dispensing with any requirement of knowledge of the contents of the book on the part of the seller, the ordinance tends to impose a severe limitation on the public's access to constitutionally protected matter. For if the bookseller is criminally liable without knowledge of the contents, and the ordinance fulfills its purpose, he will tend to restrict the books he sells to those he has inspected; and thus the State will have imposed a restriction upon the distribution of constitutionally protected as well as obscene literature. . . . The bookseller's self-censorship, compelled by the State, would be a censorship affecting the whole public, hardly less virulent for being privately administered.[59]

Finally, in the context of tort liability for "false light" privacy, the Court in *Hill* conceptualized the problem as one of triggering self-censorship; it thus would give the publisher a conditional privilege defeasible only by actual malice:

> We create grave risk of serious impairment of the indispensable service of a free press in a free society if we saddle the press with the impossible burden of verifying to a certainty the facts associated in a news article with a person's name, picture or portrait, particularly as related to nondefamatory matter. Even negligence would be a most elusive standard especially when the content of the speech itself affords no warning of prospective harm to another through falsity.

---

55. 357 U.S. 513 (1958).
56. 361 U.S. 147 (1959).
57. 385 U.S. 374 (1967).
58. 357 U.S. 513, 526 (1958).
59. 361 U.S. 147, 153-54 (1959).

. . . Fear of large verdicts in damage suits for innocent or merely negligent misstatement, even the fear of expense involved in their defense, must inevitably cause publishers "to steer . . . wider of the unlawful zone . . . ."[60]

The Court is thus in command of a versatile concept which represents, I think, a fascinating addition to the vocabulary of first amendment doctrine. It should perhaps be acknowledged that the opinions in all three cases were written by Justice Brennan.

One other potentially powerful idea of the Warren Court should be noted: the principle that strict economy of means is required when communication is regulated. It is not enough that the end be legitimate; the means must not be wasteful of first amendment values. The seeds of this notion first appeared in *Schneider v. New Jersey*,[61] decided in 1939, which invalidated a prohibition against distributing leaflets where the governmental objective was to prevent littering the streets. But the idea was given its fullest expression by the Warren Court in *Shelton v. Tucker*,[62] which voided a state statute requiring each school teacher as a condition of employment to file annually an affidavit listing every organization to which he had belonged or contributed in the preceding five years. The Court found that, although the state had a legitimate interest in the organizational commitments of its teachers, the statute gratuitously overshot its target. Justice Stewart stated the principle this way:

> In a series of decisions this Court has held that, even though the governmental purpose be legitimate and substantial, that purpose cannot be pursued by means that broadly stifle fundamental personal liberties when the end can more narrowly be achieved. The breadth of legislative abridgment must be viewed in the light of less drastic means for achieving the same basic purpose.[63]

It remains to be seen whether this principle, too, will be seminal. There is more than a suggestion in it of a preferred-position thesis. Legislation regulating communication may not be presumptively unconstitutional today, but under the economy principle it will not be entitled to, in Holmes' phrase, "a penumbra" of legislative convenience.[64]

---

60. 385 U.S. 374, 389 (1967).
61. 308 U.S. 147.
62. 364 U.S. 479 (1960).
63. 364 U.S. at 479.
64. Dissenting in Schlesinger v. Wisconsin, 270 U.S. 230, 241 (1926): ("But the law allows a penumbra to be embraced that goes beyond the outline of its object in order that the object may be secured.") There is another group of related cases dealing with vagueness and requiring precision in phrasing to avoid ambiguity. *See, e.g.,* Elfbrandt v. Russell, 384 U.S. 11 (1966); Keyishian v. Board of Regents, 385 U.S. 589 (1967); Aptheker v. United States, 378 U.S. 500 (1964); United States v. Robel, 389

III.

The momentum of the Warren Court in other areas of constitutional law has been the source of sustained controversy and criticism.[65] Without attempting to assess the merits of such criticism in general, I should like to explore whether in the special area of free speech the Court's work is subject to similar disapproval.

It has frequently been objected that the Court has moved too fast and in giant steps rather than with the gradual deliberation appropriate to the judicial process, that its opinions have often displayed inadequate craftsmanship, that it has failed to confront the issues and to rationalize its results with appropriate rigor. However, if we consider for a moment the work of the Court in two important areas—obscenity and the scope of the power of congressional investigating committees—these criticisms do not appear warranted. To be sure there had been, as we noted, no constitutional decisions whatsoever on the obscenity issue prior to 1957. But that was simply because such cases had not come before the Court; there was no general consensus that such regulation was constitutional. In fact, there had long been recognized a tension between obscenity regulation and the first amendment. It is enough to cite the widespread praise of Judge Woolsey's decision and opinion in the *Ulysses* case[66] to document the tension generally seen between the regulation of obscenity and the reach of the first amendment; by the time the Supreme Court entered the field in the *Roth* case, judges in other courts had explicitly noted the constitutional shadows.[67]

Moreover, in *Roth* the Court *upheld* the constitutionality of the obscenity regulation involved. In doing so, however, it recognized and attempted to define the constitutional limitations on such regulation. While in the past decade an unusual number of obscenity cases have reached the Supreme Court, the sequence of resulting decisions can fairly be characterized as involving the gradual resolution of limited and closely related problems on a case-by-case basis. Thus, *Kingsley Pictures*[68] resolved the problems of thematic obscenity; *Butler v. Michigan*[69] resolved the problems of regulation of

U.S. 258 (1967). Perhaps on close analysis the vagueness, economy, and self-censorship criteria can be made to converge.

65. *Cf.* Kurland, *The Supreme Court 1963 Term—Foreword: "Equal in Origin and Equal in Title to the Legislative and Executive Branches of the Government"*, 78 HARV. L. REV. 143 (1964); A. Cox, *supra* note 24.

66. United States v. One Book Called "Ulysses," 5 F. Supp. 182 (S.D.N.Y. 1934), *aff'd*, 72 F.2d 705 (2d Cir. 1934).

67. *See* the opinions of Judge Curtis Bok in Commonwealth v. Gordon, 66 Pa. D. & C. 101 (1949); and the concurring opinion of Judge Jerome Frank in the court below in the *Roth* case itself, 237 F.2d 796 (2d Cir. 1956).

68. 360 U.S. 684 (1959).

69. 352 U.S. 380 (1957).

general literature distribution keyed to what is suitable for children; and *Smith*[70] dealt with permissible regulation of booksellers. Moreover, *Manual Enterprises v. Day*[71] added the element of "patent offensiveness" to the constitutional definition of obscenity, and *Jacobellis v. Ohio*[72] attached the element of "utterly without redeeming significance." If there has been a jarring note, it has come not in accelerating the liberation of arts and letters from obscenity censorship, but rather from the sudden move in the opposite direction in *Ginzburg v. United States*[73] by adding the perplexing "pandering" element to the constitutional test.

It is true that the Court has been conspicuously unsuccessful in pleasing commentators or in reaching any consensus within itself as to how to handle obscenity cases. It is possible to detect at least six different doctrinal positions among the nine Justices. But this is due, I would suggest, to the intrinsic awkwardness of the problem rather than to a judicial failure to take the cases seriously or to face the issues squarely. In any event, the Court cannot be criticized for rushing past existing precedent in order to abolish censorship altogether.

Similarly, in cases involving congressional investigating committees, and in particular the House Un-American Activities Committee, the Court, while recognizing a first amendment shadow, has inched along case by case in an attempt to develop a formula of limitation. Again, the sheer frequency of cases at the Supreme Court level within the last decade is astonishing. In a number of cases— *Barenblatt*,[74] *Uphaus*,[75] *Braden*,[76] and *Wilkinson*[77]—the Court has upheld committee power and refused to inquire into the motives of the congressmen. In *Watkins*,[78] despite the stirring rhetoric of Chief Justice Warren's opinion, the actual decision was keyed to the technical requirement that the pertinency of the committee's questions must be made clear to a witness if he is to be legally compelled to answer. In *Yellin*,[79] the decision adverse to the committee rested simply on the committee's failure to follow its own procedural rules; in *Gibson*,[80] the Court was impressed by the committee's failure to establish a sufficient nexus or foundation for its questions; in *DeGregory*,[81] the crucial factor was the staleness of the questions.

70. 361 U.S. 147 (1959).
71. 370 U.S. 478 (1962).
72. 378 U.S. 184 (1964).
73. 383 U.S. 463 (1966).
74. Barenblatt v. United States, 360 U.S. 109 (1959).
75. Uphaus v. Wyman, 360 U.S. 72 (1959).
76. Braden v. United States, 365 U.S. 431 (1961).
77. Wilkinson v. United States, 365 U.S. 399 (1961).
78. Watkins v. United States, 354 U.S. 178 (1957).
79. Yellin v. United States, 374 U.S. 109 (1963).
80. Gibson v. Florida Legislative Investigation Comm., 372 U.S. 539 (1963).
81. DeGregory v. Attorney General of New Hampshire, 383 U.S. 825 (1966).

Thus far, the Court has recognized that compulsory disclosure to an investigating committee may inhibit freedom of speech and association, but it has found this loss a legitimate consequence of the state's interest in finding facts. Moreover, the Court has managed to withstand the argument of four dissenters[82] who have urged repeatedly that committee inquiries into subversion violate the first amendment. Here as with obscenity the Court has not found a satisfactory solution to the problems posed, but it has worked at them steadily, with circumspection, and without taking giant libertarian steps.

The congressional committee cases suggest one final point about the Warren Court and its critics—a point on which Archibald Cox recently commented.[83] Not infrequently the Court has been criticized for usurping power from other branches of government, for failing to seek solutions that would accommodate the separation of political power in our society. Yet in the congressional committee cases, although the Court has made evident its distaste for the excesses of committee inquiry, it has been careful when deciding against the committee to place its decision on grounds that would leave the power ultimately in Congress. Thus *if* the committee follows its own rules of procedure, *if* it makes the pertinency of its questions clear to the witness, *if* it avoids stale inquiries, and *if* it lays some foundation for examining the particular witness, the Supreme Court, as matters now stand, will ratify its power to compel answers to its questions.

We noted at the start that the topic of the Warren Court is an oblique, elusive one. Surely it would be easier to discuss straight away the substantive issues the Court has dealt with rather than to probe for some pattern of positions distinctive to the personality of this particular Court. Nevertheless, as we also said at the outset, there does seem to be a special trademark to this Court's work in the area of freedom of speech, press, and assembly. There is a zest for these problems and a creative touch in working with them. It has been noted that there are overtones of Alexander Meiklejohn in the Court's idiom. It may, therefore, not be inappropriate to turn to Mr. Meiklejohn for a final comment. Speaking of the principle of the first amendment, he once said: "We must think for it as well as fight for it."[84] The Warren Court in its enriching gloss on the amendment over the past fifteen years has done a good deal to help us do both.

---

82. *See* the dissents of Justices Black, Douglas, Brennan, and the Chief Justice in *Barenblatt, Uphaus, Braden,* and *Wilkinson.*

83. A. Cox, THE WARREN COURT 104-08 (1968).

84. A. MEIKLEJOHN, POLITICAL FREEDOM 6 (1960).

THE WARREN COURT AND THE PRESS

*John P. MacKenzie**

THE conventional wisdom about the relationship between the Warren Court and the news media runs something like this: With a few exceptions, the press corps is populated by persons with only a superficial understanding of the Court, its processes, and the values with which it deals. The Court has poured out pages of legal learning, but its reasoning has been largely ignored by a result-oriented news industry interested only in the superficial aspects of the Court's work. The Court can trace much of its "bad press," its "poor image," to the often sloppy and inaccurate work of news gatherers operating in mindless deadline competition. The competition to be first with the story has been the chief obstacle in these critical years to a better public understanding of the Court and of our liberties and laws.

The difficulty with this characterization is that it contains just enough truth to appear reasonably complete. This picture of the press, because it is plausible, unfortunately may actually mask difficulties that lie deeper both in the structure of complex news media and in the Court's practices as they affect both the media and the general public—difficulties which, if recognized, may provide some opportunities for better understanding of the Court. If the Warren Court has received an especially bad press, there is blame enough to go around for it; the Court and the press should each accept shares of the blame, but within each institution the blame must be reallocated.

If the ultimate history of the Warren Court includes a judgment that the press has been unfair to the institution, this surely ought to be labeled as ingratitude of the highest order. *New York Times Co. v. Sullivan*[1] and its progeny have carved out press freedoms to print news without fear of libel judgments under standards more generous and permissive to the fourth estate than the standards set by responsible newspapers for themselves. It is well that the Court has done so, and it is especially appropriate in a period when executive officials and political candidates have expressed mounting hostility toward the news media. Not only ideas, but men dealing in

---

* Supreme Court Reporter, *The Washington Post.* A.B. 1952, Amherst College; special student, Harvard University (Law School), 1964-1965.—Ed.
    1. 376 U.S. 254 (1964).

ideas and words, need breathing space to survive.[2] These great first amendment decisions contemplated that judges, like other public men, would suffer considerable personal abuse and that they must be rugged enough to take most of it,[3] but the Court surely did not mean to invite press treatment of itself that was unfair as well as highly critical.

Before discussing what the Court and the press have done to injure each other, it is worth noting that each has thrived somewhat on the developing relationships of the past decade and a half. By any definition of that elusive concept known as "news," an activist and innovative Supreme Court makes news and thus provides grist for the press. In turn, to an increasing degree, the press has been expanding its resources to cope with the flow of judicial news. Thus, the media have been giving the Court more exposure to the public.[4]

It must be stated, however, that the relationships between press and Court have been complex and difficult. Some of the problems are built into the systems of both institutions. The Court begins as a mystery, and the reporter or editor who fails to appreciate the fact that certain things about the Supreme Court will remain unknowable and consequently unprintable simply does not understand the situation. The Court's decisions are the start of an argument more often than they are the final, definitive word on a given subject. Opinions often are written in such a way that they mask the difficulties of a case rather than illuminate them. New decisions frequently cannot be reconciled with prior rulings because "policy considerations, not always apparent on the surface, are powerful agents of decision."[5]

Certainly not all the turmoil of the conference room spills over into the delivery of opinions. Secrecy at several levels both protects and obscures the Court and its work. The process of marshalling a Court, of compromise, of submerging dissents and concurrences, or

---

2. Libel plaintiffs usually sue newspapers—and not newsmen—for obvious reasons; but the pain felt by corporations at becoming libel defendants is often communicated to their employees.

3. *See* Garrison v. Louisiana, 379 U.S. 64 (1964).

4. *The New York Times, The Washington Post, The Washington Star,* and other newspapers have been represented at the Supreme Court for many years, as have the principal wire services, Associated Press and United Press International. In the past few years the *Los Angeles Times* and the Newhouse chain of newspapers, among others, have assigned specialist reporters to the Court. Ordinarily these reporters are also assigned to cover the Justice Department and other legal matters.

5. Malone v. Bowdoin, 369 U.S. 643, 650 (1962) (Douglas, J., dissenting).

of bringing them about, can only be imagined or deduced by the contemporary chronicler of the Court; history lags decades behind with its revelations of the Court's inner workings. This is not to say that newsmen need be privy to the Court's inner dealings, helpful as that might be, to describe its decisions accurately and well. But I would suggest that murky decision-reporting may be the reporting of murky decisions as well as the murky reporting of decisions.[6]

The handling of petitions for certiorari—a process replete with elements of subjectivity and perhaps even arbitrariness—eludes the attempts of newsmen to fathom, much less to communicate to the general public, the sense of what the Court is doing.[7] Certiorari action is the antithesis of what the Opinion of the Court is supposed to represent: a reasoned judicial action reasonably explained. Yet when the Court does speak through opinions, the press is frequently found lacking both in capacity for understanding and capacity for handling the material. Precious newspaper space, when it is available, often is wasted on trivia at the expense of reporting a decision's principal message and impact. Newspapers often fail to adjust to the abnormally large volume of material produced on a "decision day,"[8] or to the task of reporting the widespread implications of a landmark decision.[9]

Some of the demands made by the flow of Supreme Court news are beyond the capabilities of all newspapers; some are beyond the capacities of all but the newspapers most dedicated to complete coverage of the institution. For example, the actions of the last two

---

6. *See* the discussion of Reitman v. Mulkey, 387 U.S. 369 (1967), in A. Cox, THE WARREN COURT 43-50 (1968).

7. Editorial opinion by student law review writers or by journalists does not labor under the same handicaps that beset daily news reporting. *See, e.g.,* the caustic remarks about Johnson v. New Jersey, 384 U.S. 719 (1966), in *The Supreme Court, 1965 Term,* 80 HARV. L. REV. 91, 141 (1966); MacKenzie, *Equal Justice for a Lucky Few,* Washington Post, July 14, 1966, at page A 16, col. 8.

8. "Decision Monday," a tradition of opinion delivery dating back to the Civil War, has been modified somewhat by the Court's announcement of April 5, 1965, that henceforth it "will no longer adhere to the practice of reporting its decisions only at Monday sessions, and that in the future they will be reported as they become ready for decision at any session of the Court. As in the past, no announcement of decisions to be reported will be made prior to their rendition in open Court." However, the phrase "any session of the Court" has meant any day the Court has met to hear oral arguments, so that the final heavy load of a term's decisions still falls on the Mondays of May and June, after the oral arguments are completed.

9. The word "landmark" as applied to Supreme Court decisions should be eliminated from journalistic usage and perhaps English usage generally. Another candidate for extinction is the phrase "in effect," as in "The Court ruled in effect that . . . ." This phrase, at least as used by journalists, is nearly always followed by a mistake.

Mondays of the October 1963 term consume all of Volume 378 of the United States Reports. The decisions and orders of June 12, 1967, the final day of that term, are printed in Volume 388, which exceeds 580 pages. Many of these decisions have remained under advisement until the end of a term precisely because of their difficulty and complexity, elements that frequently correlate with newsworthiness. Many of them are sufficiently interesting to warrant substantial newspaper coverage, which often includes printing their full texts or excerpts. Many decisions generate, or should generate, "sidebar" or feature stories of their own on the same day. Supreme Court stories compete with each other for available column space, and all the Court news of a given day must in turn compete with all the other news from everywhere else in the world.

Between the Court and the press stands perhaps the most primitive arrangement in the entire communications industry for access to an important source of news material and distribution of the information generated by that source. On days of decision delivery, two dozen newsmen and newswomen gather in the press room on the ground floor of the Supreme Court Building to receive opinions in page proof form as they are delivered orally in the courtroom one floor above. Each Justice's contribution is passed out one opinion at a time, so that if there are, for example, several separate opinions in a cluster of three related cases,[10] the news reporter will not be able to tell what has happened until he has assembled his entire bundle of opinions one by one.

Upstairs in the courtroom, at a row of desks between the high bench and the counsel's podium, sit six newsmen (several more are seated elsewhere in the audience), three of whom represent the Associated Press, United Press International, and the Dow-Jones financial ticker. As opinions are delivered orally, Court messengers deliver printed copies to the six desks. The two wire service reporters send their copies through pneumatic tubes to fellow workers waiting in cubicles below. The AP reporter there, aided by an assistant, types out his stories and dictates them over the telephone to a stenographer at the office of the service's Washington bureau. The UPI reporter does essentially the same thing, but hands his copy to a tele-

---

10. *E.g.*, in the related cases of A Book Named "John Cleland's Memoirs of a Woman of Pleasure" v. Massachusetts, 383 U.S. 413 (1966), Ginzburg v. United States, 383 U.S. 463 (1966), and Mishkin v. New York, 383 U.S. 502 (1966), there were seventeen separate opinions.

type operator for direct transmission to the bureau office for editing. Reporters for the major afternoon newspapers must devise methods of their own for getting copy to their main offices. Reporters for morning papers do not have "all day" to perform the same tasks, but they have a much easier time of it at the moment of decision delivery. For example, they need not resort to the device used by their more time-pressed colleagues—that of preparing "canned" stories about petitions for certiorari that are released automatically when the Court announces its action granting or denying review. Such articles are prepared so that they can be transmitted with the insertion or change of a few words depending on the Court's order.[11]

The Court's clerical and semiclerical workings pose problems of their own. In the day-to-day coverage of the Supreme Court the reporter may encounter secrecy at every stage, not all of it necessary to the independent performance of the judicial function. There may be secret pleadings, of which one minor but colorful example will suffice. On December 4, 1967, the Court denied review to two topless, and by definition newsworthy, young ladies from Los Angeles, whose petition claimed first amendment protection for their chosen form of expression.[12] The ladies sought relief from the toils of prosecution by means of a petition for a writ of habeas corpus—a remedy that was intriguing in itself—but had been spurned by the lower courts. Unbeknownst to the press, which was inclined to take the petition at face value, the Court was in receipt of a letter, actually a responsive pleading, notifying the Justices that the defendants were pursuing normal appellate remedies at the same time. This information made their petition much less urgent and it might well have chilled the press interest in the case as well as the Court's. Only Justice Douglas noted his vote in favor of review. The letter was lodged in a correspondence file, a fact which this reporter learned by accident after his and other news stories about the case had been printed.

There also may be secret correspondence which does not amount to a pleading but which nevertheless may shape the outcome of a case or materially affect the writing of an opinion. In *Rees v. Peyton*,[13] a court-appointed attorney in a capital case communicated to

---

11. For a fuller discussion of the mechanics of the decision-distributing process, *see* Newland, *Press Coverage of the United States Supreme Court*, 17 W. POL. Q. 15 (1964); D. GREY, THE SUPREME COURT AND THE NEWS MEDIA (1968).

12. Bennett v. California, 389 U.S. 985 (1967).

13. 384 U.S. 312 (1966), *held over until further order*, 386 U.S. 989 (1967).

the Court by letter the fact that his client wanted to dismiss his petition, a suicidal step which counsel was understandably resisting. Again, the communication was placed in a correspondence file apart from the remainder of the record. A request to see the correspondence was denied by the Clerk's office, initially on grounds that it might invade the lawyer-client relationship and later on no grounds at all. At length the letter was released. Similarly, it might be noted that the celebrated communication from J. Edgar Hoover, Director of the Federal Bureau of Investigation, regarding FBI interrogation practices—one which figured importantly in the Chief Justice's opinion in *Miranda v. Arizona*[14]—has not been made public despite requests for access to it.

There may also be secret exhibits, such as the one requested from the bench by the Chief Justice in *Giles v. Maryland*,[15] which may prove decisive in a case. There may even be secret petitions for certiorari in a controversy not involving national security; this occurred recently in a bitterly fought domestic relations case from Maryland.[16] And, although the Court's press room is supposed to have available all briefs that are filed, the word "filed" is a term of art meaning "accepted for filing with the Court." This excludes many papers which the Justices see, including many amicus curiae briefs lodged with the Court pending its disposition of a motion for leave to file when one or both parties has objected to the filing. The "deferred appendix" method authorized by the 1967 revisions in the Supreme Court's rules[17] means that more major briefs will be formally on file with the Court in proof form; however, the briefs, while available for inspection if the fact of filing is known to the news reporter, do not become available generally until later when printed copies are delivered to the Court.

In what way, then, have these ingredients—the nature of the Court's work, the lack of capacity on the part of the press, and the Court's own administrative habits—combined to influence the public's view of the Supreme Court? Examples abound in which the principal cause of public confusion must be laid to one or another

---

14. 384 U.S. 436, 483-86 (1966). The author does not claim that the Hoover correspondence or that of Solicitor General Marshall contains anything not summarized in the opinion.

15. 386 U.S. 66, 74-80 (1967).

16. *In re* Malmstedt, 385 U.S. 976 (1966), denying certiorari and granting respondent's motion to "seal the records and preserve anonymity."

17. *See, e.g.,* Rule 36, 388 U.S. 967.

of these elements.[18] The examples are to be found primarily in the areas of deepest controversy: race relations, use of confessions in criminal cases, reapportionment, obscenity, and religion.[19]

In the area of the Warren Court's central achievement, the promotion of equal treatment for racial minorities, the Court must take some share of the blame for the bad press it received. One source of difficulty was the famous footnote 11 in *Brown v. Board of Education*,[20] which cited "modern authority" as to the state of psychological knowledge about the detrimental effects of state-imposed segregated education. The importance of the gratuitous footnote was emphasized out of all proportion by segregationists, and at least by hindsight it seems to have been inevitable that this should be so. The press contributed to the difficulty not so much by misreporting the opinion as by failing to muster the depth of understanding to place the footnote in perspective by comparing "modern authority" with the amateur sociology used by the nineteenth century Court.[21]

In the field of criminal law, another area in which the Warren Court has made headlines, one may again see the difficulty of attributing blame. As with civil rights, it is virtually certain that most members of the general public literally know about the Supreme Court's work in this area only what they have read in the newspapers,

---

18. Accusations of slanted reporting pure and simple are beyond the intended scope of this discussion, partly because, while the Court may have suffered in peculiar ways from press bias, it is not unique among governmental institutions as a victim. Unquestionably, one might cite examples such as the contrasting ways in which the controversial labor case, Textile Workers v. Darlington Co., 380 U.S. 263 (1965), was described at the time of oral argument. *Compare* N.Y. Times, Dec. 10, 1964, at 46, col. 4 ("The right of management to terminate a business operation on grounds of its own choosing was confronted by its most direct legal challenge in the Supreme Court today.") *with* N.Y. Times, Dec. 10, 1964, at 54, col. 4 ("As framed in proceedings before the National Labor Relations Board, the case before the Court did not present the basic question of a company's desire to go out of business altogether. The issue was, rather, the right to close one unit in a multi-unit enterprise.")

19. *See, e.g.,* the discussion of the public school prayer and Bible-reading cases and the press treatment of them in J. CLAYTON, THE MAKING OF JUSTICE 15-23 *et passim* (1964).

20. 347 U.S. 483, 494-95 (1954).

21. A journalist has placed the footnote in better perspective. *See* A. LEWIS, PORTRAIT OF A DECADE 15-31 (1964). The sequels to *Brown*, which opened other areas of government action and human experience to scrutiny under the equal protection clause, were no less susceptible of misunderstanding and speculation in the press. The use of per curiam opinions to deal with segregation in parks, swimming pools, and the like has been commented upon for years by legal specialists. *E.g.,* H. WECHSLER, PRINCIPLES, POLITICS OF FUNDAMENTAL LAW 31 (1961). The fact that academicians registered complaints and expressed confusion months and years later ought to give some comfort to the newsmen who tried to explain these orders to the public the same day they were issued.

heard on the radio, or seen on television. Mixed though the picture may be, it has become clear at least to this writer that press misinterpretation of *Escobedo*,[22] *Miranda*,[23] and *Wade*,[24] to name several of the most controversial decisions, has not been the fault of the "regular" reporters at the Supreme Court, whether writers for wire services or daily newspapers. These decisions probably were reported more accurately under the deadline pressure of decision day than they have been reported since that time.

In *Escobedo*, for example, it was widely and correctly reported at the time of decision that the suspect's incriminating statements had been ruled inadmissible because he had been denied access to counsel who had already been retained and who was figuratively beating on the interrogation room door while the petitioner was being questioned in disregard of his express wish to consult his lawyer. Since his release from the murder charge against him, Danny Escobedo has been embroiled with the law many times; finally, in 1968, he was convicted on federal criminal charges. Yet, in most of the news accounts about the later life of Danny Escobedo, the Court's initial decision has been described as one which threw out his confession on grounds that police refused to let him see *"a lawyer."*[25] *Miranda* may have mooted the distinction, at least for trials starting after June 13, 1966, but surely the fact that Escobedo was denied permission to consult a previously retained attorney makes a difference to an evaluation of the situation that confronted the now-notorious petitioner. Given the actual factual setting, the ruling seems less based on a "technicality"[26] or excessive solicitude for a criminal.

Fairness demands acknowledgment that writers of subsequent news reports dealing with any Supreme Court decision may them-

---

22. Escobedo v. Illinois, 378 U.S. 478 (1964).
23. Miranda v. Arizona, 384 U.S. 436 (1966).
24. United States v. Wade, 388 U.S. 218 (1967).
25. *See, e.g.*, Washington Post, Feb. 21, 1968, at A21, col. 1 (Associated Press dispatch); editorial, Huntington Herald-Dispatch (W. Va.), quoted in 114 Cong. Rec. 1236 (daily ed. Feb. 14, 1968).
26. "Technicality" is another term that should be eliminated from the journalist's vocabulary. In newspaper usage the term, properly translated, usually means that the reporter did not understand the basis for the decision or considered it too complicated for the reader. But "technicality" is actually a loaded word. Justice Frankfurter extolled procedural safeguards as the basis of liberty, while Senator Thurmond of South Carolina berated Justice Fortas for the Court's decision in Mallory v. United States [354 U.S. 449 (1957)] which he described as the use of "technicalities." *Hearings on the Nominations of Abe Fortas and Homer Thornberry Before the Senate Comm. on the Judiciary*, 90th Cong., 2d Sess. 191 (1968).

selves be working under considerable deadline pressure, and usually they suffer from the added handicap of not having immediate access to the written texts of the Court's opinions. An after-dinner speaker may opine that the Supreme Court would throw out the confession of a man who walked up to a policeman on a street corner and told him of a crime he had just committed. The speaker might also say, as indeed members of the United States Senate were fond of saying during the battle over the nomination of Justice Fortas to replace Chief Justice Warren, that the Court "has made it impossible to prohibit or punish the showing of indecent movies to children."[27] What does the reporter do when confronted by such statements while on an otherwise routine assignment to cover the speech? His only source of help may be the newspaper's legal correspondent, if there is one and if he is sufficiently knowledgeable in such matters; the legal correspondent may be able to furnish information for a brief statement in the story, telling, for the benefit of the uninformed reader, what the Court actually did or said.

Inaccuracies of this nature are not the product solely of newspapers which are short on resources and reporting personnel or lack a regular correspondent at the Supreme Court. For example, *The New York Times* printed an editorial summarizing a number of post-*Miranda* confession rulings in the courts of New York. The editorial deplored the release of the confessed murderer of his wife and five children who was "freed under the rules laid down by the United States Supreme Court."[28] The newspaper came close to pinpointing the problem that the case presented. The defendant's confession had been elicited *before* the date of the *Miranda* decision but his trial occurred *afterward*. The editorial stated:

> These confessions fell into a twilight zone that unpredictably blanketed defendants under charges and awaiting trial when the Supreme Court decided the landmark Miranda case last June. In an unusual—and, in our judgment, unwise—protective innovation, the Court applied retroactively to these defendants its mandate for notice to all newly arrested suspects of their rights to counsel.[29]

The rule of *Miranda's* companion case of *Johnson v. New Jersey*[30]

---

27. *See* remarks of Senator Long of Louisiana, 114 Cong. Rec. 11,340 (daily ed. Sept. 25, 1968). Such statements ignored the decision in Ginsberg v. New York, 390 U.S. 629 (1968).

28. N.Y. Times, Feb. 23, 1967, at 34, col. 1.

29. *Id.*

30. 384 U.S. 719 (1966).

was indeed an "innovation," but not because of its lenity. It was in fact an unprecedented limitation of the retroactive effect of a constitutional ruling, more severely restricting *Miranda*'s application to past cases than even the fairly recent decisions limiting the retroactive impact of *Mapp v. Ohio*[31] and *Griffin v. California*.[32] In fact, there was confusion about this point later in Congress. Much of the legislative response to *Miranda* expressed in Title II of the Omnibus Safe Streets and Crime Control Act of 1968[33] appears to have been based on press reports about accused persons who benefited from the very limited retroactive impact of that decision.[34] That is, the accused came to trial after June 13, 1966—the date *Miranda* was decided—and the prosecution could not use the incriminating statements already elicited in violation of the *Miranda* rules. Although these examples were offered by the Senate critics of *Miranda* to show that police would be hopelessly "handcuffed" in solving crimes, they were inapposite for that purpose. A fair test of the decision's impact could come, if at all, only in subsequent cases when the police attempted to solve crimes with full knowledge of the constitutional

---

31. 367 U.S. 643 (1961). In *Johnson*, the applicability of *Miranda* was limited to those cases which came to trial after the date on which the *Miranda* decision was rendered by the Court. 384 U.S. at 721. In contrast, Linkletter v. Walker, 381 U.S. 618 (1965), held that the exclusionary rule announced in *Mapp* was inapplicable only to those cases in which the conviction had become final before *Mapp* was decided. 381 U.S. at 620. A conviction was defined as final "where the judgment of conviction was rendered, the availability of appeal exhausted, and the time for petition for certiorari had elapsed" before the Court's decision in *Mapp*. 381 U.S. at 622 n.5. The Court did not disturb prior decisions which had applied *Mapp* to cases which were still pending on direct review at the date *Mapp* was rendered although the trial had been held prior to the *Mapp* decision 381 U.S. at 622.

32. 380 U.S. 609 (1965). In Tehan v. Shott, 382 U.S. 406 (1966), the Court announced a rule containing the same restrictions on the retroactive application of *Griffin* as those imposed by Linkletter v. Walker, 381 U.S. 618 (1965), on the retroactivity of *Mapp*. *See* note 31 *supra*. Subsequently the Court has cut back itself more severely on the retroactivity of a new constitutional ruling. *See* Fuller v. Alaska, 37 U.S.L.W. 3157 (Oct. 28, 1968), holding that the exclusionary rule of Lee v. Florida, 392 U.S. 378, 3158 (1968), "is to be applied only to *trials* in which the evidence is sought to be introduced after the date of our decision in Lee" (emphasis added). The most severe restriction on retroactivity, of course, occurred in Stovall v. Denno, 388 U.S. 293 (1967), applying new safeguards on police identification procedures only to *cases* involving confrontation for identification purposes that occurred after the date of the decision in United States v. Wade, 388 U.S. 218 (1967), and Gilbert v. California, 388 U.S. 263 (1967). All this belt-tightening on the part of the Court took place, of course, too late to spare it the political criticism it received from reporters during the debate on the Omnibus Crime Control bill and the Fortas nomination.

33. Pub. L. No. 90-351 (June 19, 1968).

34. *See, e.g.*, 114 CONG. REC. 3329 (daily ed. April 25, 1968) (remarks of Senator Tydings). *See* note 31 *supra*.

warning and waiver requirements and when the courts began to apply the new rules to cases that had been investigated under them.

Like the *Escobedo* decision, *Miranda* has suffered more in subsequent news treatment than it did in the initial reporting of the case. The "spot stories" that were handled by on-the-scene Supreme Court specialists made reasonably clear the Court's stated reasons for the new safeguards for criminal suspects. Many of them mentioned that station-house questioning was deemed "inherently coercive" and required at least the limited protection of a police warning of the accused's rights. Many of them mentioned Chief Justice Warren's citation of FBI practice as evidence that, in the majority's view, police could "live with" the new requirements. Most accounts carefully noted the citation of police training manuals as evidence that psychological coercion had replaced physical force as a means of defeating the individual's privilege against compulsory self-incrimination. Most of these elements, which had given depth and meaning to the spot stories, were missing from later accounts that were stripped to the barest bones of the ruling, often necessarily so, because of the demands of space and the structure of the articles.

These, then, are some of the components of the massive communications failure that grew worse as the Warren era drew to a close, or rather, as the era tried to draw to a close with the attempt of the Chief Justice to retire. At the last, the critics of the Court drowned out, with their cries of "law and order" and slogans about "handcuffing the police," both the principles underlying the Court's unpopular decisions and the very existence of some rulings that should have been more popular.[35]

One of the crowning ironies of the recent confirmation struggle was that the stated reason for the last-minute defection of Senate Minority Leader Everett M. Dirksen from the supporters of the

---

35. *E.g.*, Terry v. Ohio, 392 U.S. 1 (1968) (upheld a criminal conviction based on evidence obtained through a "stop and frisk" even though the police officer did not have probable cause for arrest); Ginsberg v. New York, 390 U.S. 629 (1968) (upheld a state statute prohibiting sale of obscene material to minors even though sale of the same material could be made to adults); Katz v. United States, 389 U.S. 347 (1967) (indicated that evidence obtained by an electronic listening device pursuant to a carefully circumscribed court order would be admissible); Warden v. Hayden, 387 U.S. 294 (1967) (reversed a lower court order in a criminal trial which barred as "mere evidence" defendant's clothing seized during a search of his house, and held that the "mere evidence" distinction was no longer viable; thus, a lawful search is no longer limited to the "fruits and instrumentalities" of the crime). I do not concede that the press gave these decisions too little attention at the time they were rendered.

nomination of Abe Fortas to be Chief Justice was the decision of the Court in *Witherspoon v. Illinois*[36] and its anticipated impact on the case of Richard Speck, the condemned murderer of eight Chicago nurses.[37] In *Witherspoon*, the Court vacated a death sentence imposed by a "stacked" jury from which veniremen had been automatically eliminated when they expressed reservations about imposing the death penalty. *Witherspoon* is a decision which, unless I seriously misread it, is grounded in significant part on a Gallup Poll estimate of contemporary attitudes toward capital punishment.[38]

The failure of communications, so at odds with the Court's necessary function as a constitutional teacher, had worthy origins. The school desegregation cases would doubtless have been excoriated by segregationists no matter what form of words the Court had chosen, and segregationist officials clearly would have defied the rulings just as vigorously. Perhaps *Brown v. Board of Education*, besides being a catalyst for other constitutional breakthroughs, set the pattern for the Warren Court's judicial conduct in the face of conservative hostility. The Court sent the message out that segregation was unlawful; the message came back that unlawfulness would persist in parts of the land; and the Court became determined to do whatever justice it could on its own. Similarly, in the criminal law field, Earl Warren and some of his colleagues ultimately expressed doubts that the Court could issue a constitutional exclusionary rule that would be effective in actual police practice;[39] however, they undertook to lay down the rules anyway, although quite possibly the Justices were conditioned to some disappointment about the level of compliance.

Under Chief Justice Warren significant advances were made in the techniques of communicating the Court's work to the public, although the advances were outstripped by events. Starting soon after *Brown*, the press at its best began to reach new levels of competence. The Court made the press' job a bit easier by meeting at ten a.m. instead of at noon. The Association of American Law Schools began a helpful program of issuing background memoranda for the press on major cases which had been argued before the Court. The Court

---

36. 391 U.S. 510 (1968).

37. 114 Cong. Rec. 11687-88 (daily ed. Oct. 1, 1968)(Remarks of Senator Dirksen explaining his vote against cloture).

38. *See* 391 U.S. at 520.

39. Terry v. Ohio, 392 U.S. 1, 4-7 (1968). *See* the interpretation of the stop-and-frisk cases advanced in La Fave, *"Street Encounters" and the Constitution; Terry, Sibron, Peters, and Beyond*, 67 Mich. L. Rev. 39, 59-60 (1968).

also began to space out the delivery of some of its opinions. Some often-mentioned experiments were not tried, however—most notably the proposal to supply the press with opinions a few hours in advance of delivery in order to give reporters time to compose more careful articles. Apparently the deterrent has been fear that some decisions, especially important economic ones, might be compromised by early release no matter what precautions were taken by the short-handed Court staff. The experiment should be tried anyway, if necessary with the specific exclusion of such economic cases. In the future, the Court must also seriously consider some *rapprochement* with television and re-examination of its ban on cameras in the courtroom. Television will certainly not invest money, manpower, and air time to cover a subject that will not reward the medium pictorially, and more and more Americans seem to receive all or most of their news over that medium.

During his confirmation hearings, Justice Fortas offered in broad outline a mixture of proposals for study of many of these problems.[40] He mentioned the already-accomplished revision of the "Decision Monday" procedure[41] and noted that the burden on the press had been relieved somewhat but perhaps could be relieved more. He suggested expanding the Association of American Law Schools' project (now supported by the American Bar Foundation), which supplies helpful memoranda about most of the argued cases to the press at the time of argument, to the post-decision phase of the Court's work.[42] He also recommended that statistical information be compiled for newsmen; as an example of a little-reported fact, he cited the results of a survey showing that 92 or 93 per cent of all criminal cases presented to the Court for review during the October 1967 term had been rejected.[43] He commended the formation of

---

40. Letter from Abe Fortas to Chairman Eastland of the Senate Judiciary Committee, *Hearings, supra* note 27, at 253.

41. *See* note 8 *supra.*

42. A brief experiment relating to the announcement of decisions was tried in 1965, whereby a law teacher from the Washington, D.C., area was available to newsmen in the press room. This practice was abandoned when it became apparent that the reporters were too busy making their own analyses and writing their own stories to consult with the expert in residence. Leaders in the AALS project began discussion late in 1968 of the possibility of additional, post-decision memoranda that could be distributed within a week or so of major decisions.

43. Several newsmen saw this as an unfelicitous example of the value of increased information services. Most of the reporters are fully aware of this sort of statistic and many have reported routinely that only about one in twenty petitioners ever wins review. The dangers of "news management" are apparent but they are far over the horizon.

an organization of practitioners before the Court. And, he suggested coming to grips with the pressing problems of radio and television coverage.

Perhaps Justice Fortas will help to implement some of these general ideas, though not, of course, as Chief Justice. His sympathetic concern for the problems of the press, and similar feelings on the part of other members of the Court, have been evident. The cornerstone for constructing any improvements is that the Supreme Court must be an open institution—as open as is truly consistent with proper adjudication and as open as the democratic society the Warren Court sought so earnestly to fashion.

JUDICIAL VALOUR AND THE WARREN COURT'S LABOR DECISIONS

*Theodore J. St. Antoine**

LAWYERS who practice regularly before the Supreme Court are likely to prepare their arguments with a specific Justice in mind. The choice does not necessarily turn on who might be the swing vote in a given case. Often it is just a matter of which Justice can be relied upon, because of his particular interests and his insight, to search out the strengths and weaknesses of the opposing positions, and to see that all the hard questions are asked. In a labor case during the early years of the Warren Court, that would usually have meant Justice Frankfurter. Later on, depending on the circumstances, it might have been Justice Harlan or Brennan or Fortas. It has probably never been the Chief Justice.

Yet now as I look back upon the whole sweep of the Warren Court's labor decisions over the past decade and a half, I am struck by the sudden suspicion that many members of the Supreme Court's labor bar[1] may have outsmarted themselves. They were, perhaps, like the fabled fox who knew many things; they failed to recognize that it was the Chief Justice who knew the One Big Thing. For the major contribution of the Warren Court to the development of labor law has not depended on the kind of subtle statutory interpretation that is needed to wend one's way through the labyrinthine secondary boycott passages of the Taft-Hartley Act. Instead, the Court's main achievement in the labor field involved a simple but fundamental restructuring of intergovernmental relations. What the Court did, in a series of decisions that were hotly controverted at the time but have quietly won general acceptance since, was to nationalize the regulation of labor relations in industries affecting interstate commerce. The Court's action reflected the same characteristically audacious Warren approach toward established state institutions which was displayed in dealing with reapportionment and civil rights.

The importance in the Court's eyes of "federal pre-emption"—the exclusion of state substantive law from areas regulated by Congress—can be shown to an extent simply in quantitative terms. Some-

---

* Associate Professor of Law, University of Michigan. A.B. 1951, Fordham College; J.D. 1954, University of Michigan.—Ed.
1. In fairness I should mention that I was a junior member of this group (as union counsel) for about half the span of the Warren Court. No one could be more guilty than I of the accusation in the text.

what arbitrarily, I have labelled about 110 labor decisions of the Warren era as "important." Of these, almost forty—or over a third —deal either directly with the metes and bounds of the pre-emption doctrine, or with issues which would not have arisen but for the displacement of state law by federal.[2] I shall discuss the cases in two categories: those decisions concerned with the extent to which state law may still operate in areas subject to federal regulation; and those decisions concerned with the development of federal law to replace state law as the basis for enforcing collective bargaining agreements. Thereafter, I shall add a few words about some of the other significant labor decisions of the Warren Court.

At the time Chief Justice Warren assumed office, the pre-emption doctrine in its application to labor relations was still in its adolescence. The well-nigh axiomatic principle had been established that a state could not directly impede the exercise of federal rights of self-organization, for example, by imposing onerous licensing requirements on union agents.[3] But states were still free to regulate such labor activities as "quickie" strikes, which technically were neither protected nor prohibited under federal law.[4] More important, no clear rationale had been evolved to justify conclusions that particular kinds of conduct fell either within or without the ambit of state regulation. And there had been little airing of the underlying policy considerations which go to the very heart of our federal system: the balancing of the need for a uniform national policy in matters affecting the country as a whole against the need to accommodate regional differences and desires for local experimentation.

The first term of the Warren Court ushered in the vanguard elements of today's pre-emption theory. In *Garner v. Teamsters Union*[5] the Court held that a state injunction could not duplicate a federal remedy by forbidding conduct proscribed under the National Labor Relations Act. Diversity of procedures was said to be as apt to produce conflicting adjudications as diversity of substantive rules. It soon became apparent, however, that a majority of the Court regarded a deficiency in the federal remedy as a sufficient reason for sustaining state jurisdiction. Thus, employees or employers suffering monetary losses through tortious conduct that was also an unfair

---

2. Chief Justice Warren himself authored eleven opinions in the approximately 110 cases I surveyed; five dealt with pre-emption. His opinions included four dissents, three on this subject. The Chief Justice has consistently been one of the most pro-pre-emption members of the Court.

3. Hill v. Florida, 325 U.S. 538 (1945).

4. UAW-AFL v. WERB [*Briggs & Stratton Corp.*], 336 U.S. 245 (1949). For a more recent approach, *see* Teamsters Local 20 v. Morton, 377 U.S. 252 (1964).

5. 346 U.S. 485 (1953).

labor practice could maintain a state court action for damages, since the National Labor Relations Board had no general power to award full compensatory relief.[6] At this juncture Chief Justice Warren stepped in to protest a state's awarding damages, especially punitive damages, for conduct regulated by the federal labor statutes. As he saw it, the uniformity of regulation by which Congress sought to secure nationwide industrial peace would be undermined by the numerous variations in state laws and the "provincialism" of local juries.[7]

The Warren views did not entirely prevail, but their influence was plainly felt in *San Diego Building Trades Council v. Garmon*,[8] which remains the Court's most definitive statement on pre-emption. There the Court in handling the pre-emption issue shifted from an emphasis on the nature of the state relief sought (was it more adequate than the federal remedy?) to an emphasis on the nature of the activity in question (was it regulated under federal law?). The now-famous test was enunciated that if conduct is "arguably" protected by section 7 of the NLRA, or "arguably" prohibited by section 8, exclusive primary jurisdiction rests in the NLRB and state (or federal) courts are precluded from acting. Earlier decisions which had appeared to rely on the deficiency of the federal remedy were explained as upholding state court jurisdiction because violence or threatened violence was present, or because the activity was of "merely peripheral concern" to the federal statutory scheme.[9]

The soundness of all this surely is not self-evident. Under the expansive pre-emption doctrine, states have been sharply limited in the role they can play as "laboratories" for social experiment. Numerous restrictions have been imposed on customary state functions. Thus, although the states can still assert their police power to maintain public order, they cannot take over a public utility to halt a strike.[10] Laws not dealing specifically with labor relations, such as state antitrust statutes[11] and even traditional common-law libel doctrines,[12] may also run afoul of the pre-emption principle. This is so

---

6. United Constr. Workers v. Laburnum Constr. Corp., 347 U.S. 656 (1954); UAW v. Russell, 356 U.S. 634 (1958).

7. UAW v. Russell, 356 U.S. 634, 650-51 (1958) (dissenting opinion).

8. 359 U.S. 236 (1959).

9. 359 U.S. at 241-43, citing United Constr. Workers v. Laburnum Constr. Corp., 347 U.S. 656 (1954) (threatened violence); UAW v. Russell, 356 U.S. 634 (1958) (mass picketing); IAM v. Gonzales, 356 U.S. 617 (1958) (wrongful expulsion of member from union).

10. Street, Elec. Ry. & Motor Coach Employees Div. 1287 v. Missouri, 374 U.S. 74 (1963).

11. Teamsters Local 24 v. Oliver, 358 U.S. 283 (1959).

12. *Cf.* Linn v. Plant Guard Workers Local 114, 383 U.S. 53 (1966) (libel action

even though it is by no means clear that Congress is as eager as the Supreme Court would suggest to ensure the unsullied uniformity of federal regulation.[13] In extending the pre-emption doctrine, the Court nonetheless moved boldly ahead, willing to risk local losses to achieve national gains, and willing too, it would seem, to risk congressional displeasure for reading more into the statute than the legislature may have intended.

On balance, I think the Court has acted wisely. Labor law continues to be one of our most divisive domestic issues, and much of the divisiveness runs along regional lines. Federally enforced uniformity thus seems peculiarly necessary, lest either unions or employers be unduly favored in particular states. Such regional variations could hardly fail to have an adverse impact on the nation's economy. For example, plants might be lured from place to place while labor bitterness constantly deepened. The present healthy trend toward a leveling of wage rates for similar jobs across the country could well be reversed. Of course, a different result in almost any given Supreme Court pre-emption decision would doubtless not have had dire consequences. But by now we probably have sufficient experience under the Court's broad pre-emption doctrine to conclude that vital local interests have in fact suffered no serious injury. This alone may be enough to indicate that the Court was right when it began to tip the scales, as a matter of general policy, in favor of national interests rather than local concerns.

The Warren Court's vigor in furthering the primacy of federal law was demonstrated even more strikingly in its rulings on the enforcement of collective bargaining agreements. Labor contracts were traditionally enforced in accordance with state substantive law. It was often hard to sue a union in the state courts, however, because of the difficulty of obtaining jurisdiction over an unincorporated association. Therefore, in 1947, Congress wrote section 301 into the Taft-Hartley Act[14] to provide that suits on contracts between unions and employers could be brought in the federal district courts. Unions were explicitly made competent to sue or be sued as entities.

But what was the substantive law to be applied in 301 suits—federal or state? If section 301 were to be treated as merely procedural, with state substantive law applicable, the provision would

---

maintainable only if defamation in course of labor dispute is malicious and actually injurious).

13. When Congress enacted the Landrum-Griffin Act in 1959 to provide the first comprehensive federal regulation of internal union affairs, it specifically negated any general intent to exclude concurrent state regulation. See 29 U.S.C. § 523 (1964).

14. 29 U.S.C. § 185 (1964).

be of dubious constitutionality; article III of the Constitution confines the jurisdiction of the federal district courts to cases involving diversity of citizenship or a federal question. Yet section 301 was silent on the question of applicable law, and Congress had furnished no clear guidance.

After one earlier inconclusive skirmish,[15] the Supreme Court came to grips with the problem in *Textile Workers Union v. Lincoln Mills*.[16] A union sued an employer in federal court for specific performance of the arbitration provisions in the parties' collective contract. Jurisdiction was contested. Justice Douglas, for the Court, cut the constitutional knot with one swift stroke, declaring that "the substantive law to apply in suits under § 301(a) is federal law which the courts must fashion from the policy of our national labor laws."[17] Once this was established, jurisdiction could constitutionally be reposed in the federal judiciary.

Perhaps the magnitude of the Court's undertaking in *Lincoln Mills* can best be gauged by attending to the highly literate criticism leveled at the decision in a classic article by Professors Alexander Bickel and Harry Wellington of the Yale Law School.[18] The authors point out, quite correctly, that Justice Douglas' previously quoted conclusion, "which intrudes upon state power, which finds no support in the language of the statute and insignificant support in the legislative history, received no explanation in the opinion."[19] But their ultimate objection to *Lincoln Mills* is far more profound. With an almost mystical concern for the institutional integrity of the judiciary, Bickel and Wellington argue that section 301, as read by the Supreme Court, demands of the federal courts a task to which they are "enormously unequal," and "its imposition on them is therefore capable of damaging their usefulness for the essential duties that they are suited to perform."[20] The authors concluded that when Congress confers responsibilities upon the federal courts which are beyond their institutional capabilities, the proper disposition is a "remand" of the matter to Congress for further consideration. Remand is to be achieved through "any form of dismissal for lack of jurisdiction which does no violence to the statutory language."[21]

15. Association of Westinghouse Salaried Employees v. Westinghouse Elec. Corp., 348 U.S. 437 (1955).

16. 353 U.S. 448 (1957).

17. 353 U.S. at 456. Justice Frankfurter dissented in a massively documented eighty-six-page opinion in which he sought to show that § 301 did not create substantive rights but was only procedural. 353 U.S. at 460.

18. *Legislative Purpose and the Judicial Process: The Lincoln Mills Case*, 71 Harv. L. Rev. 1 (1957).

19. *Id.* at 35-36.

20. *Id.* at 22-23.

21. *Id.* at 35.

The task shouldered by the Supreme Court, despite the grave apprehensions of Bickel and Wellington, was the task of fashioning a body of federal contract law to govern the enforcement of collective agreements. Its sources were to be the policies of the federal labor statutes, state contract law where appropriate, arbitrators' decisions, and so on. Bickel and Wellington looked at these "bits and pieces" and were aghast; the Court had faith that "judicial inventiveness" would find a way.[22] Perhaps that is the difference between professors and practical men. By hindsight, at any rate, it is hard to find justification for the fears of the two perceptive Yale critics.

Possibly an explanation for the easy survival of the federal judiciary lies in the next maneuver executed by the Warren Court. Having boldly staked out a claim in *Lincoln Mills* to the whole of the labor contract domain, the Court then turned around in the *Warrior* trilogy[23] and delegated to arbitrators the principal responsibility for interpreting and applying collective bargaining agreements. Courts are to order arbitration of grievances under a contract "unless it may be said with positive assurance that the arbitration clause is not susceptible of an interpretation that covers the asserted dispute."[24] Moreover, an arbitrator's award is to be enforced by a court without a review on the merits, so long as the award is not the product of fraud or capriciousness. Thus, through the *Warrior* approach, the Court may have finessed many of the problems envisaged by Bickel and Wellington.

Even so, the Warren Court has managed to build up a fairly substantial body of basic contract doctrine. For instance, a labor agreement may be binding on a successor employer even though he has not signed it.[25] Available grievance and arbitration machinery has to be exhausted before there can be resort to a court suit on a contract.[26] And in the absence of a federal statute of limitations, state statutes apply to section 301 actions.[27] These are the kinds of questions one might have anticipated the Court would have to resolve. They hardly seem a threat to its institutional capacities.

Perhaps the most nettlesome current issue of labor contract enforcement is the impact of the Norris-La Guardia Act. Here, more than anywhere else, the Supreme Court may be open to the charge

22. Textile Workers Union v. Lincoln Mills, 353 U.S. 448, 457 (1957).
23. United Steelworkers v. American Mfg. Co., 363 U.S. 564 (1960); United Steelworkers v. Warrior & Gulf Nav. Co., 363 U.S. 574 (1960); United Steelworkers v. Enterprise Wheel & Car Corp., 363 U.S. 593 (1960).
24. United Steelworkers v. Warrior & Gulf Nav. Co., 363 U.S. 574, 582-83 (1960).
25. John Wiley & Sons, Inc. v. Livingston, 376 U.S. 543 (1964).
26. Drake Bakeries, Inc. v. Bakery Workers, Local 50, 370 U.S. 254 (1962); Republic Steel Corp. v. Maddox, 379 U.S. 650 (1965).
27. UAW v. Hoosier Cardinal Corp., 383 U.S. 696 (1966).

that it failed to think through the implications of applying federal substantive law to suits brought under section 301. So far, the Court has held that the Norris-La Guardia injunction ban does not prevent specific enforcement of an agreement to arbitrate,[28] but that it does prevent an injunction by a federal court against a strike in breach of contract.[29] Two embarrassing questions are left. Does Norris-La Guardia prevent a decree ordering specific performance of an arbitrator's award directing a union to halt a strike? And, does Norris-La Guardia apply to prevent a *state* court injunction against a strike in breach of contract?[30] If the last question is answered "yes," that will be an ironic denouement to the Taft-Hartley Congress' efforts to *increase* the range of employer remedies against unions. If the question is answered "no," the anomaly may be that state courts will become, by employer choice, the principal formulators of *federal* law in this important area.[31] These logical difficulties could have been avoided if the Supreme Court had applied state substantive law in *Lincoln Mills*. The chances are, however, the Court would have come out the same way even if it had foreseen these problems. For the policy tug of having uniform federal law govern contract enforcement would have remained. And in a conflict between logic and policy, the Warren Court has never been prone to favor logic.

Several other labor doctrines of the Warren Court mirror the libertarian philosophy that has permeated the Chief Justice's tenure. At least two should be mentioned—free speech and individual rights.

After being in eclipse for almost a decade,[32] the concept of peaceful picketing as a form of free speech protected by the first amendment enjoyed a resurgence in the late years of the Warren Court. In one case the Court engaged in some rather strained statutory interpretation to reach the conclusion that the 1959 amendments to the Taft-Hartley Act do not forbid consumer picketing aimed at a particular nonunion product being distributed by a neutral retailer;[33] otherwise, difficult constitutional questions might have been raised. In another case the Court held that a state court injunction

---

28. Textile Workers Union v. Lincoln Mills, 353 U.S. 448 (1957).

29. Sinclair Ref. Co. v. Atkinson, 370 U.S. 195 (1962).

30. State courts retain jurisdiction to enforce collective agreements, but they must apply federal substantive law under § 301. Teamsters Local 174 . v. Lucas Flour Co., 369 U.S. 95 (1962).

31. Union removal of § 301 suits from state to federal court may solve this dilemma. *See* Avco Corp. v. Machinists Aero Lodge 735, 390 U.S. 557 (1968).

32. *See, e.g.,* Teamsters Local 695 v. Vogt, Inc., 354 U.S. 284 (1957).

33. NLRB v. Fruit & Vegetable Packers & Warehousemen Local 760 [*Tree Fruits*], 377 U.S. 58 (1964).

against the peaceful picketing of a business in a privately owned shopping center violated the first amendment.[34] The Court went on to say that ordinarily picketing can be forbidden only when it has an illegal end, and rejected the notion that the nonspeech aspects of picketing render the first amendment completely inapplicable. The Court also rewrote the legislative history of the union security provisions of the Railway Labor Act for the purpose of avoiding first amendment issues. In two different cases the Court held that the Act prevented railroad unions from using dues money collected from employees under a union shop agreement for political purposes, if the employees objected.[35]

One of the most dramatic developments of the last half decade has been the rapid extension of employees' rights to fair representation in the negotiation and administration of collective bargaining agreements. An individual employee now may sue his employer for breach of contract, and may join the union or sue it alone if it has treated him arbitrarily, capriciously, or in bad faith.[36] An employee has no absolute right to have a grievance arbitrated,[37] however, and he must first pursue any remedies available under the contract before he can file suit.[38] Important questions in this area await the Court's future attention. Do honesty and conscientiousness excuse any union blunder? Do certain employee rights "vest" so as to be immune from further union-employer bargaining? To what extent may the courts intrude to protect individual rights without impairing effective collective bargaining? This may well be the area in which the Warren Court has left the most unfinished business.

In a celebrated little essay Sir Frederick Pollock remarked, "Caution and valour are both needed for the fruitful constructive interpretation of legal principles."[39] I suspect that others besides Professors Bickel and Wellington have doubts about the Warren Court on the score of caution. My own feeling, however, is that most of its forays are set off by retrenchments. States may not regulate conduct covered by the NLRA; but an exception is carved out for malicious and harmful libel. The courts shall assume responsibility for writing a body of federal contract law; but the day-to-day task is delegated to the arbitrators. Is that not "caution" as well as "valour"? In any event, if I must choose between the two in a field like labor law, the choice is plain.

---

34. Food Employees Local 590 v. Logan Valley Plaza, Inc., 391 U.S. 308 (1968).
35. IAM v. Street, 367 U.S. 740 (1961); Brotherhood of Ry. & S.S. Clerks v. Allen, 373 U.S. 113 (1963).
36. Humphrey v. Moore, 375 U.S. 335 (1964); Vaca v. Sipes, 386 U.S. 171 (1967).
37. Vaca v. Sipes, 386 U.S. 171 (1967).
38. Republic Steel Corp. v. Maddox, 379 U.S. 650 (1965).
39. *Judicial Caution and Valour*, in JURISPRUDENCE IN ACTION 367, 373 (1953).

THE "WARREN COURT" AND THE ANTITRUST LAWS: OF ECONOMICS, POPULISM, AND CYNICISM

*Thomas E. Kauper**

No one could quarrel with the simple assertion that the so-called "Warren Court" has had a significant, if indeed not extraordinary, impact on the development of the antitrust laws. It could hardly have been otherwise. The fifteen years since 1953 represent virtually one-fourth of the total history of the Clayton and Federal Trade Commission Acts,[1] and one fifth of the time which has elapsed since passage of the Sherman Act.[2] Every Supreme Court decision under the 1950 amendments to section 7 of the Clayton Act,[3] the so-called antimerger law, has come after the accession of Chief Justice Warren to the bench.

Moreover, these fifteen years have been unlike any other consecutive fifteen years in the history of antitrust enforcement. Government and the public have remained committed to antitrust concepts—to a firm belief in the efficacy of the free market as a regulator of business behavior.[4] It has not always been so. Historically, there has been a questioning of the assumptions underlying antitrust and correlative lack of enforcement during periods of grave economic or military crisis.[5] But no such crises have existed since 1953.[6] The enforcement agencies remained reasonably well-funded and active during this period. Private litigants have brought more treble damage actions, with a higher degree of success, than ever before. An expanding economy, characterized by extraordinary technological development, has created an array of

---

* Associate Professor of Law, University of Michigan. A.B. 1957, J.D. 1960, University of Michigan.—Ed.
  1. Clayton Act, 15 U.S.C. §§ 12-27 (1964); Federal Trade Commission Act, 15 U.S.C. §§ 41-58 (1964).
  2. 15 U.S.C. §§ 1-7 (1964).
  3. 15 U.S.C. § 18 (1964).
  4. There are of course those who do not share this belief. *See, e.g.,* J. GALBRAITH, THE NEW INDUSTRIAL STATE (1967).
  5. The NRA codes of the early thirties, and the use of wage and price controls and rationing of consumer goods during World War II are but two illustrations of this phenomenon.
  6. The government's need to meet the demands of the Vietnam war and its desire to curb inflationary pressures have led to some deviations from market self-regulation, as demonstrated by the periodic confrontations between the White House and the steel industry over proposed price increases, and the government's attempts to secure voluntary compliance with its wage and price guidelines. But there has not been an extended, considered departure from basic antitrust concepts.

new problems. In such circumstances, it would be astonishing if the Court, with its peculiar responsibility for formulation of antitrust doctrine,[7] had not contributed much to its development.

Many of the Court's post-1953 antitrust decisions are simply reaffirmations of pre-existing doctrine. This has been particularly true of cases involving conspiratorial conduct, where the Court has continued zealously to condemn price-fixing, horizontal market division, and group boycotts as per se violations of section 1 of the Sherman Act.[8] But in other areas, new standards reflecting a strong enforcement philosophy have been applied. The most striking, most publicized, and most criticized decisions have been the extended series of decisions holding mergers in violation of section 7 of the Clayton Act. Beginning with the *Brown Shoe* case,[9] which perhaps remains the most radical of the antimerger rulings, the Court has moved to a virtual per se prohibition of horizontal mergers between firms with substantial market shares.[10] In dealing with conglomerate acquisitions, where structural effects cannot normally be measured by reference to market shares or changes in concentration ratios, the Court has proceeded with greater caution, but violations have been found in each case.[11]

Of at least equal significance has been the Court's treatment of a wide variety of vertical restraints. The Court has extended the long-standing ruling that vertical price-fixing is a per se violation of section 1 of the Sherman Act by closing a number of avenues previously used, with judicial blessing, to achieve the same end. The *Colgate*[12] doctrine—which in effect permitted a seller to implement a program of resale price maintenance by refusing to deal with buyers who failed to comply with the seller's pre-announced policy—has been severely curtailed, although it is too much to assert that it has been completely overruled. The Court's expansion of vertical conspiracy doctrine, together with its unwillingness to countenance reliance on *Colgate* if the

---

7. Under the Expediting Act, 15 U.S.C. § 29 (1964), appeals in civil antitrust actions brought by the Department of Justice must be taken directly to the Supreme Court.

8. *See, e.g.,* United States v. Sealy, Inc., 388 U.S. 350 (1967); Klor's, Inc. v. Broadway-Hale Stores, Inc., 359 U.S. 207 (1959).

9. Brown Shoe Co. v. United States, 370 U.S. 294 (1962).

10. *See, e.g.,* United States v. Pabst Brewing Co., 384 U.S. 546 (1966); United States v. Von's Grocery Co., 384 U.S. 270 (1966); United States v. Aluminum Co. of America, 377 U.S. 271 (1964); United States v. Philadelphia Natl. Bank, 374 U.S. 321 (1963). *See also* United States v. Continental Can Co., 378 U.S. 441 (1964).

11. FTC v. Consolidated Foods Corp., 380 U.S. 592 (1965); FTC v. Procter & Gamble Co., 386 U.S. 568 (1967). The merger condemned in United States v. El Paso Natural Gas Co., 376 U.S. 651 (1964), is perhaps best described as a market extension conglomerate.

12. United States v. Colgate & Co., 250 U.S. 300 (1919).

seller goes in any way beyond a naked refusal to deal, makes the immunized path a narrow one indeed.[13] The immunity once conferred upon bona fide consignment relationships, where the seller dictated the price at which its agent sold, has met a similar fate. At least in those cases where a seller operates through a sizeable distribution network, such arrangements have been brought within the per se vertical price fixing rule.[14] Finally, the Court's hostility toward vertical price-fixing is manifest in its narrow construction of the McGuire Amendment,[15] which legislatively permits some sellers operating in so-called fair trade states to engage in resale price maintenance.[16]

Other vertical restrictions have been similarly treated. Tie-ins and compulsory package arrangements are now virtually per se illegal.[17] After some initial hesitation in *White Motor*,[18] the Court has apparently held that contractual restraints upon the ability of a purchasing dealer to resell the manufacturer's product where and to whom the dealer pleases are per se violations of the Sherman Act, although in a curious twist the Court has not applied a per se rule where such restrictions are placed upon a manufacturer's agents.[19] Indeed, virtually the only vertical arrangement between seller and purchaser other than outright merger to come before the Court during this period and escape per se or near per se condemnation has been the simple requirements contract.[20]

There have been other significant developments. Apparent conflicts between the patent and antitrust laws have been resolved in favor of the latter.[21] The patent misuse doctrine has been extended.[22] With its holding that a firm may violate the Sherman Act through the exercise of a patent procured through active

---

13. For examples of decisions which have narrowed the *Colgate* doctrine, *see* Albrecht v. Herald Co., 390 U.S. 145 (1968); United States v. Parke, Davis & Co., 362 U.S. 29 (1960). *Cf.* United States v. General Motors Corp., 384 U.S. 127 (1966).

14. Simpson v. Union Oil Co., 377 U.S. 13 (1964). *But cf.* United States v. Arnold, Schwinn & Co., 388 U.S. 365 (1967).

15. 15 U.S.C. § 45 (1964).

16. *See* United States v. McKesson & Robbins, Inc., 351 U.S. 305 (1956).

17. United States v. Loew's, Inc., 371 U.S. 38 (1962); Northern Pacific Ry. Co. v. United States, 356 U.S. 1 (1958).

18. White Motor Co. v. United States, 372 U.S. 253 (1963).

19. United States v. Arnold, Schwinn & Co., 388 U.S. 365 (1967). *But see* Albrecht v. Herald Co., 390 U.S. 145, 154 (1968) (concurring opinion).

20. Tampa Elec. Co. v. Nashville Coal Co., 365 U.S. 320 (1961). The Court has not passed upon the validity of the simple exclusive franchise, *i.e.*, a promise by the seller not to sell to others in the franchisee's area. Such an arrangement was present in *White Motor*, but was not attacked by the government.

21. *See* United States v. Singer Mfg. Co., 374 U.S. 174 (1963).

22. Brulotte v. Thys Co., 379 U.S. 29 (1964).

fraud, the Court has brought the antitrust laws directly into the Patent Office itself.[23]

On still another front, the Court's fundamental faith in the efficacy of antitrust has been reflected in its continuing rejection of arguments for industry-wide exemption from the antitrust laws. Exempting legislation has been narrowly construed, except in the case of labor activities.[24] Doubts about the applicability of antitrust to professional sports other than baseball have been removed.[25] In a number of regulated industries, the fact of regulation has been held insufficient grounds for immunization from the antitrust laws.[26]

Finally, special note should be taken of the Court's willingness to defer to the discretion of the Federal Trade Commission, which surely had not been accustomed to such favored treatment. Despite a marked propensity for disagreeing with district court findings, the Court has shown little inclination to go behind the findings of the Commission. But deference to the Commission has not been limited to its factual determinations alone. In a series of decisions culminating in *FTC v. Brown Shoe Co.*,[27] the Court has recognized to an unprecedented extent a broad authority in the Commission to declare conduct conflicting with the policies of the Sherman and Clayton Acts unlawful without proof of actual or probable anticompetitive effects. So far as the Supreme Court is concerned, the Commission now stands at its high water mark.

The role played by Chief Justice Warren in these developments has not been highly visible. He has authored few Court opinions in leading antitrust cases, and has written even fewer dissents. (The latter is in part because he has generally been with the majority.) Best known of his opinions for the Court is the enigmatic opinion in the *Brown Shoe* merger case.[28] The result—holding unlawful the acquisition of a retailer with at most 1.2 per cent of national retail shoe sales by a manufacturer producing some 4

---

23. Walker Process Equip., Inc. v. Food Mach. & Chem. Corp., 382 U.S. 172 (1965).

24. *E.g.*, Case-Swayne Co. v. Sunkist Growers, Inc., 389 U.S. 384 (1967), *rehearing denied*, 390 U.S. 930 (1968); Carnation Co. v. Pacific Westbound Conference, 383 U.S. 213 (1966); Maryland & Virginia Milk Producers Assn. v. United States, 362 U.S. 458 (1960). *But see* Sunkist Growers, Inc. v. Winckler & Smith Citrus Prods. Co., 370 U.S. 19 (1962).

25. Radovich v. National Football League, 352 U.S. 445 (1957); United States v. International Boxing Club, Inc., 348 U.S. 236 (1955).

26. *E.g.*, United States v. Philadelphia Natl Bank, 374 U.S. 321 (1963); Silver v. New York Stock Exchange, 373 U.S. 341 (1963). *See* California v. FPC, 369 U.S. 482 (1962).

27. 384 U.S. 316 (1966). *See also* Atlantic Ref. Co. v. FTC, 381 U.S. 357, *rehearing denied*, 382 U.S. 873 (1965).

28. 370 U.S. 294 (1962). The best-known dissent by the Chief Justice is in the *DuPont Cellophane* case. United States v. E. I. duPont de Nemours & Co., 351 U.S. 377, 414 (1956).

per cent of national footwear—is startling indeed. But the outcome is obscured by an opinion which, seemingly by design, contains something for everyone. The call for a broad economic inquiry, the recognition of the failing-company doctrine, and several
other statements, suggested moderation in the Court's approach.
At the same time, the Court expressed fears about increasing
concentration, emphasized the need for halting merger trends in
their "incipiency," and stressed the desirability of protecting small
business. Each of these emphases gave comfort to those calling
for a strict antimerger policy and, as it turned out, set the
tenor for decisions which followed. The *Brown Shoe* opinion is
perhaps less reflective of the Chief Justice's substantive views than
of his capacity as a judicial statesman. Since *Brown Shoe* was the
first major decision under the amended section 7, its widespread
acceptance by the bar and the business community was essential
to the antimerger movement. In achieving this acceptance, it seems
to me, the Chief Justice succeeded. But like all successes, this one
had its price. In later cases, critics would accuse the Court of
departing from the moderate standards of *Brown Shoe*.

The Chief Justice has had a considerable impact simply as
one of nine voting members of the Court. His voting record, in
terms of result, is remarkably consistent: he has voted "for liability"
more than any other member of the Court during his fifteen year
tenure.[29] But any suggestion that the Chief Justice has had an impact *beyond* the weight of his vote would be sheer speculation at
this point. It seems more likely that he has followed the views of
others, particularly Justices Black and Douglas, than that they
have followed him. The antitrust work of the Warren Court, like
its work in other areas, is the work of a Court over which a given
Chief Justice has happened to preside. The doctrines developed
by the majority may be identified with him, for he has generally
been part of the majority, but he is neither solely nor, apparently,
primarily responsible for them.

Substantively, the antitrust opinions of the Warren Court have
reflected a peculiar blend of modern economic theory and Populism. The increasing use of economic theory as a basis for, or
at least an explanation of, decisions in merger cases has been particularly apparent; opinions in merger cases now speak the language and rely upon the writings of economists. The antitrust
lawyer in a merger case finds himself talking about concentration
ratios, barriers to entry, elasticity of supply and demand, and po-

---

29. *See* Arnold, *The Supreme Court and the Antitrust Laws 1953-1967*, 34 A.B.A.
ANTITRUST L.J. 2, 7 (1967).

tential competition. The Court's fear of increased concentration, and the rules enunciated to prevent it, do reflect increasing sophistication in the use of oligopoly theory.[30] Yet even here the Court has continued on occasion to express a concern for particular competitors, small businesses, and consumer choice—a concern beyond that justified by economic theory.

Continued reliance on the knowledge of economists is essential to the antitrust practitioner, and lawyers who continually assert that they cannot understand economics or economists must go back and learn. It is foolhardy to ignore an extremely significant part of human knowledge because it seems difficult to comprehend. But, while the Court's recognition of such knowledge is a healthy development in the abstract, it also presents a number of questions. First, and most obvious, is whether the Court has simply used economic doctrine to support decisions arrived at upon other grounds. This is not an easy question to answer. There is often no single applicable economic theory; economists disagree about the results in particular cases just as frequently as lawyers do. Hence, as a necessary by-product of any reliance on economic doctrine, the Court has recited the views of some economists in preference to the views of others. In its first section 7 cases, and particularly in the *Philadelphia Bank* case, the Court did rely upon oligopoly theory as a basis for formulating broad general rules to deal with the effects of increased concentration in particular markets.[31] The rules created could be justified by reference to the theory relied upon. But the Court has not purported to rest its decision in every case upon the dictates of such economic analysis. Subsequent cases have interjected other values; for example, the emphasis on the protection of small business as an end in itself in the *Brown Shoe*[32] and *Von's Grocery*[33] cases. At other times, the Court has stressed the need for simple rules which can be understood and easily applied. These cases represent less a misuse of economic doctrine than an unwillingness to make results dependent upon it. One can quarrel with such divergence from the dictates of strict economic reasoning; perhaps the teachings of economic theory should be conclusive. But this is a question to be confronted head on, and not by accusing the Court of misusing doctrine it has not purported to apply.

---

30. *See generally* Brodley, *Oligopoly Power Under the Sherman and Clayton Acts— From Economic Theory to Legal Policy*, 19 STAN. L. REV. 285 (1967).

31. United States v. Philadelphia Natl. Bank, 374 U.S. 321 (1963). *See also* United States v. Continental Can Co., 378 U.S. 441 (1964); United States v. Aluminum Co. of America, 377 U.S. 271 (1964).

32. Brown Shoe Co. v. United States, 370 U.S. 294, 344 (1962).

33. United States v. Von's Grocery Co., 384 U.S. 270 (1966).

If there has been a real abuse of economic analysis—a conscious or unconscious manipulation of economic concepts to fit an apparently pre-ordained result—it has been in the process of market definition. More will be said of this subsequently. But whatever the defects in the Court's process of market definition, the blame cannot be placed entirely with the Justices. Economists have labored to develop theories which are ultimately dependent upon market definition, but they have furnished far less guidance in outlining the definitional process itself.[34]

The use of economic analysis by the Court raises a number of additional questions: How is the Court to "know" such theory? Is it, or can it be, sufficiently sophisticated in economic principles to apply them at all? Half a theory, when the balance is not comprehended, may be more dangerous than none at all. Moreover, the interjection of noneconomic values into a structured system of economic analysis, unless done with great skill, may make the analysis meaningless. And economic theory must be applied consistently; it cannot be used today and forgotten tomorrow. Otherwise distortions will appear.

Few of these questions arise in connection with the Court's opinions involving vertical restraints; here economic theory is conspicuous by its absence. The growing body of economic knowledge concerning the effects of vertical integration, resale price maintenance, territorial and other restrictions on distributors, and tying arrangements have been virtually ignored.[35] The Court has generally dealt with such vertical restraints in a manner more familiar to common-law lawyers. Decisions in this area often rest upon grounds whose antecedents trace far back into the history of the antitrust laws. The Court's per se condemnation of the territorial and customer restrictions imposed by Arnold Schwinn & Co. upon its purchaser-dealers rested on the common-law rule against restraints on alienation,[36] employed as far back as the *Dr. Miles Medical* case[37] in connection with vertical price-fixing. Other essentially vertical restraints have been held unlawful through expanded concepts of vertical conspiracy, thereby obviating, at least

---

34. One notable exception is Lozowick, Steiner, & Miller, *Law and Quantitative Multivariate Analysis: An Encounter*, 66 MICH. L. REV. 1641 (1968). *See generally* Steiner, *Markets and Industries*, in 9 INTERNATIONAL ENCYCLOPEDIA OF THE SOCIAL SCIENCES 575 (1968).

35. *See, e.g.*, Bork, *The Rule of Reason and the Per Se Concept: Price Fixing and Market Division II*, 75 YALE L.J. 373 (1966); Bowman, *Tying Arrangements and the Leverage Problem*, 67 YALE L.J. 19 (1957); Burstein, *A Theory of Full-Line Forcing*, 55 Nw. U. L. REV. 62 (1960). These works have a similar, highly controversial outlook, and I do not mean to suggest that the courts should necessarily adopt their analysis. But they should at least be confronted.

36. United States v. Arnold, Schwinn & Co., 388 U.S. 365, 377-79 (1967).

37. Dr. Miles Medical Co. v. John D. Park & Sons Co., 220 U.S. 373 (1911).

in the Court's judgment, any necessity for determining the actual impact of the restraint and the legality of similar restraints unilaterally imposed.[38] The legality of vertical acquisitions, requirements contracts, and, to a lesser degree, tying arrangements, depends in large measure upon the percentage of the market foreclosed to competitors of the seller by the arrangement.[39] This standard was further simplified by the assumption in *Brown Shoe* that competitors of the seller would as the result of a vertical acquisition necessarily be foreclosed from *all* sales to the acquired customer. The mere fact of substantial foreclosure is not always conclusive of illegality. Economies created by the arrangement *may* be taken into account.[40] New firms, or firms with other peculiar problems, may be treated differently. But substantial foreclosure, rather than an increase in concentration or horizontal market power, has become the measure of the injury to competition called for by the Clayton Act.

Why this should be so has not been made altogether clear. One cannot assume that substantial foreclosure necessarily reflects or results in increased concentration or market power at the seller level. Foreclosure through various forms of vertical integration may create unduly high barriers to entry, but this is not so in every case and may not be particularly relevant if the industry is highly competitive anyway. Some of these arrangements, particularly tie-ins, may be used by a seller with market power to obtain additional monopoly profit, but such an effect can hardly be measured by reference to degree of market foreclosure. Apparently uncertain about the effect of such vertical arrangements upon concentration in the market and not confident that in all cases such effects can be determined on a case-by-case basis, the Court has proceeded with a method of analysis placing primary emphasis on equality of opportunity, free access to markets by competing sellers, and complete freedom of choice by buyers. If it can be proved that the challenged practice is likely to increase concentration or create high barriers to entry, so much the better. But in any event, the practice may be condemned as an unwarranted limitation on buyer and/or seller opportunities.

Preservation of free and unrestricted markets comprised of a large number of buyers and sellers is of course perfectly consistent with the economic goal of workable competition. But the

---

38. *See* United States v. General Motors Corp., 384 U.S. 127 (1966).

39. *Compare* Brown Shoe Co. v. United States, 370 U.S. 294 (1962) (vertical merger) *with* United States v. Loew's, Inc., 371 U.S. 38 (1962) (tying arrangement) *and* Tampa Elec. Co. v. Nashville Coal Co., 365 U.S. 320 (1961) (requirements contract).

40. *Compare* Brown Shoe Co. v. United States, 370 U.S. 294, 344 (1962), *with* Tampa Elec. Co. v. Nashville Coal Co., 365 U.S. 320 (1961).

Court has often seemed less concerned with the economically necessary level of rivalry within the market than with what may be described as the "rights" of the individual firms which comprise the market: their independence and right to be treated as other firms are treated have become values to be protected as ends in themselves. This necessarily shifts the focus away from the market to the allegedly injured firm or group of firms.

The preoccupation in *Von's Grocery*,[41] a horizontal merger case, with the dual need to preserve a large number of competitors and to protect small business indicates that such concerns have found expression in cases other than those involving vertical restraints. But it is in cases challenging vertical restraints that these themes have been most persistent and most determinative of the outcome. The "foreclosure" standard so frequently used in vertical restraint cases partially reflects this emphasis on the preservation of numerous competitors and protection of small businessmen. This concern is also evident, in a somewhat different dimension, in the Court's frequent assertions that unlawful ᵢrestraints have been "imposed" on buyers (usually distributors) as the result of inequality of bargaining power between buyer and seller. One of the commonly stated vices of tying arrangements is that they "coerce" the buyer into purchasing a product he does not want.[42] In *Brown Shoe*, the Court noted that the acquired firm would be "forced" to buy Brown's shoes.[43] Similar findings of "coercion," "compulsion," or other economic pressure appear regularly in cases involving contractual arrangements between manufacturers and distributors with respect to prices, territories, and customers. This suggests that it is the manner in which the restraint is imposed, rather than the effect of the arrangement upon the market, which is the reason for its condemnation.[44] "Coercion" is a slippery concept, and the Court has used the word rather loosely. In some cases, it appears to mean that the buyer is peculiarly dependent upon a given seller as a source of supply and may simply be a shorthand expression denoting market power in the seller. But at other times, the word seems to mean little more than the seller is somehow "bigger" than the buyer, a condition which generally prevails when the buyer is an independent distributor. However unrealistically, the distributor is viewed as an independent economic unit whose very independence is itself

41. United States v. Von's Grocery Co., 384 U.S. 270 (1966).
42. *See, e.g.*, United States v. Loew's, Inc., 371 U.S. 38, 48 n.6 (1962).
43. Brown Shoe Co. v. United States, 370 U.S. 294, 332 (1962).
44. Simpson v. Union Oil Co., 377 U.S. 13, 21 (1964); United States v. Parke, Davis & Co., 362 U.S. 29, 42 (1960). *Cf.* Atlantic Ref. Co. v. FTC, 381 U.S. 357, 368 (1964).

a value to be protected. The antitrust laws have become the vehicle for redressing the imbalance of bargaining power which threatens the exercise of his independent judgment.

The Court's increasing emphasis on the preservation of equal individual opportunity and on uncoerced, fully independent decision-making can hardly be said to be alien to the history and tradition of the antitrust laws. The values reflected are more social and political than economic, but this is in itself no basis for condemnation of the Court, particularly at a time when similar values have become increasingly important in other areas. Equality of opportunity—the right of every man to make his own decisions and to go as far as his talents will take him—has been the dominant concern of our time. It has also been the primary concern of the Warren Court. These values cannot be left behind when the Court proceeds from a civil rights or criminal case to an antitrust case. On the other hand, such values cannot simply be transposed from controversies pitting blacks against whites to those between "big" business and "small" business; obviously the values may be qualitatively different and more important in one setting than in the other. Moreover, even in civil rights some have argued that the Court has gone too far—that it has created more than equality between black and white, poor and rich, and that it has failed to give proper weight to other societal values. This does not mean that equality as a social and political value is unimportant. It merely suggests that in a given case its cost may come too high.

The question of cost—of the proper weighing of competing values—is now the critical one for antitrust. The teachings of economic theory may not be determinative of the outcome, but they are not irrelevant. Through the use of economic analysis, the costs of competing antitrust values can be identified with considerable accuracy. If protection of independent judgment, individual initiative, and equality of opportunity is achieved at the cost of economic efficiency, the price may be too great. Society may value small business, for example, but not to the point of subsidizing it. It is in the proper weighing of these values, it seems to me, that the Court has often failed. It has too often been intolerant of arguments predicated upon the efficiency-creating nature of the conduct before it.[45] While perhaps not all conduct resulting in economic efficiency should be approved, the Court must accurately appraise the cost of prohibiting a practice before condemning it.

---

45. The clearest example is Brown Shoe Co. v. United States, 370 U.S. 294, 344 (1962).

Apart from what the Court has said and done in specific cases, what has been the practical effect of its antitrust work? To a considerable degree, the answer must await the passage of time. It is surely too early to determine whether there has been any restructuring of American industry in a manner more likely to assure competitive results. We might assume, for example, that horizontal mergers have been significantly impeded and still conclude that alternative means of expansion have brought about just as much, if not more, concentration in the market. But some noneconomic effects are already apparent, and worth noting.

First, both directly and through its encouragement of public and private enforcement, the Court has made the business community more aware of antitrust than ever before. No major American corporation would consider a merger today without first consulting antitrust counsel. Businessmen now commonly talk about antitrust; internal compliance programs have been initiated and carried out. One cynical friend suggests that antitrust is now the second most talked about subject among businessmen, the favorite still being prices!

Second, the broad prohibitory rules established by the Court, particularly in merger cases, have gradually but perceptibly worked significant institutional changes in the Antitrust Division of the Department of Justice. Prosecutors always have some degree of discretion in deciding whether to prosecute. But under the standards of recent horizontal merger cases, the decision by the Department to proceed in a given case is viewed as virtually determinative of the outcome. As a result, attention has focused on this initial decision. Formally or informally, hearing procedures are developing; argument by counsel may be heard before a complaint is issued. Recent months have also seen the announcement of Department guidelines for enforcement of section 7 of the Clayton Act.[46] What all this suggests is that the decision-making forum is shifting and that the Department is acting increasingly like an administrative agency—a development which warrants more attention than it has so far received.

Finally, the Court's work has resulted in an increasing cynicism about its methods and results which threatens to foreclose realistic assessment of its accomplishments and ultimately to jeopardize acceptance of its commands. This is admittedly a harsh statement. Hopefully I overstate the problem. I would be delighted to be wrong. But anyone dealing daily with antitrust knows that a growing attitude exists among antitrust lawyers that no purpose

---

46. United States Department of Justice, Merger Guidelines, May 30, 1968.

is served either by analyzing opinions or by preparing factual records and arguments. There is, in short, a far too common belief that whatever the language of previous Court opinions, the findings of the district court, or the merits of the case in general, the result is preordained. Defense lawyers expect to lose, and are likely to view the litigation as a useless gesture. I have heard government lawyers express similar views, except that they expect to win. Combatting this same attitude in law students is, in my judgment, the most difficult part of teaching antitrust. As an immediate matter, the effectiveness of the litigation process may be impaired. Such an attitude may also lead to an increasing assumption of decision-making responsibility by the Congress, thereby further impairing the credibility of the judicial process.[47]

The attitude with which I am concerned is something more than fundamental disagreement with the results reached by the Court; there is obviously a difference between good faith criticism and cynicism. The cynicism of which I speak concerns the Court's methods—the decision-making process itself. This is not to suggest that it is an attitude wholly unconcerned with the result of cases, or that, indeed, it does not reflect some good faith disagreement with the policies being applied. But for the most part, cynicism has developed because of the one-sidedness of the decisions, not because of their merits.

The tendency of many critics to focus on the manner in which the Court has decided cases, rather than upon the ultimate merits of the decisions, seemed deplorable to me when I began teaching antitrust three years ago. Obviously some opinions were less than clear and seemed lacking in candor. There were occasions when the Court ignored or abused precedent to reach a particular result. But the same was true in many earlier opinions, and there have often been sound reasons for these deficiencies. It was equally true that the Court had formulated broad prohibitory rules in cases where such rules were not necessary to the outcome. But in my view it seemed clear that the interests of antitrust policy could not always best be served by deciding particular cases on the narrowest possible grounds. Broader rules which are stated with some certainty afford needed guidance to the business community. I was even willing to concede that the Court was result-oriented. After all, the antitrust laws virtually direct the Court to formulate economic policy; to suggest that a Court so charged by the statute was result-oriented was virtually a truism. If in a

---

47. *Cf.* Bank Merger Act of 1966, 12 U.S.C. § 1828(c) (Supp. II, 1967).

particular case the result happened to favor the Government, it was simply because the Government's position was in accord with the policies being applied by the Court. I still have considerable faith in these answers, but every year they are less satisfying. I now find myself being infected with the same cynicism, hopefully to a lesser degree, that has infected my students. I do not think the explanation is as simple as contagion. Whatever the explanation, it is disturbing that those of us who should know better are catching the disease.

The explanation for this cynical attitude is complex. It begins with statistics. During the 1953 through 1967 terms, the Court wrote full opinions in forty-five antitrust cases in which the Government was plaintiff. Forty-two cases were decided in the Government's favor. Of twenty-five cases decided with full opinion involving the Federal Trade Commission, twenty-three decisions have been in favor of the Commission. Private plaintiffs in treble damage suits have not fared quite as well; they obtained favorable results in only twenty of thirty-one cases decided with full opinion during this same period.[48] To be sure, there have been landmark decisions in favor of defendants. *Tampa Electric*,[49] upholding a long-term requirements contract, and *Noerr*,[50] virtually immunizing what may be loosely described as lobbying practices from the antitrust laws, may be cited as examples. But these decisions came in treble damage suits to which the Government was not a party. There have been but two major decisions in government cases favorable to defendants. One, the *DuPont Cellophane* case,[51] came early in the history of the Warren Court, and the other, *White Motor*,[52] apparently has been superseded.

Among many laymen, and indeed many lawyers, the basic concept of evenhanded justice has come to be reflected in the view that some kind of score—a measure of justice if you like—can be kept in won-lost columns. When the columns get too far out of balance in either direction, something is wrong. The columns in antitrust are now hopelessly out of balance. But such a won-lost

48. These figures are based upon those in Arnold, *supra* note 29, at 18, which cover the Court's 1953 through 1965 terms. To these I have added figures for the 1966 term, as set out in *The Supreme Court, 1966 Term*, 81 HARV. L. REV. 69, 128-29 (1967), and figures for the 1967 term based on my own count. There may of course be disagreement over who "won" a particular case. The *Schwinn* case, for example, is identified as a Government victory, a debatable conclusion. But such disagreements can extend to very few cases.

49. Tampa Elec. Co. v. Nashville Coal Co., 365 U.S. 320 (1961).

50. Eastern R.R. Presidents Conference v. Noerr Motor Freight, Inc., 365 U.S. 127 (1961).

51. United States v. E. I. duPont de Nemours & Co., 351 U.S. 377 (1956).

52. White Motor Co. v. United States, 372 U.S. 253 (1963).

analysis has little utility, for it says nothing about why the imbalance has occurred. The figures may whet one's curiosity—may even raise doubts—but doubts can be erased by adequate explanation. Some explanation may be found in the high selectivity exercised by the Solicitor General over cases carried by the Government to the Supreme Court. But ultimately, explanation of the Court's actions must come from the Court itself. The observer who is dissatisfied with the Court's own explanations of its actions is left to speculate for himself.

Others have catalogued in detail the deficiencies in many of the Court's opinions, and I do not intend to repeat that here.[53] The cases about to be discussed are simply illustrative; they are ones which have particularly troubled my students as well as myself. They do not typify all of the Court's antitrust opinions (for some have been outstanding), but they are illustrative in the sense that other cases could be substituted to make the same points. Nor, it should be understood, do I intend to be critical for the sake of criticism. But the reasons for a widely prevalent attitude must be understood if it is to be corrected. What follows is in a sense a plea for the Court to give its defenders more help than it has given them in the past.

The Court's merger decisions have contributed disproportionately to the growing concern with the Court's methodology. *Brown Shoe* was well received, primarily because of the moderate tenor of the opinion. And there was an appealing practical candor to the opinion in *Philadelphia Bank* (at least that portion of the opinion dealing with the merits of the section 7 violation). But subsequent decisions, particularly those in which market definition has been critical, have caused many to concur with Justice Stewart's observation that the only consistent pattern discernible in the Court's merger decisions is that "the Government always wins."[54] This attitude rests in part on the fact that the Government *has* always won, and in part on the Court's ability to place increasing emphasis on the preservation of small business and a wide range of buyer choice as the market shares in the cases before it have grown smaller.

The *Brown Shoe* opinion itself has been a contributing factor to the growing sense of cynicism. For as the Court has moved closer to a per se prohibition of horizontal mergers, its apparent departure from the approach suggested in *Brown Shoe* has led some to conclude that the Court did not mean what it initially said. This

---

53. *See, e.g.,* Handler, *The Supreme Court and the Antitrust Laws (From the Viewpoint of the Critic)*, 34 A.B.A. ANTITRUST L.J. 21 (1967).

54. United States v. Von's Grocery, 384 U.S. 270, 301 (1966) (dissenting opinion).

is the kind of self-perpetuating suspicion which is easily carried over to other cases. It is not inconceivable that the Court *has* had a more severe prohibition in mind all along, or at least that it has concluded that the antimerger movement desired by Congress would be substantially impeded by a single pro-merger decision. If so, *Brown Shoe* may be explained as a tactical effort to achieve initial maximum acceptance. Any subsequent open announcement of a harsher rule would have been too much of a departure from *Brown Shoe,* particularly since the same message could be communicated on a case-by-case basis. Moreover, adopting a harsher rule might have placed undue pressure to prosecute on the Department of Justice. If the Court *has* reasoned in such a manner, one might simply suggest that the cost in terms of impairment of its credibility has been too great. But while some members of the Court may have had such a preconceived plan, the more plausible explanation is that the Court meant what it said in *Brown Shoe* and that its position has changed, if at all, only as it gained experience with subsequent cases. Indeed, I do not agree that there has been a substantial departure from *Brown Shoe.*

The most common specific attack on the Court's methodology in merger cases has been directed at its definitions of markets. On the whole, given the complexity of market definition and the lack of adequate expert guidance furnished to the Court, it has handled the process as well as can be expected. But market definitions *can* be manipulated to reach a particular result. Each party in merger litigation has a tactical reason for preferring one market definition over another. The Court has persistently accepted the market definitions proposed by or favorable to the Government, often setting aside district court findings to do so. In such circumstances, it takes only one or two cases in which the Court's reasoning is clearly inadequate to cast doubt on the entire definitional process. *Alcoa-Rome Cable*[55] is such a case. The Supreme Court, having concluded contrary to the findings of the district court that insulated aluminum conductor was in a market apart from its copper counterpart, went on to define the relevant market to include both bare and insulated aluminum cable. The inclusion of these two products in a single market is particularly astonishing. While noting that both bare and insulated aluminum cable are used to carry electricity, the Court's primary justification for this curious result was that it was simply "a logical extension of the District Court's findings."[56] But it clearly is not. It hardly follows that because aluminum in-

---

55. United States v. Aluminum Co. of America, 377 U.S. 271 (1964).
56. 377 U.S. at 277 n.4 (1964).

sulated conductor and copper insulated conductor do not compete that bare and insulated aluminum conductor do. With what explanation is the reader left?

The Court's treatment of precedent has often lacked candor and interjected confusion concerning the meaning of its rulings. In *Simpson v. Union Oil Co.*,[57] for instance, the Court held unlawful a series of consignment contracts pursuant to which Union Oil fixed the price to be charged by its dealer-consignees. The Court's opinion is clouded with unnecessary uncertainty: although proceeding on the assumption that there was a valid consignment, the Court emphasized the "coercion" of dealers, and its constant use of quotation marks around the word "agency" suggests that it doubted the good faith of the arrangement. Holding the arrangement unlawful seems to conflict with the old *G.E.* case,[58] which permitted a manufacturer to control its consignees' prices. *Simpson* distinguished *G.E.* on the ground that a patented article was involved in the latter,[59] a distinction far too transparent. The rationale of *G.E.* in no way relied upon the presence of a patent. In asserting that it did, the Court quoted portions of the *G.E.* opinion dealing with a completely different issue—the right of a patent holder to set the price at which its manufacturing licensees sell (a fact pointed out by the dissent).

Simpson, in turn, was treated in an almost inexplicable manner in *Schwinn*,[60] as was the Court's earlier decision in *White Motor*.[61] At issue in *Schwinn* were (1) agreements preventing distributors from selling bicycles purchased from Schwinn to anyone other than retailers franchised by Schwinn; (2) agreements preventing franchised retailers from selling bicycles purchased from Schwinn to nonfranchised retailers; (3) a series of similar restrictions, including territorial restrictions, imposed on distributors who did not purchase but acted as Schwinn's agents or consignees. Agreements confining resale by purchasing distributors to specific territories had been held unlawful by the district court, and no review of this holding was sought. Schwinn's restraints upon purchasing distributors and retailers were similar to those before the Court in *White Motor*. In that case, which came on motion for summary judgment, the Court refused to apply a per se rule to the restraints, explaining that it did "not know enough of the economic

57. 377 U.S. 13 (1964).
58. United States v. General Elec. Co., 272 U.S. 476 (1926).
59. 377 U.S. at 23.
60. United States v. Arnold, Schwinn & Co., 388 U.S. 365 (1967).
61. White Motor Co. v. United States, 372 U.S. 253 (1963).

and business stuff out of which these arrangements emerge to be certain of their purpose and effect."[62] Yet in *Schwinn*, the Court seemed to hold that all agreements placing customer or territorial limitations upon purchasing retailers are per se violations of the Sherman Act. What then became of *White Motor*? *White Motor* was cited *in support* of the Court's per se rule. Perhaps by the time *Schwinn* was decided the Court did know more of the purpose and effect of such arrangements, but this was not demonstrated. The Court's holding rested on the common-law rule against restraints on alienation, a rule without necessary relationship to anticompetitive effect and as much available in *White Motor* as in *Schwinn*. Recognizing that this common-law rule afforded no basis for condemnation of Schwinn's contractual arrangements placing similar restraints on consignees or agents, the Court next concluded that these restraints were not only not per se violations, but were entirely lawful on the record before it. The Court's distinction between agency and sale brought *Schwinn* into apparent conflict with *Simpson*, where the Court seemed to say that the application of antitrust rules is in no way dependent upon such a distinction. To be sure, *Simpson* emphasized that dealers had been "coerced" into the consignment; such coercion was apparently lacking in *Schwinn*. The dealers in *Simpson* handled no competing products; Schwinn's dealers did sell other bicycles. And, *Simpson* involved price-fixing. But the Court in *Schwinn* made virtually no effort to distinguish *Simpson*. The result in *Schwinn* may well be sound, but the Court's own explanation, together with its treatment of *White Motor* and *Simpson*, puts the matter in doubt.

Finally, note should be taken of a number of cases in which the Court has adopted strained statutory constructions thought justified by broad antitrust policy considerations. The constructions of the jurisdictional provisions of section 7 in *Philadelphia Bank*[63] and the interpretation of the All Writs Act[64] in *Dean Foods*[65] may be cited as examples. Most disturbing, however, has been the Court's holding that under section 5(b) of the Clayton Act the pendency of Federal Trade Commission proceedings will toll the statute of limitations on treble damage actions involving the same matter.[66] Dealing with statutory language which was on its face quite clearly

---

62. 372 U.S. at 263 (1963).
63. United States v. Philadelphia Natl. Bank, 374 U.S. 321, 335-49 (1963).
64. 28 U.S.C. § 1651(a) (1964).
65. FTC v. Dean Foods Co., 384 U.S. 597 (1966).
66. New Jersey Wood Finishing Co. v. Minnesota Mining and Mfg. Co., 381 U.S. 311 (1965).

inapplicable, the Court's only specific reference to the language was a statement that it "does not clearly encompass Commission proceedings."[67] Such decisions, whether right or wrong in terms of antitrust policy, are particularly disturbing to lawyers who may feel uneasy in criticizing substantive decisions because they do not fully comprehend economic doctrine, but who regard statutory interpretation as their own domain.

Alcoa-Rome Cable, Simpson, Schwinn, and the other cases just discussed are of course but single cases. Each decision may be explained, and its inadequacies may be justified. But it is the impression and attitude derived from a series of such cases that is troublesome. Too often the burden of explanation has been left to those of us who would defend the Court. The task grows increasingly difficult.

The antitrust accomplishments of the Warren Court have been many. As in other substantive areas it has led, not followed. It has led reluctant lower courts and, on occasion, a reluctant Department of Justice. But methodology is an important aspect of leadership, even for those in positions of power. A leader with a just cause may fail not because his cause is unacceptable but because his methods are wrong. This is the dilemma the Court now faces. Faced with increasing cynicism and distrust among many of those it seeks to lead, there is at least some danger that it may become a Pied Piper with an unheeded tune.

---

67. New Jersey Wood Finishing Co. v. Minnesota Mining and Mfg. Co., 381 U.S. 311, 321 (1965). *See* P. AREEDA, ANTITRUST ANALYSIS 42 n.97 (1967).

THE WARREN COURT AND THE
POLITICAL PROCESS

*William M. Beaney**

I. THE COURT BEFORE WARREN

Our complex political system creates endless opportunity to
debate the proper roles and powers of each of our principal
political institutions. Students of the Supreme Court who quarrel
over the proper role of the Court sometimes forget that the powers
of the President and the proper place of Congress have also been
subject to fierce controversy throughout our history, and that the
political tension between the national government and the states
has provided a persistent theme from the beginning of the Republic.
It must never be forgotten that the system provided by the Framers
was not designed to produce efficient government, but rather was
intended, through the positing of power against power, to create a
"free" government, one in which property and the other minority
rights might be reasonably secure against the weight of popular
majorities. Yet, they did not—and in the nature of things they could
not—set forth a detailed permanent model, one in which the role of
each of our great political institutions was rigorously defined for all
times. James Madison, speculating about the probable strength of
each of the three branches of the new government, gave the palm to
the legislature, which, in his judgment, tended to draw "all power
into its impetuous vortex."[1] His fellow commentator, Hamilton,
awarded third place to the Supreme Court, "beyond comparison
the weakest of the three."[2] The relationship between national and
state governments conceived by Madison envisaged the popular and
powerful states as fully capable of resisting national power; thus,
the task of the newly established national government was to attract
sufficient support to enable it to serve as a counterweight to the
divisive tendencies of the states.[3]

In tracing historically the relationships of each branch of the

---

* Professor of Politics, Princeton University; Visiting Professor of Law (1968-1969),
University of Denver. A.B. 1940, Harvard University; LL.B. 1947, Ph.D. 1951, University of Michigan.—Ed.

1. THE FEDERALIST No. 48, at 333 (J. Cooke ed. 1961). In the same number, Madison
observed that "it is against the enterprising ambition of this department [the legislature], that the people ought to indulge all their jealousy and exhaust all their precautions." *Id.* at 334.

2. *Id.* No. 78, at 523. To Hamilton, the Court would "always be the least dangerous
to the political rights of the constitution . . . ." *Id.* at 522.

3. *Id.* Nos. 45, 46.

national government to the others, one notes both long-term and short-term changes in the relative power of each. Certain Presidents, notably Jackson and Lincoln, expanded presidential power during a century marked by strong congressional action. The Supreme Court, under Marshall, strengthened national powers against state pretensions and established the Court's role as the pre-eminent interpreter of the Constitution. Yet, the Court was usually generous toward state action until the last decade of the nineteenth century, and the *Dred Scott* decision[4] in 1857, which frustrated congressional efforts to compromise the slavery issue, marked only the second time the Court had faulted an act of Congress.

The present century has been marked not only by short-range ebbing and flowing of executive power, but also by congressional acceptance of a largely ratifying and checking role in its relationship with the President.[5] The twentieth century clearly is the age of executive initiative and administrative government. The great era of Congress lies in the past.

To point out that the Supreme Court has also had a checkered career since the turn of the century is to state the obvious. Over the protests of Justices Holmes, Brandeis, and occasionally others, the Court read into the Constitution an economic and social philosophy which made it a frequent and effective censor of state and national legislation.[6] Progressive political leaders increasingly viewed the Court, which allied itself in spirit with the dominant laissez-faire philosophy of powerful business leaders, as a barrier against needed social change. When the forces pressing for large-scale social reform found a powerful spokesman in Franklin D. Roosevelt, the Court was brought under siege. Although the President's ill-conceived Court-packing plan was defeated, the Court, sensing the dangers confronting it, withdrew from its censorious role. The power to govern was returned to Congress and the President. No longer would the Court use the tenth amendment to frustrate national commerce and taxing power.[7] Also abandoned was the ready use of the due process clauses to inhibit state and national social legislation.[8]

---

4. Scott v. Sanford, 60 U.S. (19 How.) 393.

5. E. CORWIN, THE PRESIDENT, OFFICE AND POWERS (4th rev. ed. 1957); J. HARRIS, CONGRESSIONAL CONTROL OF ADMINISTRATION (1964); R. NEUSTADT, PRESIDENTIAL POWER (1960); N. POWELL, RESPONSIBLE PUBLIC BUREAUCRACY IN THE UNITED STATES (1967).

6. E. CORWIN, LIBERTY AGAINST GOVERNMENT (1948); A. MASON, THE SUPREME COURT FROM TAFT TO WARREN (rev. ed. 1968); R. McCLOSKEY, THE AMERICAN SUPREME COURT ch. VI (1960).

7. *See* United States v. Darby, 312 U.S. 100 (1941).

8. A. MASON, HARLAN FISKE STONE, esp. pt. V (1956); R. McCLOSKEY, *supra* note 6, ch. VII; C. PRITCHETT, THE ROOSEVELT COURT (1948).

In the period from 1937 to 1953, the Court's role contracted as it proceeded to undo some of its earlier handiwork, concentrating on the staples of appellate review.[9] For, even when its role is conceived in the most modest terms, the Court always has duties of the highest importance; interpreting and applying the provisions of increasingly complex congressional enactments, reviewing decisions of myriad federal agencies, and resolving clashes of state and national power still leave the Court, in James Bradley Thayer's phrase, "a great and stately jurisdiction."[10] But the post-1937 Court did not wholly abandon its role as censor. Other potentially explosive areas of judicial concern had emerged even before the Court revolution of 1937. First amendment issues involving the national government came before the Court as early as 1919,[11] and with the *Gitlow* decision[12] in 1925, state actions affecting first amendment freedoms became amenable to Supreme Court review on the judicially evolved theory that the "liberty" protected by the fourteenth amendment's due process clause included freedom of speech and, by implication, the other enumerated rights of the first amendment. In 1931 freedom of press,[13] in 1937 freedom of assembly,[14] in 1940 freedom of religion,[15] and in 1947 the religious establishment provision[16] were incorporated into the fourteenth amendment. Since state and local governments had been far more diligent than the national government in suppressing dissenters and harassing unpopular minorities, large-scale judicial intervention depended on the manner in which the Court chose to regard its new opportunities.[17]

In the celebrated footnote 4 of *United States v. Carolene Products Co.*,[18] Justice Stone suggested—in highly tentative language—that the Court might properly employ more stringent tests when reviewing legislation or official action that affected specific first amendment

---

9. C. Pritchett, Civil Liberties and the Vinson Court 240 (1954), concluded that "[t]he Vinson Court's solution was almost entirely within the tradition of the strong legislature-weak judiciary formula which Holmes developed for the quite different purpose of controlling judicial review over state economic legislation."

10. *The Origin and Scope of the American Doctrine of Constitutional Law*, 7 Harv. L. Rev. 129, 152 (1893).

11. Abrams v. United States, 250 U.S. 616 (1919); Schenck v. United States, 249 U.S. 47 (1919).

12. Gitlow v. New York, 268 U.S. 652 (1925).

13. Near v. Minnesota, 283 U.S. 697.

14. DeJonge v. Oregon, 299 U.S. 353.

15. Cantwell v. Connecticut, 310 U.S. 296.

16. Everson v. Board of Educ., 330 U.S. 1.

17. The opportunities were certain to arise because of the increasing public and legal activities of organized groups in the 1930's. *See generally* R. Horn, Groups and the Constitution (1956).

18. 304 U.S. 144, 152 (1938).

rights, restricted normal political processes, or focused upon "discrete or insular" minorities.

This conception of a preferred position for certain freedoms was firmly adopted by some of the Justices, particularly Black, Douglas, Rutledge, and Murphy, and was followed on occasion by others. In opposition, Justice Frankfurter, adhering to the teachings of his Harvard Law School mentor James Bradley Thayer, saw no reason to concede a preference to the Bill of Rights.[19] Reiterating a political philosophy expressed decades earlier, Frankfurter viewed the Supreme Court as an essentially undemocratic institution, one that should defer to the decisions of the representative branches on virtually all occasions.[20] With the exception of the second John M. Harlan, no other Justice in the modern era has foresworn judicial power in such positive terms. Although classed by most observers with Frankfurter and Harlan as "conservatives," Justices Jackson, Clark, Reed, Minton, Whittaker, White, Stewart, and Chief Justice Vinson were less impressed with the dangers of judicial intervention; their numerous votes in support of governmental action reflected their conclusion that, on balance, such action was reasonable.

Yet during the period from 1937 to 1953, there were three constitutional areas in which the Court demonstrated particular interest, and in many cases, invalidated governmental action. Jehovah's Witnesses won a number of triumphs, most notably in the second

---

19. Speaking of the preferred-position concept, he argued that it was "a mischievous phrase, if it carries the thought, which it may subtly imply, that any law touching communication is infected with presumptive invalidity." Kovacs v. Cooper, 336 U.S. 77, 90 (1949).

20. Justice Frankfurther's majority opinion in Minersville School Dist. v. Gobitis, 310 U.S. 586 (1940), and his dissent in West Virginia Board of Educ. v. Barnette, 319 U.S. 624, 646 (1943) are excellent examples of his antireview attitude. Arthur E. Sutherland suggests that between 1938 and 1943 a profound change in our political philosophy may have occurred, a revision of thought about majoritarian institutions. *All Sides of the Question, Felix Frankfurter and Personal Freedom* in 2 FELIX FRANKFURTER: THE JUDGE 109 (W. Mendelson, ed. 1964). If this insight is correct, it is clear that Frankfurter remained a true believer to the end. Clearly the Justice has a romantic and rather elementary conception of the role of our representative institutions and the nature of their functioning, which seems surprising in one who was so close to the seats of power in the 1930's. But perhaps that experience served to reinforce his bias against judicial review, since Frankfurter's principal position was that in a world of relative values the legislature was at least more representative than the Court. Frankfurter had written in 1934, "[T]he process of constitutional interpretation compels the translation of policy into judgment, and the controlling conceptions of the Justices are their 'idealized political picture' of the existing social order." *The Supreme Court of the United States*, in XIV ENCYCLOPEDIA OF THE SOCIAL SCIENCES 424 (1934), reprinted in LAW AND POLITICS: FELIX FRANKFURTER 21, 30 (E. Prichard & A. Macleish ed. 1939). Apparently he had little respect for the argument that Supreme Court Justices also have a representative role.

flag salute case.[21] The *Duncan* case,[22] invalidating martial rule in Hawaii during World War II, and *Thornhill v. Alabama*,[23] drawing peaceful picketing under the protection of free-speech guarantees, were other libertarian victories. Second, by insisting on a realistic assessment of the "equality" afforded by "separate but equal" facilities,[24] and by stressing the importance of the intangible detriments flowing from a segregated education,[25] the pre-Warren Court rendered inevitable the decision in the school desegregation cases.[26] Similarly, the pre-Warren Court began in the 1930's to evince interest in the process of criminal justice in the states. As the Court chose to look more closely at the realities of criminal justice, it discovered that racial minorities and indigent and inexperienced defendants were subject to law enforcement and trial practices that fell short of due process of law.[27]

Despite its new judicial concerns, it is fair to say that the pre-Warren Court had slipped into a secondary role in the political system, and its decisions, on the whole, did not arouse serious public criticism. The decision in the steel seizure cases[28] was popular, primarily because President Truman's standing with the American people was not high. The decision upholding the convictions of the Communist Party leaders[29] was widely applauded, as were other decisions supporting actions restricting Communists.[30]

By 1953, then, when Earl Warren stepped down as Governor of California to accept a recess appointment from President Eisenhower, the Court was already embarked on new judicial paths. But the nation, troubled by its thorny relations with the Soviet Union and frustrated by its seemingly inconclusive involvement in Korea only five years after the conclusion of a major war, seemed in no mood to deal forthrightly with the pressing problem of civil rights, and reacted with some impatience to claims on behalf of political dissenters. And law enforcement agencies, as well as the public in general, had traditionally been hostile to more considerate treatment

---

21. West Virginia Bd. of Educ. v. Barnette, 319 U.S. 624 (1943).

22. Duncan v. Kahanamoku, 327 U.S. 304 (1946).

23. 310 U.S. 88 (1940).

24. Sweatt v. Painter, 339 U.S. 629 (1950).

25. McLaurin v. Oklahoma State Regents for Higher Educ., 339 U.S. 637 (1950).

26. Brown v. Board of Educ., 347 U.S. 483 (1954). *See* R. Harris, The Quest of Equality (1960); C. Pritchett, Civil Liberties and the Vinson Court ch. 7 (1954).

27. *See* D. Fellman, The Defendant's Rights (1958).

28. Youngstown Sheet & Tube Co. v. Sawyer, 343 U.S. 579 (1952).

29. Dennis v. United States, 341 U.S. 494 (1951).

30. American Communication Assn. v. Douds, 339 U.S. 382 (1950); Adler v. Board of Educ. of the City of New York, 342 U.S. 485 (1952), among others.

for criminal defendants, whether by overly generous judicial doctrine or the use of legal "technicalities."

II. The Warren Era

President Eisenhower's nomination of Earl Warren as Chief Justice of the United States represented an awareness that the Supreme Court was, and necessarily remains, a political organ as well as a court of law. If legal experience and technical skill were prime requisites for a Justice or Chief Justice, it would have been difficult to justify the Warren appointment. Apart from discharging a major political debt, the appointment—concurred in by United States Attorney General Brownell and presumably by other leaders of the Eastern wing of the Republican Party—promised to bring to the Court a mildly liberal leader who could be counted on to play a part in reinforcing the image of no-nonsense, businesslike government which the new Administration hoped to maintain.[31]

In the very first term of Warren's tenure the Court handed down its opinion in the school desegregation cases,[32] which had been before the Court in the last term of Vinson's leadership, only to be set for reargument in the following term. The predictable reaction to the Court's pronouncement in these cases and to the implementing decision that followed in 1955,[33] despite the Court's unanimity, was a barrage of violent criticism from political leaders and other spokesmen in the "deep South." More concrete resistance soon followed: legislative "interposition" resolutions were adopted, and various laws and administrative measures to thwart, or at least delay, implementation of the *Brown* decision were enacted. Almost all Southern members of Congress joined in 1956 in issuing a "Declaration of Constitutional Principles," which concluded with an appeal for resistance by "all lawful means."[34] Other decisions applying the desegregation rule to various activities and facilities further inflamed Southern sensibilities.

It cannot be overstressed that this violent and persistent attack on the Court by the political leaders of a substantial section of the nation has affected public reaction to other important Court decisions. For here was a large, vocal minority eager to discredit the

---

31. *See* the account of the appointment in J. Weaver, Warren: The Man, the Court, the Era ch. 13 (1968).

32. Brown v. Board of Educ., 347 U.S. 483 (1954).

33. Brown v. Board of Educ., 349 U.S. 294.

34. The legal resistance is chronicled in various issues of the *Race Relations Law Reporter. See also* J. Greenberg, Race Relations and American Law (1959).

Court in every conceivable way; and, given the range of controversial subjects that inevitably challenged the Court, the opportunities for public denunciation were numerous. In addition to the
steaming racial issues, the Court had to pass on antiobscenity measures, the rights of criminal defendants, sit-ins and other controversial forms of free expression, prayers and Bible-reading in schools,
and questions involving apportionment and districting for state and
national elections. When decisions favorable to individuals and
groups claiming these rights were handed down, the Southern bloc
could be counted on for bitter comment and intense efforts to inform news media of the disastrous consequences of the Court's chosen
path.[35] Because Southern Senators and Representatives held important committee positions as a result of the seniority system, they were
able to use Congress as a forum for their anti-Court crusade. Many
non-Southern members of Congress, whose mood has been one of
frustration arising from running battles with the bureaucracy, constant presidential prodding, and widespread criticism of Congress,
joined in the chorus of denunciation, eager to point the finger of
blame at another institution. It was especially pleasant for Congressmen to assume stances that were certain to please substantial numbers of constituents, and many of the Warren Court's decisions were
unpopular with large segments of the population for reasons that
seem obvious. How many citizens, after endless instruction that
Communism was a great and imminent threat to the nation's security, would applaud a decision favorable to Communists?[36] And,
clearly, the number of parents outraged by obscene literature exceeded the number of libertarians who applauded the Court's stand
favoring literary freedom.[37] Citizens who were alarmed by the growing crime rate were also quick to join the chorus of disapproval
generated by law enforcement representatives. Millions of good people were shocked by the decision banning prayers and Bible-reading,
and only a massive counterattack beat off the effort to reverse the

---

35. The bitter struggle to curb the jurisdiction of the Supreme Court is brilliantly
described in W. MURPHY, CONGRESS AND THE COURT (1962), a work crucial to our
understanding of congressional attitudes in the 1950's and 1960's.

36. *See* Stumpf, *Congessional Response to Supreme Court Rulings: The Interaction
of Law and Politics*, 14 J. PUB. L. 377 (1965) for a study of Court "reversal" bills in
Congress. *See also* Lytle, *Congressional Response to Supreme Court Decisions in the
Aftermath of the School Segregation Cases*, 12 J. PUB. L. 290 (1963); *Hearings on
S. 2646, Limitation of Appellate Jurisdiction of the United States Supreme Court
Before the Subcomm. of the Senate Comm. on the Judiciary*, 85th Cong., 2d Sess.
(1958).

37. *See* S. KRISLOV, THE SUPREME COURT AND POLITICAL FREEDOM 39-53 (1968) for an
analysis of the antilibertarian cast of American public opinion.

Court by means of the Becker Amendment.[38] Even the relatively popular reapportionment decisions aroused militant opponents who stood to lose by a fairer system of representation.[39] And of course, the cry of "states' rights" was raised not only in response to the desegregation decisions, but also in opposition to all decisions that found fault with state laws or practices. When the Conference of State Chief Justices issued its curiously unjudicial report in 1958,[40] ticking off grievances against the United States Supreme Court, it merely confirmed for many citizens their own vague fear that in an increasingly confusing and rapidly changing world, the Supreme Court seemed determined to render innovative and therefore distressing decisions.

In retrospect, it seems obvious that when the Court chose to hand down decisions favorable to racial minorities, political dissenters, criminal defendants, and protagonists of unpopular causes, it could hardly expect cheers from the majority of people. Empirical studies of popular attitudes consistently reveal deep-rooted popular opposition to many provisions of the Bill of Rights, and ingrained hostility toward dissenters and advocates of change.[41] Only strong stands by political and social leaders and by the popular media could offset this antilibertarian sentiment of the majority, but rarely were such stands taken. The Congress, as mentioned above, found the Court a convenient target. President Eisenhower assumed a remarkably dispassionate attitude toward the desegregation decisions, and withheld the massive reinforcement which the prestige of his name and office might have provided.[42] Presidents Kennedy and Johnson were willing to speak out on racial matters, but, in the nature of politics, they could not be expected to defend the Court on every

---

38. *See* Beaney & Beiser, *Prayer and Politics: The Impact of Engel and Schemp on the Political Process*, 13 J. Pub. L. 475 (1964). Of course, the simple focused type of question may yield deceptive results; *see* the preliminary findings of Murphy & Tanenhaus, *Public Opinion and the United States Supreme Court*, 2 Law & Society Rev. 357 (1968). Given an open-ended question about the Court concerning their likes and dislikes, the majority of respondents come up with nothing. Nevertheless, racial issues and school prayer, and to a lesser but growing degree, criminal-justice matters did evoke responses from a substantial minority.

39. On the Dirksen Amendment campaign *see* R. Dixon, Democratic Representation (1968) chs. 15, 16; Dixon, *Article V: The Comatose Article of Our Living Constitution*, 66 Mich. L. Rev. 931 (1968).

40. Report of the Committee on Federal-State Relations as Affected by Judicial Decisions.

41. *See* S. Krislov, *supra* note 37.

42. *See* R. Harris, *supra* note 26, at 155-57. That "you cannot change people's hearts merely by laws," was one of President Eisenhower's cherished beliefs. J. Weaver, *supra* note 31, at 217.

issue.[43] The American bar, which furnished heroic support to the embattled Court of the 1930's, has, on the whole, taken a less sympathetic position toward the Warren Court, which it views as too controversial and excessively disrespectful toward precedent.

It has often been remarked that the Court should, and usually does, follow the election returns. The argument is that although the Court is not an elective body, it must in its own way behave as a representative institution. If one takes this argument seriously, the Warren Court has, perhaps, been wrong on most of the controversial issues for which it has provided answers. If the function of the Court is to please the majority and displease as few groups and interests as possible, then Chief Justice Warren and the other politically sophisticated members of the Court have badly misconceived their role and deserve the criticism that they have received. But there is another view of the Supreme Court's role that casts the work of the Warren Court in a more favorable light. If the role of the representative branches is to give voice to—as well as shape and lead—public opinion, it may well be the proper function of the Supreme Court to voice the best aspirations of our people, to give reality to the ideals we profess in our Constitution and Declaration of Independence, and to provide justice for those who otherwise have difficulty claiming it. Who can deny that a viable society requires reasonably prompt and appropriate attention to important social problems? It is the Court, not the representative branches, which has tried to eliminate the racial cancer which still threatens America. Only well after the Court's first efforts did Congress and the President see fit to act. And, without traversing the ground covered in other Articles in this Symposium, is it not clear that the dominant theme running through the other controversial decisions of the Warren Court is the necessity of equal rights for all, protection of the underdog, and respect for the dignity of man in a confusingly complex society? One can, of course, argue that the Warren Court has tried to move forward on too many fronts in a period of social change and unrest. A cautious political strategist might conclude that in the light of the troubles stirred up by the desegregation decisions, the Court would have been wiser to allow Bible-readings and prayers in the schools, avoid restrictions on the police, assist in the crackdown on smut

---

43. President Kennedy's espousal of a comprehensive Civil Rights Act in 1963, enacted into law under President Johnson in 1964, might be regarded as the great exception. But Congress was driven, not led, to this action in 1964 and to other rights bills in subsequent years. By 1968 all had returned to normal.

peddlers, let Communists take their lumps, and stay out of the reapportionment thicket; but the Court has chosen a more embattled way.

Writing in 1941, Robert H. Jackson observed that the Supreme Court was "almost never a really contemporary institution . . . . The judiciary is thus the check of a preceding generation on the present one; a check of conservative legal philosophy upon a dynamic people; and nearly always a check of a rejected regime on the one in being."[44] The mistake of the Warren Court, according to its critics, is that it insists on moving too fast—on advancing far beyond the needs and expectations of the present generation. One of the most perceptive commentators has warned that the Court should not ignore history "in determining how judicial control should be exercised and when it should be brought to bear." Surely, he admonishes, "the record teaches that no useful purpose is served when the judges seek all the hottest political caldrons of the moment and dive into the middle of them."[45] It is hardly a daring speculation to suggest that a post-Warren Court may move somewhat cautiously in the conservative atmosphere of the late 1960's. Yet, the doctrines of equality, freedom, and respect for human dignity laid down in the numerous decisions of the Warren Court cannot be warped back to their original dimensions. The attitude of more and more Americans, particularly the members of the young and better-educated generation, is one of intense commitment to human rights. Generations hence it may well appear that what is supposedly the most conservative of American political institutions, the Supreme Court, was the institution that did the most to help the nation adjust to the needs and demands of a free society.[46]

---

44. THE STRUGGLE FOR JUDICIAL SUPREMACY 315.
45. R. McCLOSKEY, THE AMERICAN SUPREME COURT 229 (1960).
46. Archibald Cox has written:
Only history will know whether the Warren Court has struck the balance right. For myself, I am confident that historians will write that the trend of decisions during the 1950's and 1960's was in keeping with the mainstream of American history—a bit progressive but also moderate, a bit humane but not sentimental, a bit idealistic but seldom doctrinaire, and in the long run essentially pragmatic— in short, in keeping with the true genius of our institutions.
THE WARREN COURT 133-34 (1968).

EARL WARREN, THE "WARREN COURT," AND THE WARREN MYTHS

Philip B. Kurland[*]

"IT is not enough for the knight of romance," Justice Holmes once reminded us, "that you agree that his lady is a very nice girl—if you do not admit that she is the best that God ever made or will make, you must fight."[1] So, too, with the admirers of the Chief Justice and their "fair lady." For the moment, Earl Warren is enjoying the lavish praise that is not uncommonly ladled out when a man voluntarily decides to end a long and important government career. The contents of this issue of the *Michigan Law Review* may be taken as representative of the prevalent attitude, especially in the law school world, about the greatness of Chief Justice Warren.

Indeed, it was clear from the tone of the invitation to participate in this Symposium that the editors were requesting me to play a part in a sort of secular canonization of the great man, and that my role was to be that of the devil's advocate. As an amateur in canon history, I have been unable to discover an instance in which the devil's advocate has prevailed. I assume, therefore, that the function I am expected to fulfill is that of making out a good case against the miracles that Warren is supposed to have performed, but not a good enough case to be convincing. Thus, I must align myself neither with President Eisenhower's rumored reference to his appointment of Warren as the "biggest damfool mistake I ever made"[2] nor with President Johnson's assessment of Warren as "the greatest Chief Justice of them all."[3] My proposition here is rather that Warren is deserving neither of the simpering adulation of his admirers nor of the vitriolic abuse of his detractors. It is too early to sanctify him.

I should say early on, however, that if a "great Chief Justice" is one who has presided over a Court that has written, rewritten, and repealed large segments of the law of the land—constitutional as well as statutory and judicial—then Warren clearly qualifies for the accolade. If, on the other hand, reliance is to be placed on Warren's individual contributions to American jurisprudence as revealed in his opinions, it will be difficult indeed to justify such laurels.

---

* Professor of Law, University of Chicago, A.B. 1942, University of Pennsylvania; LL.B. 1944, Harvard University.—Ed.

1. *Natural Law*, in COLLECTED LEGAL PAPERS 310 (1920).
2. J. WEAVER, WARREN: THE MAN, THE COURT, THE ERA 342-43 (1967).
3. *See* J. WEAVER, *supra* note 2, at 335-36.

The Warren myths, I submit, whether one finds them in the vast demonology or extensive hagiography devoted to the subject, are dependent upon identification of the Chief Justice with the institution over which he presides, an identification that has not been valid since the time of John Marshall, if it was valid then. A Chief Justice, despite the public image, has little authority that is not shared by his colleagues on the Court, except that which inheres in his personal capacities. Harlan Stone, for example, lent no more direction to the Court's actions as Chief Justice than he did as an Associate Justice.

The Chief Justice of the United States differs in function from an Associate Justice of the Supreme Court in that he is treated as the senior member of the Court no matter how short his tenure and, therefore, assigns the opinions when he is a member of the majority. And he presides at the conferences and during the presentations of oral arguments. It is certainly true that a strong Chief Justice can use these roles as devices for framing the issues to which the Court will address itself, but that function has as often been performed by an occupant of a side chair as by the possessor of the center chair.

There is no evidence that Warren's influence has extended beyond the power of the one vote that is conferred upon him as a member of the Court. Unlike Stone and Charles Evans Hughes before him, Warren can hardly be regarded as the intellectual or forensic superior of any of his brethren. Indeed, a far more accurate estimate is that Warren has not formed the Court but rather that the Court has formed him. Certainly Warren the Chief Justice has revealed a very different set of values than did Warren the district attorney, Warren the state attorney general, or Warren the governor.

As a district attorney and attorney general in California, he engaged in and endorsed the very prosecutorial practices that the "Warren Court" has so thoroughly condemned: extorting confessions, although allegedly not by physical violence; depriving indigents of counsel, although allegedly not at trial; bugging homes and offices and conducting illegal searches and seizures, although, it is said, the illegally secured evidence was not used at trial.[4] Nor, during this period, did he abstain from the kind of Red-baiting that characterized the McCarthy era.[5] As Governor of California he led the racist attack that resulted in the evacuation of the Japanese-Americans from the West Coast.[6] And, he successfully fought legislative re-

---

4. *Id.* at 76-94.
5. *Id.* at 62-75.
6. *Id.* at 105-14.

apportionment[7] that would have brought his state closer to the simplistic "one man—one vote" formula that he later thought should be imposed on all states, not merely as a desirable standard but rather as a constitutionally compelled one.[8] It is readily evident that the Supreme Court gave the new values to the Chief Justice; he certainly did not impose his standards upon the Court.

A second of the Warren myths is dependent on the proposition that his genial personality—and there is none who would deny him this—has been a cohesive force, drawing together the disparate views of his brethren into a unified whole. Unfortunately, the facts are to the contrary. Under Warren's presidency, the Court has been the most divided, if not the most divisive, in American history. A glance at a few statistics will make this point clear.

A comparison of the last five years of the Warren Court (excluding the 1967 term) with the last five-year period in the life of the equally embattled New Deal Court of the "Nine Old Men," which included such noteworthy dissenters as Justices Brandeis, Stone, and Cardozo, reveals the following:

	"The Nine Old Men"				"The Warren Court"		
Term	Majority Opinions	Concurring Opinions	Dissenting Opinions	Term	Majority Opinions	Concurring Opinions	Dissenting Opinions
1932-33	168	1	17	1962-63	117	40	76
1933-34	158	4	18	1963-64	127	30	77
1934-35	156	1	14	1964-65	101	46	71
1935-36	146	3	20	1965-66	107	37	74
1936-37	149	1	17	1966-67	119	26	97
Totals	777	10	86		571	179	395
Average	155	2	17		114	36	79

If one looks only at the dissenting *votes*, the figures are these:

	"The Nine Old Men"			"The Warren Court"	
Term	Dissenting Votes	Number of Cases	Term	Dissenting Votes	Number of Cases
1932-33	70	168	1962-63	234	117
1933-34	67	158	1963-64	320	127
1934-35	60	156	1964-65	173	101
1935-36	76	146	1965-66	168	107
1936-37	78	149	1966-67	322	119
Totals	351	777		1217	571
Average	70	155		243	114

7. *Id.* at 239-42.
8. Baker v. Carr, 369 U.S. 186 (1962).

This is not to suggest that there is anything wrong with a Court that chooses to express individual views by way of concurring and dissenting opinions and dissenting votes. It is offered only to indicate that the Chief Justice was perhaps not the great conciliating force that so many have suggested him to be.

This particular Warren myth, as indeed almost all of them, began with the unanimous opinion in the first of the school desegregation cases, *Brown v. Board of Education*.[9] The argument assumes that Warren is responsible, if not for the judgment in that case and its companions, at least for the unanimity with which the judgment was announced. It takes no occult powers to recognize that the *Brown* decision was the result of a careful, step-by-step process in which Warren participated only at the ultimate stage of authoring the *Brown* opinion—a step that would have been taken even with Fred Vinson still occupying the office of Chief Justice. Nor was the presence of Warren on the Supreme Court and that tribunal's unanimity any more than coincidental. It is safe to say that the façade of unanimity was due at least as much to the persuasive capacities of Hugo Black and Felix Frankfurter as to the benign presence of Earl Warren. (Perhaps, however, it may be said that Warren's visit to Justice Jackson while the latter was in the hospital with a heart attack was designed to prevent the filing of a separate opinion by Jackson.)

Warren's "greatness" depends, therefore, upon the erroneous identification of the Chief Justice with the institution over which he presides, as if a Chief Justice is responsible for the work of the Court as a President is held responsible for the actions of all his subordinates in the executive branch. That this is an erroneous concept of the Chief Justice's role should be clear. That it is the public concept, however, has only recently been underlined by the confirmation hearings and Senate debate on the nomination of Associate Justice Fortas to the Chief Justiceship.[10] And so, because the error is so pervasive, history may well measure Warren's place by the work of the Court on which he served rather than by his individual contributions to constitutional jurisprudence. Thus, a quick look at the work of the Court may be in order.

The acclaim for the Warren Court rests largely on five areas of its work: the school desegregation cases,[11] the criminal procedure

---

9. 347 U.S. 483 (1954).

10. *See, e.g.,* N.Y. Times, Oct. 4, 1968, § 2, at 53, col. 7.

11. *See* Carter, *The Warren Court and Desegreation,* 67 MICH. L. REV. 237 (1968).

cases,[12] the reapportionment cases,[13] the church-state cases,[14] and the obscenity cases.[15] I shall not touch upon the last because in that area Warren was more likely to be found on the side of censorship than against it.

I think that few but racial or religious bigots would reject the objectives of the Court in the school desegregation cases and the church-state cases. Objections to the reapportionment decisions may rest either on different philosophies of democracy than that of the Levellers,[16] or on notions of the impropriety and lack of wisdom in the Court's intervention in this political area.[17] And only a tyrant would object to the goals of due process that underlie the criminal procedure cases, however much legitimate exception may be taken to the Court's methods of securing these goals. In short, the Court's good intentions cannot be gainsaid. Indeed, if, as has been suggested, the road to hell is paved with good intentions, the Warren Court has been among the great roadbuilders of all time.

History, however, has a nasty way of measuring greatness in terms of success rather than in terms of goodness. Marshall, for example, is applauded because his Court contributed to the centralization of governmental power at a time when the centrifugal philosophy of Jeffersonian democracy might have destroyed the nation or kept it from coming into being. Roger Taney, on the other hand, has gone down in infamy, despite some noteworthy contributions to American constitutional jurisprudence, because he defended the institution of slavery in the *Dred Scott*[18] case when the forces of history proved to be on the other side—the side of the Union Army.

If we measure the Warren Court's efforts in terms of specifics, they do not augur well for history's halo. As of today, we have little more integration in the public school systems than we did when *Brown* was decided in 1954. (Congressional ratification and implementation of the Court's goals may change the tide, but not soon.) School prayers and Bible-reading are uninhibited, despite the

---

12. *See* Pye, *The Warren Court and Criminal Procedure,* 67 Mich. L. Rev. 249 (1968).

13. *See* MacKay, *Reapportionment: Success Story of the Warren Court,* 67 Mich. L. Rev. 223 (1968).

14. *See* P. Kauper, *The Warren Court: Religious Liberty and Church-State Relations,* 67 Mich. L. Rev. 269 (1968).

15. *See* Kalven, *"Uninhibited, Robust, and Wide-Open"—A Note on Free Speech and the Warren Court,* 67 Mich. L. Rev. 289 (1968).

16. *See, e.g.,* Dirksen, *The Supreme Court and the People,* 66 Mich. L. Rev. 837, 854 (1968).

17. *See, e.g., id.* at 839.

18. Dred Scott v. Sanford, 60 U.S. (19 How.) 393 (1857).

Court's decisions, except in those few places where a direct judicial mandate has been imposed or threatened. If we have achieved widespread reapportionment of state legislatures, it must be recognized that, for the most part, the politicians rather than the people have controlled such reapportionment. But worse, to the extent that voting power has been shifted, it has been shifted from the rural areas and, in some cases, the cities, to suburbia—a politically more reactionary constituency than even the farm groups. But the success of reapportionment is most likely to be discounted because the state legislatures have become relatively unimportant instruments in a country in which power is essentially divided between the national government and the cities. Police brutality seems not to be reduced, although a number of guilty defendants have been freed to attempt their escapades again.

On the other hand, if one views the Court's efforts from a broader perspective, looking at the woods rather than the trees, the Court may ultimately appear to be much more successful. Certainly the Court must be given credit for helping to spark the Negro revolution that engulfs us at the moment. Certainly, too, the Court has contributed to the egalitarian ethos that is becoming so dominant. But we do not yet know whether the Court's efforts have enhanced the rule of law in our society or have diminished it. And ultimately, I suspect, the verdict of history will depend upon the outcome of these three manifestations of the Court's business.

To restate my thesis then, it is too early to tell whether history is on the side of the Warren Court. If the Court has chosen the right side, and history credits it with contributing to that side's success, then history may use for Earl Warren the words Holmes once used for another jurist who, alas, has now been forgotten: "Great places make great men. The electric current of large affairs turns even common mould to diamond, and traditions of ancient honor impart something of their dignity to those who inherit them."[19] As of now, I submit, even these words would be extravagant and premature.

---

19. O. HOLMES, SPEECHES 54 (1913).

APPENDIX

BAKER ET AL. *v.* CARR ET AL.

APPEAL FROM THE UNITED STATES DISTRICT COURT FOR THE MIDDLE DISTRICT OF TENNESSEE.

No. 6. Argued April 19–20, 1961.—Set for reargument May 1, 1961.— Reargued October 9, 1961.—Decided March 26, 1962.

Appellants are persons allegedly qualified to vote for members of the General Assembly of Tennessee representing the counties in which they reside. They brought suit in a Federal District Court in Tennessee under 42 U. S. C. §§ 1983 and 1988, on behalf of themselves and others similarly situated, to redress the alleged deprivation of their federal constitutional rights by legislation classifying voters with respect to representation in the General Assembly. They alleged that, by means of a 1901 statute of Tennessee arbitrarily and capriciously apportioning the seats in the General Assembly among the State's 95 counties, and a failure to reapportion them subsequently notwithstanding substantial growth and redistribution of the State's population, they suffer a "debasement of their votes" and were thereby denied the equal protection of the laws guaranteed them by the Fourteenth Amendment. They sought, *inter alia,* a declaratory judgment that the 1901 statute is unconstitutional and an injunction restraining certain state officers from conducting any further elections under it. The District Court dismissed the complaint on the grounds that it lacked jurisdiction of the subject matter and that no claim was stated upon which relief could be granted. *Held:*

  1. The District Court had jurisdiction of the subject matter of the federal constitutional claim asserted in the complaint.

  2. Appellants had standing to maintain this suit.

  3. The complaint's allegations of a denial of equal protection presented a justiciable constitutional cause of action upon which appellants are entitled to a trial and a decision.

179 F. Supp. 824, reversed and cause remanded.

Charles S. Rhyne and *Z. T. Osborn, Jr.* reargued the cause for appellants. With them on the briefs were *Hobart F. Atkins, Robert H. Jennings, Jr., J. W. Anderson, C. R. McClain, Walter Chandler, Harris A. Gilbert, E. K. Meacham* and *Herzel H. E. Plaine.*

BAKER v. CARR.

Jack Wilson, Assistant Attorney General of Tennessee, reargued the cause for appellees. With him on the briefs were *George F. McCanless,* Attorney General, and *Milton P. Rice* and *James M. Glasgow,* Assistant Attorneys General.

Solicitor General Cox, by special leave of Court, 365 U. S. 864, reargued the cause for the United States, as *amicus curiae,* urging reversal. With him on the briefs were *Assistant Attorney General Marshall, Acting Assistant Attorney General Doar, Bruce J. Terris, Harold H. Greene, David Rubin* and *Howard A. Glickstein.*

Briefs of *amici curiae,* in support of appellants, were filed by *J. Howard Edmondson,* Governor of Oklahoma, and *Norman E. Reynolds, Jr.* for the Governor; *W. Scott Miller, Jr.* and *George J. Long* for the City of St. Matthews, Kentucky; *Roger Arnebergh, Henry P. Kucera, J. Elliott Drinard, Barnett I. Shur, Alexander G. Brown, Nathaniel H. Goldstick* and *Charles S. Rhyne* for the National Institute of Municipal Law Officers; *Eugene H. Nickerson* and *David M. Levitan* for John F. English et al.; *Upton Sisson, Clare S. Hornsby, Walter L. Nixon, Jr.* and *John Sekul* for Marvin Fortner et al.; and *Theodore Sachs* for August Scholle.

Mr. Justice Brennan delivered the opinion of the Court.

This civil action was brought under 42 U. S. C. §§ 1983 and 1988 to redress the alleged deprivation of federal constitutional rights. The complaint, alleging that by means of a 1901 statute of Tennessee apportioning the members of the General Assembly among the State's 95 counties,[1] "these plaintiffs and others similarly situated,

---

[1] Public Acts of Tennessee, c. 122 (1901), now Tenn. Code Ann. §§ 3–101 to 3–107. The full text of the 1901 Act as amended appears in an Appendix to this opinion, *post,* p. 237.

are denied the equal protection of the laws accorded them by the Fourteenth Amendment to the Constitution of the United States by virtue of the debasement of their votes," was dismissed by a three-judge court convened under 28 U. S. C. § 2281 in the Middle District of Tennessee.[2] The court held that it lacked jurisdiction of the subject matter and also that no claim was stated upon which relief could be granted. 179 F. Supp. 824. We noted probable jurisdiction of the appeal. 364 U. S. 898.[3] We hold that the dismissal was error, and remand the cause to the District Court for trial and further proceedings consistent with this opinion.

The General Assembly of Tennessee consists of the Senate with 33 members and the House of Representatives with 99 members. The Tennessee Constitution provides in Art. II as follows:

"Sec. 3. Legislative authority—Term of office.— The Legislative authority of this State shall be vested in a General Assembly, which shall consist of a Senate and House of Representatives, both dependent on the people; who shall hold their offices for two years from the day of the general election.

"Sec. 4. Census.—An enumeration of the qualified voters, and an apportionment of the Representatives in the General Assembly, shall be made in the year one thousand eight hundred and seventy-one, and within every subsequent term of ten years.

"Sec. 5. Apportionment of representatives.—The number of Representatives shall, at the several

---

[2] The three-judge court was convened pursuant to the order of a single district judge, who, after he had reviewed certain decisions of this Court and found them distinguishable in features "that may ultimately prove to be significant," held that the complaint was not so obviously without merit that he would be justified in refusing to convene a three-judge court. 175 F. Supp. 649, 652.

[3] We heard argument first at the 1960 Term and again at this Term when the case was set over for reargument. 366 U. S. 907.

BAKER v. CARR.

periods of making the enumeration, be apportioned among the several counties or districts, according to the number of qualified voters in each; and shall not exceed seventy-five, until the population of the State shall be one million and a half, and shall never exceed ninety-nine; Provided, that any county having two-thirds of the ratio shall be entitled to one member.

"Sec. 6. Apportionment of senators.—The number of Senators shall, at the several periods of making the enumeration, be apportioned among the several counties or districts according to the number of qualified electors in each, and shall not exceed one-third the number of representatives. In apportioning the Senators among the different counties, the fraction that may be lost by any county or counties, in the apportionment of members to the House of Representatives, shall be made up to such county or counties in the Senate, as near as may be practicable. When a district is composed of two or more counties, they shall be adjoining; and no county shall be divided in forming a district."

Thus, Tennessee's standard for allocating legislative representation among her counties is the total number of qualified voters resident in the respective counties, subject only to minor qualifications.[4] Decennial reapportionment

---

[4] A county having less than, but at least two-thirds of, the population required to choose a Representative is allocated one Representative. See also Tenn. Const., Art. II, § 6. A common and much more substantial departure from the number-of-voters or total-population standard is the guaranty of at least one seat to each county. See, e. g., Kansas Const., Art. 2, § 2; N. J. Const., Art. 4, § 3, ¶ 1.

While the Tennessee Constitution speaks of the number of "qualified voters," the exhibits attached to the complaint use figures based on the number of persons 21 years of age and over. This basis seems to have been employed by the General Assembly in apportioning legislative seats from the outset. The 1870 statute providing for the first enumeration, Acts of 1870 (1st Sess.), c. 107, directed the courts of

in compliance with the constitutional scheme was effected
by the General Assembly each decade from 1871 to 1901.
The 1871 apportionment[5] was preceded by an 1870
statute requiring an enumeration.[6] The 1881 apportionment involved three statutes, the first authorizing an
enumeration, the second enlarging the Senate from 25 to

---

the several counties to select a Commissioner to enumerate "all the
male inhabitants of their respective counties, who are twenty-one years
of age and upward, who shall be resident citizens of their counties on
the first day of January, 1871 . . . ." Reports compiled in the several
counties on this basis were submitted to the General Assembly by the
Secretary of State and were used in the first apportionment. Appendix
to Tenn. S. J., 1871, 41–43. Yet such figures would not reflect the
numbers of persons qualified to exercise the franchise under the then-
governing qualifications: (a) citizenship; (b) residence in the State 12
months, and in the county 6 months; (c) payment of poll taxes for
the preceding year unless entitled to exemption. Acts of 1870 (2d
Sess.), c. 10. (These qualifications continued at least until after 1901.
See Shan. Tenn. Code Ann., §§ 1167, 1220 (1896; Supp. 1904).)
Still, when the General Assembly directed the Secretary of State to do
all he could to obtain complete reports from the counties, the Resolution spoke broadly of "the impossibility of . . . [redistricting] without
the census returns of the voting population from each county . . . ."
Tenn. S. J., 1871, 46–47, 96. The figures also showed a correla-
tion with Federal Census figures for 1870. The Census reported
259,016 male citizens 21 and upward in Tennessee. Ninth Census of
the United States, 1870, Statistics of the Population 635 (1872). The
Tennessee Secretary of State's Report, with 15 counties not reported,
gave a figure of 237,431. Using the numbers of actual votes in the
last gubernatorial election for those 15 counties, the Secretary arrived
at a total of 250,025. Appendix to Tenn. S. J., 1871, 41–43. This
and subsequent history indicate continued reference to Census figures
and finally in 1901, abandonment of a state enumeration in favor of
the use of Census figures. See notes 7, 8, 9, *infra*. See also Williams,
Legislative Apportionment in Tennessee, 20 Tenn. L. Rev. 235, 236,
n. 6. It would therefore appear that unless there is a contrary showing at the trial, appellants' current figures, taken from the United
States Census Reports, are apposite.

  [5] Acts of 1871 (1st Sess.), c. 146.
  [6] Acts of 1870 (1st Sess.), c. 107.

33 members and the House from 75 to 99 members, and
the third apportioning the membership of both Houses.[7]
In 1891 there were both an enumeration and an apportionment.[8] In 1901 the General Assembly abandoned separate enumeration in favor of reliance upon the Federal
Census and passed the Apportionment Act here in controversy.[9] In the more than 60 years since that action,
all proposals in both Houses of the General Assembly for
reapportionment have failed to pass.[10]

---

[7] The statute authorizing the enumeration was Acts of 1881 (1st
Sess.), c. 124. The enumeration commissioners in the counties were
allowed "access to the U. S. Census Reports of the enumeration of
1880, on file in the offices of the County Court Clerks of the State,
and a reference to said reports by said commissioners shall be legitimate as an auxiliary in the enumeration required . . . ." *Ibid.,* § 4.

The United States Census reported 330,305 male citizens 21 and
upward in Tennessee. The Tenth Census of the United States, 1880,
Compendium 596 (1883). The Tennessee Secretary of State's Report
gave a figure of 343,817, Tenn. H. J. (1st Extra. Sess.), 1881, 12–14
(1882).

The General Assembly was enlarged in accordance with the constitutional mandate since the State's population had passed 1,500,000.
Acts of 1881 (1st Extra. Sess.), c. 5; and see, *id.,* S. J. Res. No. III;
see also Tenth Census of the United States, 1880, Statistics of the
Population 77 (1881). The statute apportioning the General Assembly was Acts of 1881 (1st Extra. Sess.), c. 6.

[8] Acts of 1891, c. 22; Acts of 1891 (Extra. Sess.), c. 10. Reference
to United States Census figures was allowed just as in 1881, see
supra, n. 7. The United States Census reported 402,476 males 21
and over in Tennessee. The Eleventh Census of the United States,
1890, Population (Part I) 781 (1895). The Tennessee Secretary of
State's Report gave a figure of 399,575. 1 Tenn. S. J., 1891, 473–474.

[9] Acts of 1901, S. J. Res. No. 35; Acts of 1901, c. 122. The
Joint Resolution said: "The Federal census of 1900 has been very
recently taken and by reference to said Federal census an accurate
enumeration of the qualified voters of the respective counties of the
State of Tennessee can be ascertained and thereby save the expense
of an actual enumeration . . . ."

[10] For the history of legislative apportionment in Tennessee, including attempts made since 1901, see Tenn. S. J., 1959, 909–930;

Between 1901 and 1961, Tennessee has experienced substantial growth and redistribution of her population. In 1901 the population was 2,020,616, of whom 487,380 were eligible to vote.[11]   The 1960 Federal Census reports the State's population at 3,567,089, of whom 2,092,891 are eligible to vote.[12]   The relative standings of the counties in terms of qualified voters have changed significantly. It is primarily the continued application of the 1901 Apportionment Act to this shifted and enlarged voting population which gives rise to the present controversy.

Indeed, the complaint alleges that the 1901 statute, even as of the time of its passage, "made no apportionment of Representatives and Senators in accordance with the constitutional formula . . . , but instead arbitrarily and capriciously apportioned representatives in the Senate and House without reference . . . to any logical or reasonable formula whatever." [13]   It is further alleged

and "A Documented Survey of Legislative Apportionment in Tennessee, 1870–1957," which is attached as exhibit 2 to the intervening complaint of Mayor West of Nashville, both prepared by the Tennessee State Historian, Dr. Robert H. White.   Examples of preliminary steps are: In 1911, the Senate called upon the Redistricting Committee to make an enumeration of qualified voters and to use the Federal Census of 1910 as the basis.   Acts of 1911, S. J. Res. No. 60, p. 315.   Similarly, in 1961, the Senate called for appointment of a select committee to make an enumeration of qualified voters.   Acts of 1961, S. J. Res. No. 47.   In 1955, the Senate called for a study of reapportionment.   Tenn. S. J., 1955, 224; but see *id.*, at 1403. Similarly, in 1961, the House directed the State Legislative Council to study methods of reapportionment.   Acts of 1961, H. J. Res. No. 65.

[11] Twelfth Census of the United States, 1900, Population (Part 1) 39 (1901); (Part 2) 202 (1902).

[12] United States Census of Population: 1960, General Population Characteristics—Tennessee, Table 16 (1961).

[13] In the words of one of the intervening complaints, the apportionment was "wholly arbitrary, . . . and, indeed, based upon no lawfully pertinent factor whatever."

that "because of the population changes since 1900, and
the failure of the Legislature to reapportion itself since
1901," the 1901 statute became "unconstitutional and
obsolete." Appellants also argue that, because of the
composition of the legislature effected by-the 1901 Apportionment Act, redress in the form of a state constitutional
amendment to change the entire mechanism for reappor-
tioning, or any other change short of that, is difficult or
impossible.[14] The complaint concludes that "these plain-

---

[14] The appellants claim that no General Assembly constituted
according to the 1901 Act will ·submit reapportionment proposals
either to the people or to a Constitutional Convention. There is no
provision for popular initiative in Tennessee. Amendments proposed
in the Senate or House must first be approved by a majority of all
members of each House and again by two-thirds of the members in
the General Assembly next chosen. ˙ The proposals are then submitted
to the people at the next general election in which a Governor is to
be chosen. Alternatively, the legislature may submit to the people
at any general election the question of calling a convention to consider
specified proposals. Such as are adopted at a convention do not,
however, become effective unless approved by a majority of the
qualified voters voting separately on each proposed change or amendment at an election fixed by the convention. Conventions shall not
be held oftener than once in six years. Tenn. Const., Art. XI, § 3.
Acts of 1951, c. 130, § 3, and Acts of 1957, c. 340, § 3, provided that
delegates to the 1953 and 1959 conventions were to be chosen from
the counties and floterial districts just as are members of the State
House of Representatives. The General Assembly's call for a 1953
Constitutional Convention originally contained a provision "relating
to the appointment [sic] of representatives and senators" but this
was excised. Tenn. H. J., 1951, 784. A Resolution introduced at
the 1959 Constitutional Convention and reported unfavorably by
the Rules Committee of the Convention was as follows:
"By Mr. Chambliss (of Hamilton County), Resolution No. 12—
Relative to Convention considering reapportionment, which is as
follows:
"WHEREAS, there is a rumor that this Limited Convention has
been called for the purpose of postponing for six years a Convention
that would make a decision as to reapportionment; and

[Footnote 14 continued on p. 178]

tiffs and others similarly situated, are denied the equal protection of the laws accorded them by the Fourteenth Amendment to the Constitution of the United States by virtue of the debasement of their votes." [15]   They seek a

"WHEREAS, there is pending in the United States Courts in Tennessee a suit under which parties are seeking, through decree, to compel reapportionment; and

"WHEREAS, it is said that this Limited Convention, which was called for limited consideration, is yet a Constitutional Convention within the language of the Constitution as to Constitutional Conventions, forbidding frequent Conventions in the last sentence of Article Eleven, Section 3, second paragraph, more often than each six years, to-wit:

" 'No such Convention shall be held oftener than once in six years.'

"Now, THEREFORE, BE IT RESOLVED, That it is the consensus of opinion of the members of this Convention that since this is a Limited Convention as hereinbefore set forth another Convention could be had if it did not deal with the matters submitted to this Limited Convention.

"BE IT FURTHER RESOLVED, That it is the consensus of opinion of this Convention that a Convention should be called by the General Assembly for the purpose of considering reapportionment in order that a possibility of Court enforcement being forced on the Sovereign State of Tennessee by the Courts of the National Government may be avoided.

"BE IT FURTHER RESOLVED, That this Convention be adjourned for two years to meet again at the same time set forth in the statute providing for this Convention, and that it is the consensus of opinion of this body that it is within the power of the next General Assembly of Tennessee to broaden the powers of this Convention and to authorize and empower this Convention to consider a proper amendment to the Constitution that will provide, when submitted to the electorate, a method of reapportionment." Tenn. Constitutional Convention of 1959, The Journal and Debates, 35, 278.

[15] It is clear that appellants' federal constitutional claims rest exclusively on alleged violation of the Fourteenth Amendment. Their primary claim is that the 1901 statute violates the Equal Protection Clause of that amendment. There are allegations invoking the Due Process Clause but from the argument and the exhibits it appears that the Due Process Clause argument is directed at certain tax statutes. Insofar as the claim involves the validity of those statutes

declaration that the 1901 statute is unconstitutional and
an injunction restraining the appellees from acting to
conduct any further elections under it.   They also pray
that unless and until the General Assembly enacts a valid
reapportionment, the District Court should either decree
a reapportionment by mathematical application of the
Tennessee constitutional formulae to the most recent
Federal Census figures, or direct the appellees to conduct
legislative elections, primary and general, at large.   They
also pray for such other and further relief as may be
appropriate.

I.

THE DISTRICT COURT'S OPINION AND ORDER OF DISMISSAL.

Because we deal with this case on appeal from an order
of dismissal granted on appellees' motions, precise identi-

---

under the Due Process Clause we find it unnecessary to decide its
merits.   And if the allegations regarding the tax statutes are designed
as the framework for proofs as to the effects of the allegedly discriminatory apportionment, we need not rely upon them to support our
holding that the complaint states a federal constitutional claim of
violation of the Equal Protection Clause.   Whether, when the issue
to be decided is one of the constitutional adequacy of this particular
apportionment, taxation arguments and exhibits as now presented
add anything, or whether they could add anything however presented,
is for the District Court in the first instance to decide.

The complaint, in addition to the claims under the Federal Constitution, also alleges rights, and the General Assembly's duties, under
the Tennessee Constitution.   Since we hold that appellants have—if
it develops at trial that the facts support the allegations—a cognizable federal constitutional cause of action resting in no degree on
rights guaranteed or putatively guaranteed by the Tennessee Constitution, we do not consider, let alone enforce, rights under a State
Constitution which go further than the protections of the Fourteenth
Amendment.   Lastly, we need not assess the legal significance, in
reaching our conclusion, of the statements of the complaint that the
apportionment effected today under the 1901 Act is "contrary to the
philosophy of government in the United States and all Anglo-Saxon
jurisprudence . . . ."

fication of the issues presently confronting us demands
clear exposition of the grounds upon which the District
Court rested in dismissing the case. The dismissal order
recited that the court sustained the appellees' grounds
"(1) that the Court lacks jurisdiction of the subject matter, and (2) that the complaint fails to state a claim upon
which relief can be granted . . . ."

In the setting of a case such as this, the recited grounds
embrace two possible reasons for dismissal:

First: That the facts and injury alleged, the legal
bases invoked as creating the rights and duties relied
upon, and the relief sought, fail to come within that language of Article III of the Constitution and of the jurisdictional statutes which define those matters concerning
which United States District Courts are empowered to act;

Second: That, although the matter is cognizable and
facts are alleged which establish infringement of appellants' rights as a result of state legislative action departing from a federal constitutional standard, the court will
not proceed because the matter is considered unsuited to
judicial inquiry or adjustment.

We treat the first ground of dismissal as "lack of jurisdiction of the subject matter." The second we consider
to result in a failure to state a justiciable cause of action.

The District Court's dismissal order recited that it was
issued in conformity with the court's *per curiam* opinion.
The opinion reveals that the court rested its dismissal
upon lack of subject-matter jurisdiction and lack of a
justiciable cause of action without attempting to distinguish between these grounds. After noting that the
plaintiffs challenged the existing legislative apportionment
in Tennessee under the Due Process and Equal Protection Clauses, and summarizing the supporting allegations
and the relief requested, the court stated that

> "The action is presently before the Court upon the
> defendants' motion to dismiss predicated upon three

180

grounds: first, that the Court lacks jurisdiction of the subject matter; second, that the complaints fail to state a claim upon which relief can be granted; and third, that indispensable party defendants are not before the Court." 179 F. Supp., at 826.

The court proceeded to explain its action as turning on the case's presenting a "question of the distribution of political strength for legislative purposes." For,

"From a review of [numerous Supreme Court] . . . decisions there can be no doubt that the federal rule, as enunciated and applied by the Supreme Court, is that the federal courts, whether from a lack of jurisdiction or from the inappropriateness of the subject matter for judicial consideration, will not intervene in cases of this type to compel legislative reapportionment." 179 F. Supp., at 826.

The court went on to express doubts as to the feasibility of the various possible remedies sought by the plaintiffs. 179 F. Supp., at 827–828. Then it made clear that its dismissal reflected a view not of doubt that violation of constitutional rights was alleged, but of a court's impotence to correct that violation:

"With the plaintiffs' argument that the legislature of Tennessee is guilty of a clear violation of the state constitution and of the rights of the plaintiffs the Court entirely agrees. It also agrees that the evil is a serious one which should be corrected without further delay. But even so the remedy in this situation clearly does not lie with the courts. It has long been recognized and is accepted doctrine that there are indeed some rights guaranteed by the Constitution for the violation of which the courts cannot give redress." 179 F. Supp., at 828.

In light of the District Court's treatment of the case, we hold today only (a) that the court possessed jurisdiction of the subject matter; (b) that a justiciable cause of

action is stated upon which appellants would be entitled
to appropriate relief; and (c) because appellees raise
the issue before this Court, that the appellants have standing to challenge the Tennessee apportionment statutes.[16]
Beyond noting that we have no cause at this stage to
doubt the District Court will be able to fashion relief if
violations of constitutional rights are found, it is improper
now to consider what remedy would be most appropriate
if appellants prevail at the trial.

II.

JURISDICTION OF THE SUBJECT MATTER.

The District Court was uncertain whether our cases
withholding federal judicial relief rested upon a lack of
federal jurisdiction or upon the inappropriateness of the
subject matter for judicial consideration—what we have
designated "nonjusticiability." The distinction between
the two grounds is significant. In the instance of nonjusticiability, consideration of the cause is not wholly and
immediately foreclosed; rather, the Court's inquiry necessarily proceeds to the point of deciding whether the duty
asserted can be judicially identified and its breach judicially determined, and whether protection for the right
asserted can be judicially molded. In the instance of
lack of jurisdiction the cause either does not "arise under"
the Federal Constitution, laws or treaties (or fall within
one of the other enumerated categories of Art. III, § 2),
or is not a "case or controversy" within the meaning of
that section; or the cause is not one described by any
jurisdictional statute. Our conclusion, see pp. 208–237,
infra, that this cause presents no nonjusticiable "political
question" settles the only possible doubt that it is a case
or controversy. Under the present heading of "Jurisdic-

---

[16] We need not reach the question of indispensable parties because
the District Court has not yet decided it.

tion of the Subject Matter" we hold only that the matter
set forth in the complaint does arise under the Constitution and is within 28 U. S. C. § 1343.

Article III, § 2, of the Federal Constitution provides
that "The judicial Power shall extend to all Cases, in Law
and Equity, arising under this Constitution, the Laws of
the United States, and Treaties made, or which shall be
made, under their Authority . . . ." It is clear that the
cause of action is one which "arises under" the Federal
Constitution. The complaint alleges that the 1901 statute effects an apportionment that deprives the appellants
of the equal protection of the laws in violation of the
Fourteenth Amendment. Dismissal of the complaint
upon the ground of lack of jurisdiction of the subject
matter would, therefore, be justified only if that claim
were "so attenuated and unsubstantial as to be absolutely
devoid of merit," *Newburyport Water Co.* v. *Newburyport,* 193 U. S. 561, 579, or "frivolous," *Bell* v. *Hood,* 327
U. S. 678, 683.[17] That the claim is unsubstantial must be
"very plain." *Hart* v. *Keith Vaudeville Exchange,* 262
U. S. 271, 274. Since the District Court obviously and
correctly did not deem the asserted federal constitutional
claim unsubstantial and frivolous, it should not have dismissed the complaint for want of jurisdiction of the subject matter. And of course no further consideration of the
merits of the claim is relevant to a determination of the
court's jurisdiction of the subject matter. We said in
an earlier voting case from Tennessee: "It is obvious . . .
that the court, in dismissing for want of jurisdiction, was
controlled by what it deemed to be the want of merit in
the averments which were made in the complaint as to
the violation of the Federal right. But as the very
nature of the controversy was Federal, and, therefore,

---

[17] The accuracy of calling even such dismissals "jurisdictional" was
questioned in *Bell* v. *Hood.* See 327 U. S., at 683.

jurisdiction existed, whilst the opinion of the court as to the want of merit in the cause of action might have furnished ground for dismissing for that reason, it afforded no sufficient ground for deciding that the action was not one arising under the Constitution and laws of the United States." *Swafford* v. *Templeton*, 185 U. S. 487, 493. "For it is well settled that the failure to state a proper cause of action calls for a judgment on the merits and not for a dismissal for want of jurisdiction." *Bell* v. *Hood*, 327 U. S. 678, 682.   See also *Binderup* v. *Pathe Exchange*, 263 U. S. 291, 305–308.

Since the complaint plainly sets forth a case arising under the Constitution, the subject matter is within the federal judicial power defined in Art. III, § 2, and so within the power of Congress to assign to the jurisdiction of the District Courts.   Congress has exercised that power in 28 U. S. C. § 1343 (3):

> "The district courts shall have original jurisdiction of any civil action authorized by law[18] to be commenced by any person . . . [t]o redress the deprivation, under color of any State law, statute, ordinance, regulation, custom or usage, of any right, privilege or immunity secured by the Constitution of the United States . . . ."[19]

---

[18] 42 U. S. C. § 1983 provides: "Every person who, under color of any statute, ordinance, regulation, custom, or usage, of any State or Territory, subjects, or causes to be subjected, any citizen of the United States or other person within the jurisdiction thereof to the deprivation of any rights, privileges, or immunities secured by the Constitution and laws, shall be liable to the party injured in an action at law, suit in equity, or other proper proceeding for redress."

[19] This Court has frequently sustained District Court jurisdiction under 28 U. S. C. § 1343 (3) or its predecessors to entertain suits to redress deprivations of rights secured against state infringement by the Equal Protection and Due Process Clauses of the Fourteenth

An unbroken line of our precedents sustains the federal courts' jurisdiction of the subject matter of federal constitutional claims of this nature. The first cases involved the redistricting of States for the purpose of electing Representatives to the Federal Congress. When the Ohio Supreme Court sustained Ohio legislation against an attack for repugnancy to Art. I, § 4, of the Federal Constitution, we affirmed on the merits and expressly refused to dismiss for want of jurisdiction "In view . . . of the subject-matter of the controversy and the Federal characteristics which inhere in it . . . ." *Ohio ex rel. Davis v. Hildebrant*, 241 U. S. 565, 570. When the Minnesota Supreme Court affirmed the dismissal of a suit to enjoin the Secretary of State of Minnesota from acting under Minnesota redistricting legislation, we reviewed the constitutional merits of the legislation and reversed the State Supreme Court. *Smiley* v. *Holm*, 285 U. S. 355. And see companion cases from the New York Court of Appeals and the Missouri Supreme Court, *Koenig* v. *Flynn*, 285 U. S. 375; *Carroll* v. *Becker*, 285 U. S. 380. When a three-judge District Court, exercising jurisdiction under the predecessor of 28 U. S. C. § 1343 (3), permanently enjoined officers of the State of Mississippi from conducting an election of Representatives under a Mississippi redistricting act, we reviewed the federal questions on the merits and reversed the District Court. *Wood* v. *Broom*, 287 U. S. 1, reversing 1 F. Supp. 134. A similar decree of a District Court, exercising jurisdiction under the same statute, concerning a Kentucky redistricting act, was

Amendment. *Douglas* v. *Jeannette*, 319 U. S. 157; *Stefanelli* v. *Minard*, 342 U. S. 117; cf. *Nixon* v. *Herndon*, 273 U. S. 536; *Nixon* v. *Condon*, 286 U. S. 73; *Snowden* v. *Hughes*, 321 U. S. 1; *Smith* v. *Allwright*, 321 U. S. 649; *Monroe* v. *Pape*, 365 U. S. 167; *Egan* v. *Aurora*, 365 U. S. 514.

reviewed and the decree reversed. *Mahan* v. *Hume,* 287 U. S. 575, reversing 1 F. Supp. 142.[20]

The appellees refer to *Colegrove* v. *Green,* 328 U. S. 549, as authority that the District Court lacked jurisdiction of the subject matter. Appellees misconceive the holding of that case. The holding was precisely contrary to their reading of it. Seven members of the Court participated in the decision. Unlike many other cases in this field which have assumed without discussion that there was jurisdiction, all three opinions filed in *Colegrove* discussed the question. Two of the opinions expressing the views of four of the Justices, a majority, flatly held that there was jurisdiction of the subject matter. MR. JUSTICE BLACK joined by MR. JUSTICE DOUGLAS and Mr. Justice Murphy stated: "It is my judgment that the District Court had jurisdiction . . . ," citing the predecessor of 28 U. S. C. § 1343 (3), and *Bell* v. *Hood, supra.* 328 U. S., at 568. Mr. Justice Rutledge, writing separately, expressed agreement with this conclusion. 328 U. S., at 564, 565, n. 2. Indeed, it is even questionable that the opinion of MR. JUSTICE FRANKFURTER, joined by Justices Reed and Burton, doubted jurisdiction of the subject matter. Such doubt would have been inconsistent with the professed willingness to turn the decision on either the majority or concurring views in *Wood* v. *Broom, supra.* 328 U. S., at 551.

Several subsequent cases similar to *Colegrove* have been decided by the Court in summary *per curiam* statements. None was dismissed for want of jurisdiction of the subject matter. *Cook* v. *Fortson,* 329 U. S. 675; *Turman* v.

---

[20] Since that case was not brought to the Court until after the election had been held, the Court cited not only *Wood* v. *Broom,* but also directed dismissal for mootness, citing *Brownlow* v. *Schwartz,* 261 U. S. 216.

Duckworth, ibid.; Colegrove v. *Barrett,* 330 U. S. 804; [21]
Tedesco v. *Board of Supervisors,* 339 U. S. 940; *Remmey*
v. *Smith,* 342 U. S. 916; *Cox* v. *Peters,* 342 U. S. 936;
Anderson v. *Jordan,* 343 U. S. 912; *Kidd* v. *McCanless,*
352 U. S. 920; *Radford* v. *Gary,* 352 U. S. 991; *Hartsfield*
v. *Sloan,* 357 U. S. 916; *Matthews* v. *Handley,* 361 U. S.
127.[22]

Two cases decided with opinions after *Colegrove* like-
wise plainly imply that the subject matter of this suit is
within District Court jurisdiction. In *MacDougall* v.
Green, 335 U. S. 281, the District Court dismissed for
want of jurisdiction, which had been invoked under 28
U. S. C. § 1343 (3), a suit to enjoin enforcement of the
requirement that nominees for state-wide elections be
supported by a petition signed by a minimum number of
persons from at least 50 of the State's 102 counties.
This Court's disagreement with that action is clear since
the Court affirmed the judgment after a review of the
merits and concluded that the particular claim there was
without merit. In *South* v. *Peters,* 339 U. S. 276, we
affirmed the dismissal of an attack on the Georgia "county
unit" system but founded our action on a ground that
plainly would not have been reached if the lower court
lacked jurisdiction of the subject matter, which allegedy
existed under 28 U. S. C. § 1343 (3). The express words
of our holding were that "Federal courts consistently
refuse to exercise their equity powers in cases posing

---

[21] Compare *Boeing Aircraft Co.* v. *King County,* 330 U. S. 803
("the appeal is dismissed for want of jurisdiction"). See *Coleman* v.
Miller, 307 U. S. 433, 440.

[22] *Matthews* did affirm a judgment that may be read as a dismissal for want of jurisdiction, 179 F. Supp. 470. However, the
motion to affirm also rested on the ground of failure to state a claim
upon which relief could be granted. Cf. text following, on *MacDougall*
v. *Green.* And see text, *infra,* p. 236.

political issues arising from a state's geographical distribution of electoral strength among its political subdivisions." 339 U. S., at 277.

We hold that the District Court has jurisdiction of the subject matter of the federal constitutional claim asserted in the complaint.

III.

STANDING.

A federal court cannot "pronounce any statute, either of a State or of the United States, void, because irreconcilable with the Constitution, except as it is called upon to adjudge the legal rights of litigants in actual controversies." *Liverpool Steamship Co.* v. *Commissioners of Emigration*, 113 U. S. 33, 39. Have the appellants alleged such a personal stake in the outcome of the controversy as to assure that concrete adverseness which sharpens the presentation of issues upon which the court so largely depends for illumination of difficult constitutional questions? This is the gist of the question of standing. It is, of course, a question of federal law.

The complaint was filed by residents of Davidson, Hamilton, Knox, Montgomery, and Shelby Counties. Each is a person allegedly qualified to vote for members of the General Assembly representing his county.[23] These appellants sued "on their own behalf and on behalf of all qualified voters of their respective counties, and further, on behalf of all voters of the State of Tennessee who

---

[23] The Mayor of Nashville suing "on behalf of himself and all residents of the City of Nashville, Davidson County, . . ." and the Cities of Chattanooga (Hamilton County) and Knoxville (Knox County), each suing on behalf of its residents, were permitted to intervene as parties plaintiff. Since they press the same claims as do the initial plaintiffs, we find it unnecessary to decide whether the intervenors would have standing to maintain this action in their asserted representative capacities.

are similarly situated . . . ." [24]   The appellees are the
Tennessee Secretary of State, Attorney General, Coordi-
nator of Elections, and members of the State Board of
Elections; the members of the State Board are sued in
their own right and also as representatives of the County
Election Commissioners whom they appoint. [25]

---

[24] The complaint also contains an averment that the appellants sue
"on their own behalf and *on behalf of all other voters* in the State of
Tennessee." (Emphasis added.)   This may be read to assert a
claim that voters in counties allegedly over-represented in the General Assembly also have standing to complain.   But it is not necessary
to decide that question in this case.

[25] The duties of the respective appellees are alleged to be as follows:

"Defendant, *Joe C. Carr,* is the duly elected, qualified and acting
Secretary of State of the State of Tennessee, with his office in Nashville in said State, and as such he is charged with the duty of fur-
nishing blanks, envelopes and information slips to the County Election Commissioners, certifying the results of elections and maintaining
the records thereof; and he is further ex officio charged, together with
the Governor and the Attorney General, with the duty of examining
the election returns received from the County Election Commissioners and declaring the election results, by the applicable provisions
of the Tennessee Code Annotated, and by Chapter 164 of the Acts
of 1949, inter alia.

"Defendant, *George F. McCanless,* is the duly appointed and acting Attorney General of the State of Tennessee, with his office in
Nashville in said State, and is charged with the duty of advising the
officers of the State upon the law, and is made by Section 23–1107
of the Tennessee Code Annotated a necessary party defendant in any
declaratory judgment action where the constitutionality of statutes of
the State of Tennessee is attacked, and he is ex-officio charged,
together with the Governor and the Secretary of State, with the duty
of declaring the election results, under Section 2–140 of the Tennessee
Code Annotated.

"Defendant, *Jerry McDonald,* is the duly appointed Coordinator
of Elections in the State of Tennessee, with his office in Nashville,
Tennessee, and as such official, is charged with the duties set forth
in the public law enacted by the 1959 General Assembly of Tennessee
creating said office.

"Defendants, *Dr. Sam Coward, James Alexander,* and *Hubert
Brooks* are the duly appointed and qualified members constituting

We hold that the appellants do have standing to maintain this suit. Our decisions plainly support this conclusion. Many of the cases have assumed rather than articulated the premise in deciding the merits of similar claims.[26] And *Colegrove* v. *Green, supra,* squarely held that voters who allege facts showing disadvantage to themselves as individuals have standing to sue.[27] A num-

---

the State Board of Elections, and as such they are charged with the duty of appointing the Election Commissioners for all the counties of the State of Tennessee, the organization and supervision of the biennial elections as provided by the Statutes of Tennessee, Chapter 9 of Title 2 of the Tennessee Code Annotated, Sections 2–901, et seq.

"That this action is brought against the aforenamed defendants in their representative capacities, and that said Election Commissioners are sued also as representatives of all of the County Election Commissioners in the State of Tennessee, such persons being so numerous as to make it impracticable to bring them all before the court; that there is a common question of law involved, namely, the constitutionality of Tennessee laws set forth in the Tennessee Code Annotated, Section 3–101 through Section 3–109, inclusive; that common relief is sought against all members of said Election Commissions in their official capacities, it being the duties of the aforesaid County Election Commissioners, within their respective jurisdictions, to appoint the judges of elections, to maintain the registry of qualified voters of said County, certify the results of elections held in said County to the defendants State Board of Elections and Secretary of State, and of preparing ballots and taking other steps to prepare for and hold elections in said Counties by virtue of Sections 2–1201, et seq. of Tennessee Code Annotated, and Section 2–301, et seq. of Tennessee Code Annotated, and Chapter 164 of the Acts of 1949, inter alia."

The question whether the named defendants are sufficient parties remains open for consideration on remand.

[26] *Smiley* v. *Holm, supra,* at 361 (" 'citizen, elector and taxpayer' of the State"); *Koenig* v. *Flynn, supra,* at 379 (" 'citizens and voters' of the State") *Wood* v. *Broom, supra,* at 4 ("citizen of Mississippi, a qualified elector under its laws, and also qualified to be a candidate for election as representative in Congress"); cf. *Carroll* v. *Becker, supra* (candidate for office).

[27] Mr. Justice Rutledge was of the view that any question of standing was settled in *Smiley* v. *Holm, supra;* MR. JUSTICE BLACK stated "that appellants had standing to sue, since the facts alleged show that

BAKER v. CARR.

ber of cases decided after *Colegrove* recognized the standing of the voters there involved to bring those actions.[28]

These appellants seek relief in order to protect or vindicate an interest of their own, and of those similarly situated. Their constitutional claim is, in substance, that the 1901 statute constitutes arbitrary and capricious state action, offensive to the Fourteenth Amendment in its irrational disregard of the standard of apportionment prescribed by the State's Constitution or of any standard, effecting a gross disproportion of representation to voting population. The injury which appellants assert is that this classification disfavors the voters in the counties in which they reside, placing them in a position of constitutionally unjustifiable inequality *vis-à-vis* voters

---

they have been injured as individuals." He relied on *Coleman* v. *Miller,* 307 U. S. 433, 438, 467. See 328 U. S. 564, 568.

Commentators have suggested that the following statement in MR. JUSTICE FRANKFURTER's opinion might imply a view that appellants there had no standing: "This is not an action to recover for damage because of the discriminatory exclusion of a plaintiff from rights enjoyed by other citizens. The basis for the suit is not a private wrong, but a wrong suffered by Illinois as a polity." 328 U. S., at 552. See Jaffe, Standing to Secure Judicial Review: Public Actions, 74 Harv. L. Rev. 1265, 1298 (1961); Lewis, Legislative Apportionment and the Federal Courts, 71 Harv. L. Rev. 1057, 1081–1083 (1958). But since the opinion goes on to consider the merits, it seems that this statement was not intended to intimate any view that the plaintiffs in that action lacked standing. Nor do the cases cited immediately after the above quotation deal with standing. See especially *Lane* v. *Wilson,* 307 U. S. 268, 272–273.

[28] *MacDougall* v. *Green, supra,* at 282 ("the 'Progressive Party,' its nominees for United States Senator, Presidential Electors, and State offices, and several Illinois voters"); *South* v. *Peters, supra,* at 277 ("residents of the most populous county in the State"); *Radford* v. *Gary,* 145 F. Supp. 541, 542 ("citizen of Oklahoma and resident and voter in the most populous county"); *Matthews* v. *Handley, supra* ("citizen of the State"); see also *Hawke* v. *Smith (No. 1),* 253 U. S. 221; *Leser* v. *Garnett,* 258 U. S. 130; *Coleman* v. *Miller,* 307 U. S. 433, 437–446.

in irrationally favored counties.   A citizen's right to a vote free of arbitrary impairment by state action has been judicially recognized as a right secured by the Constitution, when such impairment resulted from dilution by a false tally, cf. *United States* v. *Classic,* 313 U. S. 299; or by a refusal to count votes from arbitrarily selected precincts, cf. *United States* v. *Mosley,* 238 U. S. 383, or by a stuffing of the ballot box, cf. *Ex parte Siebold,* 100 U. S. 371; *United States* v. *Saylor,* 322 U. S. 385.

It would not be necessary to decide whether appellants' allegations of impairment of their votes by the 1901 apportionment will, ultimately, entitle them to any relief, in order to hold that they have standing to seek it.   If such impairment does produce a legally cognizable injury, they are among those who have sustained it.   They are asserting "a plain, direct and adequate interest in maintaining the effectiveness of their votes," *Coleman* v. *Miller,* 307 U. S., at 438, not merely a claim of "the right, possessed by every citizen, to require that the Government be administered according to law . . . ." *Fairchild* v. *Hughes,* 258 U. S. 126, 129; compare *Leser* v. *Garnett,* 258 U. S. 130.   They are entitled to a hearing and to the District Court's decision on their claims.   "The very essence of civil liberty certainly consists in the right of every individual to claim the protection of the laws, whenever he receives an injury." *Marbury* v. *Madison,* 1 Cranch 137, 163.

IV.

JUSTICIABILITY.

In holding that the subject matter of this suit was not justiciable, the District Court relied on *Colegrove* v. *Green, supra,* and subsequent *per curiam* cases.[29]   The

---

[29] *Cook* v. *Fortson,* 329 U. S. 675; *Turman* v. *Duckworth, ibid.;* *Colegrove* v. *Barrett,* 330 U. S. 804; *MacDougall* v. *Green,* 335 U. S. 281; *South* v. *Peters,* 339 U. S. 276; *Remmey* v. *Smith,* 342 U. S. 916;

"discrimination is sufficiently shown, the right to relief under the equal protection clause is not diminished by the fact that the discrimination relates to political rights." *Snowden* v. *Hughes,* 321 U. S. 1, 11. To show why we reject the argument based on the Guaranty Clause, we must examine the authorities under it. But because there appears to be some uncertainty as to why those cases did present political questions, and specifically as to whether this apportionment case is like those cases, we deem it necessary first to consider the contours of the "political question" doctrine.

Our discussion, even at the price of extending this opinion, requires review of a number of political question cases, in order to expose the attributes of the doctrine— attributes which, in various settings, diverge, combine, appear, and disappear in seeming disorderliness. Since that review is undertaken solely to demonstrate that neither singly nor collectively do these cases support a conclusion that this apportionment case is nonjusticiable, we of course do not explore their implications in other contexts. That review reveals that in the Guaranty Clause cases and in the other "political question" cases, it is the relationship between the judiciary and the coordinate branches of the Federal Government, and not the federal judiciary's relationship to the States, which gives rise to the "political question."

We have said that "In determining whether a question falls within [the political question] category, the appropriateness under our system of government of attributing finality to the action of the political departments and also the lack of satisfactory criteria for a judicial determination are dominant considerations." *Coleman* v. *Miller,* 307 U. S. 433, 454–455. The nonjusticiability of a political question is primarily a function of the separation of powers. Much confusion results from the capacity of the "political question" label to obscure the need for

court stated: "From a review of these decisions there can be no doubt that the federal rule . . . is that the federal courts . . . will not intervene in cases of this type to compel legislative reapportionment." 179 F. Supp., at 826. We understand the District Court to have read the cited cases as compelling the conclusion that since the appellants sought to have a legislative apportionment held unconstitutional, their suit presented a "political question" and was therefore nonjusticiable. We hold that this challenge to an apportionment presents no nonjusticiable "political question." The cited cases do not hold the contrary.

Of course the mere fact that the suit seeks protection of a political right does not mean it presents a political question. Such an objection "is little more than a play upon words." *Nixon* v. *Herndon,* 273 U. S. 536, 540. Rather, it is argued that apportionment cases, whatever the actual wording of the complaint, can involve no federal constitutional right except one resting on the guaranty of a republican form of government,[30] and that complaints based on that clause have been held to present political questions which are nonjusticiable.

We hold that the claim pleaded here neither rests upon nor implicates the Guaranty Clause and that its justiciability is therefore not foreclosed by our decisions of cases involving that clause. The District Court misinterpreted *Colegrove* v. *Green* and other decisions of this Court on which it relied. Appellants' claim that they are being denied equal protection is justiciable, and if

---

Anderson v. *Jordan,* 343 U. S. 912; *Kidd* v. *McCanless,* 352 U. S. 920; *Radford* v. *Gary,* 352 U. S. 991.

[30] "The United States shall guarantee to every State in this Union a Republican Form of Government, and shall protect each of them against Invasion; and on Application of the Legislature, or of the Executive (when the Legislature cannot be convened) against domestic Violence." U. S. Const., Art. IV, § 4.

case-by-case inquiry. Deciding whether a matter has in any measure been committed by the Constitution to another branch of government, or whether the action of that branch exceeds whatever authority has been committed, is itself a delicate exercise in constitutional interpretation, and is a responsibility of this Court as ultimate interpreter of the Constitution. To demonstrate this requires no less than to analyze representative cases and to infer from them the analytical threads that make up the political question doctrine. We shall then show that none of those threads catches this case.

Foreign relations: There are sweeping statements to the effect that all questions touching foreign relations are political questions.[31] Not only does resolution of such issues frequently turn on standards that defy judicial application, or involve the exercise of a discretion demonstrably committed to the executive or legislature;[32] but many such questions uniquely demand single-voiced statement of the Government's views.[33] Yet it is error to suppose that every case or controversy which touches foreign relations lies beyond judicial cognizance. Our cases in this field seem invariably to show a discriminating analysis of the particular question posed, in terms of the history of its management by the political branches, of its susceptibility to judicial handling in the light of its nature and posture in the specific case, and of the possible conse-

---

[31] *E. g.,* "The conduct of the foreign relations of our Government is committed by the Constitution to the Executive and Legislative— 'the political'—Departments of the Government, and the propriety of what may be done in the exercise of this political power is not subject to judicial inquiry or decision." *Oetjen* v. *Central Leather Co.,* 246 U. S. 297, 302.

[32] See *Doe* v. *Braden,* 16 How. 635, 657; *Taylor* v. *Morton,* 23 Fed. Cas., No. 13,799 (C. C. D. Mass.) (Mr. Justice Curtis), affirmed, 2 Black 481.

[33] See *Doe* v. *Braden,* 16 How. 635, 657.

quences of judicial action. For example, though a court will not ordinarily inquire whether a treaty has been terminated, since on that question "governmental action . . . must be regarded as of controlling importance," if there has been no conclusive "governmental action" then a court can construe a treaty and may find it provides the answer. Compare *Terlinden* v. *Ames,* 184 U. S. 270, 285, with *Society for the Propagation of the Gospel in Foreign Parts* v. *New Haven,* 8 Wheat. 464, 492–495.[34] Though a court will not undertake to construe a treaty in a manner inconsistent with a subsequent federal statute, no similar hesitancy obtains if the asserted clash is with state law. Compare *Whitney* v. *Robertson,* 124 U. S. 190, with *Kolovrat* v. *Oregon,* 366 U. S. 187.

While recognition of foreign governments so strongly defies judicial treatment that without executive recognition a foreign state has been called "a republic of whose existence we know nothing," [35] and the judiciary ordinarily follows the executive as to which nation has sovereignty over disputed territory,[36] once sovereignty over an area is politically determined and declared, courts may examine the resulting status and decide independently whether a statute applies to that area.[37] Similarly, recognition of belligerency abroad is an executive responsibility, but if the executive proclamations fall short of an explicit answer, a court may construe them seeking, for example, to determine whether the situation is such that statutes designed to assure American neutrality have

---

[34] And see *Clark* v. *Allen,* 331 U. S. 503.

[35] *United States* v. *Klintock,* 5 Wheat. 144, 149; see also *United States* v. *Palmer,* 3 Wheat. 610, 634–635.

[36] *Foster & Elam* v. *Neilson,* 2 Pet. 253, 307; and see *Williams* v. *Suffolk Insurance Co.,* 13 Pet. 415, 420.

[37] *Vermilya-Brown Co.* v. *Connell,* 335 U. S. 377, 380; *De Lima* v. *Bidwell,* 182 U. S. 1, 180–200.

become operative. *The Three Friends,* 166 U. S. 1, 63, 66. Still again, though it is the executive that determines a person's status as representative of a foreign government, *Ex parte Hitz,* 111 U. S. 766, the executive's statements will be construed where necessary to determine the court's jurisdiction, *In re Baiz,* 135 U. S. 403. Similar judicial action in the absence of a recognizedly authoritative executive declaration occurs in cases involving the immunity from seizure of vessels owned by friendly foreign governments. Compare *Ex parte Peru,* 318 U. S. 578, with *Mexico* v. *Hoffman,* 324 U. S. 30, 34–35.

Dates of duration of hostilities: Though it has been stated broadly that "the power which declared the necessity is the power to declare its cessation, and what the cessation requires," *Commercial Trust Co.* v. *Miller,* 262 U. S. 51, 57, here too analysis reveals isolable reasons for the presence of political questions, underlying this Court's refusal to review the political departments' determination of when or whether a war has ended. Dominant is the need for finality in the political determination, for emergency's nature demands "A prompt and unhesitating obedience," *Martin* v. *Mott,* 12 Wheat. 19, 30 (calling up of militia). Moreover, "the cessation of hostilities does not necessarily end the war power. It was stated in *Hamilton* v. *Kentucky Distilleries & W. Co.,* 251 U. S. 146, 161, that the war power includes the power 'to remedy the evils which have arisen from its rise and progress' and continues during that emergency. *Stewart* v. *Kahn,* 11 Wall. 493, 507." *Fleming* v. *Mohawk Wrecking Co.,* 331 U. S. 111, 116. But deference rests on reason, not habit.[38] The question in a particular case may not seriously implicate considerations of finality—*e. g.,* a public program of importance

---

[38] See, *e. g., Home Building & Loan Assn.* v. *Blaisdell,* 290 U. S. 398, 426.

(rent control) yet not central to the emergency effort.[39] Further, clearly definable criteria for decision may be available. In such case the political question barrier falls away: "[A] Court is not at liberty to shut its eyes to an obvious mistake, when the validity of the law depends upon the truth of what is declared. . . . [It can] inquire whether the exigency still existed upon which the continued operation of the law depended." *Chastleton Corp.* v. *Sinclair,* 264 U. S. 543, 547–548.[40] Compare *Woods* v. *Miller Co.,* 333 U. S. 138. On the other hand, even in private litigation which directly implicates no feature of separation of powers, lack of judicially discoverable standards and the drive for even-handed application may impel reference to the political departments' determination of dates of hostilities' beginning and ending. *The Protector,* 12 Wall. 700.

Validity of enactments: In *Coleman* v. *Miller, supra,* this Court held that the questions of how long a proposed amendment to the Federal Constitution remained open to ratification, and what effect a prior rejection had on a subsequent ratification, were committed to congressional resolution and involved criteria of decision that necessarily escaped the judicial grasp.[41] Similar considerations apply to the enacting process: "The respect due to coequal and independent departments," and the need for finality and certainty about the status of a statute contribute to judicial reluctance to inquire whether, as passed, it complied with all requisite formalities. *Field* v. *Clark,* 143 U. S. 649, 672, 676–677; see *Leser* v. *Garnett,* 258 U. S. 130, 137. But it is not true that courts will never delve

---

[39] Contrast *Martin* v. *Mott, supra.*

[40] But cf. *Dakota Central Tel. Co.* v. *South Dakota,* 250 U. S. 163, 184, 187.

[41] Cf. *Dillon* v. *Gloss,* 256 U. S. 368. See also *United States* v. *Sprague,* 282 U. S. 716, 732.

into a legislature's records upon such a quest: If the enrolled statute lacks an effective date, a court will not hesitate to seek it in the legislative journals in order to preserve the enactment. *Gardner* v. *The Collector,* 6 Wall. 499. The political question doctrine, a tool for maintenance of governmental order, will not be so applied as to promote only disorder.

The status of Indian tribes: This Court's deference to the political departments in determining whether Indians are recognized as a tribe, while it reflects familiar attributes of political questions,[42] *United States* v. *Holliday,* 3 Wall. 407, 419, also has a unique element in that "the relation of the Indians to the United States is marked by peculiar and cardinal distinctions which exist no where else. . . . [The Indians are] domestic dependent nations . . . in a state of pupilage. Their relation to the United States resembles that of a ward to his guardian." *The Cherokee Nation* v. *Georgia,* 5 Pet. 1, 16, 17.[43] Yet, here too, there is no blanket rule. While

---

[42] See also *Fellows* v. *Blacksmith,* 19 How. 366, 372; *United States* v. *Old Settlers,* 148 U. S. 427, 466; and compare *Doe* v. *Braden,* 16 How. 635, 657.

[43] This case, so frequently cited for the broad proposition that the status of an Indian tribe is a matter for the political departments, is in fact a noteworthy example of the limited and precise impact of a political question. The Cherokees brought an original suit in this Court to enjoin Georgia's assertion of jurisdiction over Cherokee territory and abolition of Cherokee government and laws. Unquestionably the case lay at the vortex of most fiery political embroilment. See 1 Warren, The Supreme Court in United States History (Rev. ed.), 729–779. But in spite of some broader language in separate opinions, all that the Court held was that it possessed no original jurisdiction over the suit: for the Cherokees could in no view be considered either a State of this Union or a "foreign state." Chief Justice Marshall treated the question as one of *de novo* interpretation of words in the Constitution. The Chief Justice did say that "The acts of our government plainly recognize the Cherokee nation

" 'It is for [Congress] . . . , and not for the courts, to determine when the true interests of the Indian require his release from [the] condition of tutelage' . . . , it is not meant by this that Congress may bring a community or body of people within the range of this power by arbitrarily calling them an Indian tribe . . . ." *United States* v. *Sandoval*, 231 U. S. 28, 46. Able to discern what is "distinctly Indian," *ibid.*, the courts will strike down

---

as a state, and the courts are bound by those acts," but here he referred to their existence "as a state, as a distinct political society, separated from others . . . ." From there he went to "A question of much more difficulty . . . . Do the Cherokees constitute a foreign state in the sense of the constitution?" *Id.*, at 16. Thus, while the Court referred to "the political" for the decision whether the tribe was an entity, a separate polity, it held that whether being an entity the tribe had such status as to be entitled to sue originally was a judicially soluble issue: criteria were discoverable in relevant phrases of the Constitution and in the common understanding of the times. As to this issue, the Court was not hampered by problems of the management of unusual evidence or of possible interference with a congressional program. Moreover, Chief Justice Marshall's dictum that "It savours too much of the exercise of political power to be within the proper province of the judicial department," *id.*, at 20, was not addressed to the issue of the Cherokees' status to sue, but rather to the breadth of the claim asserted and the impropriety of the relief sought. Compare *Georgia* v. *Stanton*, 6 Wall. 50, 77. The Chief Justice made clear that if the issue of the Cherokees' rights arose in a customary legal context, "a proper case with proper parties," it would be justiciable. Thus, when the same dispute produced a case properly brought, in which the right asserted was one of protection under federal treaties and laws from conflicting state law, and the relief sought was the voiding of a conviction under that state law, the Court did void the conviction. *Worcester* v. *Georgia*, 6 Pet. 515. There, the fact that the tribe was a separate polity served as a datum contributing to the result, and despite the consequences in a heated federal-state controversy and the opposition of the other branches of the National Government, the judicial power acted to reverse the State Supreme Court. An example of similar isolation of a political question in the decision of a case is *Luther* v. *Borden*, 7 How. 1, see *infra*.

any heedless extension of that label. They will not stand impotent before an obvious instance of a manifestly unauthorized exercise of power.

It is apparent that several formulations which vary slightly according to the settings in which the questions arise may describe a political question, although each has one or more elements which identify it as essentially a function of the separation of powers. Prominent on the surface of any case held to involve a political question is found a textually demonstrable constitutional commitment of the issue to a coordinate political department; or a lack of judicially discoverable and manageable standards for resolving it; or the impossibility of deciding without an initial policy determination of a kind clearly for nonjudicial discretion; or the impossibility of a court's undertaking independent resolution without expressing lack of the respect due coordinate branches of government; or an unusual need for unquestioning adherence to a political decision already made; or the potentiality of embarrassment from multifarious pronouncements by various departments on one question.

Unless one of these formulations is inextricable from the case at bar, there should be no dismissal for non-justiciability on the ground of a political question's presence. The doctrine of which we treat is one of "political questions," not one of "political cases." The courts cannot reject as "no law suit" a bona fide controversy as to whether some action denominated "political" exceeds constitutional authority. The cases we have reviewed show the necessity for discriminating inquiry into the precise facts and posture of the particular case, and the impossibility of resolution by any semantic cataloguing.

But it is argued that this case shares the characteristics of decisions that constitute a category not yet considered, cases concerning the Constitution's guaranty, in Art. IV,

§ 4, of a republican form of government. A conclusion as to whether the case at bar does present a political question cannot be confidently reached until we have considered those cases with special care. We shall discover that Guaranty Clause claims involve those elements which define a "political question," and for that reason and no other, they are nonjusticiable. In particular, we shall discover that the nonjusticiability of such claims has nothing to do with their touching upon matters of state governmental organization.

Republican form of government: Luther v. *Borden,* 7 How. 1, though in form simply an action for damages for trespass was, as Daniel Webster said in opening the argument for the defense, "an unusual case." [44] The defendants, admitting an otherwise tortious breaking and entering, sought to justify their action on the ground that they were agents of the established lawful government of Rhode Island, which State was then under martial law to defend itself from active insurrection; that the plaintiff was engaged in that insurrection; and that they entered under orders to arrest the plaintiff. The case arose "out of the unfortunate political differences which agitated the people of Rhode Island in 1841 and 1842," 7 How., at 34, and which had resulted in a situation wherein two groups laid competing claims to recognition as the lawful government.[45] The plaintiff's right to

---

[44] 7 How., at 29. And see 11 The Writings and Speeches of Daniel Webster 217 (1903).

[45] See Mowry, The Dorr War (1901), and its exhaustive bibliography. And for an account of circumstances surrounding the decicion here, see 2 Warren, The Supreme Court in United States History (Rev. ed.), 185–195.

Dorr himself, head of one of the two groups and held in a Rhode Island jail under a conviction for treason, had earlier sought a decision from the Supreme Court that his was the lawful government. His application for original habeas corpus in the Supreme Court was

recover depended upon which of the two groups was entitled to such recognition; but the lower court's refusal to receive evidence or hear argument on that issue, its charge to the jury that the earlier established or "charter" government was lawful, and the verdict for the defendants, were affirmed upon appeal to this Court.

Chief Justice Taney's opinion for the Court reasoned as follows: (1) If a court were to hold the defendants' acts unjustified because the charter government had no legal existence during the period in question, it would follow that all of that government's actions—laws enacted, taxes collected, salaries paid, accounts settled, sentences passed—were of no effect; and that "the officers who carried their decisions into operation [were] answerable as trespassers, if not in some cases as criminals." [46]   There was, of course, no room for application of any doctrine of *de facto* status to uphold prior acts of an officer not authorized *de jure,* for such would have defeated the plaintiff's very action. A decision for the plaintiff would inevitably have produced some significant measure of chaos, a consequence to be avoided if it could be done without abnegation of the judicial duty to uphold the Constitution.

(2) No state court had recognized as a judicial responsibility settlement of the issue of the locus of state governmental authority. Indeed, the courts of Rhode Island had in several cases held that "it rested with the political power to decide whether the charter government had been displaced or not," and that that department had acknowledged no change.

---

denied because the federal courts then lacked authority to issue habeas for a prisoner held under a state court sentence. *Ex parte Dorr,* 3 How. 103.

[46] 7 How., at 39.

(3) Since "[t]he question relates, altogether, to the constitution and laws of [the] . . . State," the courts of the United States had to follow the state courts' decisions unless there was a federal constitutional ground for overturning them.[47]

(4) No provision of the Constitution could be or had been invoked for this purpose except Art. IV, § 4, the Guaranty Clause. Having already noted the absence of standards whereby the choice between governments could be made by a court acting independently, Chief Justice Taney now found further textual and practical reasons for concluding that, if any department of the United States was empowered by the Guaranty Clause to resolve the issue, it was not the judiciary:

> "Under this article of the Constitution it rests with Congress to decide what government is the established one in a State. For as the United States guarantee to each State a republican government, Congress must necessarily decide what government is established in the State before it can determine whether it is republican or not. And when the senators and representatives of a State are admitted into the councils of the Union, the authority of the government under which they are appointed, as well as its republican character, is recognized by the proper constitutional authority. And its decision is binding on every other department of the government, and could not be questioned in a judicial tribunal. It is true that the contest in this case did not last long enough to bring the matter to this issue; and . . . Congress was not called upon to decide the controversy. Yet the right to decide is placed there, and not in the courts.

---

[47] *Id.*, at 39, 40.

"So, too, as relates to the clause in the above-mentioned article of the Constitution, providing for cases of domestic violence. It rested with Congress, too, to determine upon the means proper to be adopted to fulfill this guarantee. . . . [B]y the act of February 28, 1795, [Congress] provided, that, 'in case of an insurrection in any State against the government thereof, it shall be lawful for the President of the United States, on application of the legislature of such State or of the executive (when the legislature cannot be convened), to call forth such number of the militia of any other State or States, as may be applied for, as he may judge sufficient to suppress such insurrection.'

"By this act, the power of deciding whether the exigency had arisen upon which the government of the United States is bound to interfere, is given to the President. . . .

"After the President has acted and called out the militia, is a Circuit Court of the United States authorized to inquire whether his decision was right? . . . If the judicial power extends so far, the guarantee contained in the Constitution of the United States is a guarantee of anarchy, and not of order. . . .

"It is true that in this case the militia were not called out by the President. But upon the application of the governor under the charter government, the President recognized him as the executive power of the State, and took measures to call out the militia to support his authority if it should be found necessary for the general government to interfere . . . . [C]ertainly no court of the United States, with a knowledge of this decision, would have been justified in recognizing the opposing party as the lawful gov-

ernment . . . . In the case of foreign nations, the
government acknowledged by the President is always
recognized in the courts of justice. . . ." 7 How.,
at 42–44.

Clearly, several factors were thought by the Court in
Luther to make the question there "political": the commitment to the other branches of the decision as to which
is the lawful state government; the unambiguous action
by the President, in recognizing the charter government
as the lawful authority; the need for finality in the
executive's decision; and the lack of criteria by which a
court could determine which form of government was
republican.[48]

---

[48] Even though the Court wrote of unrestrained legislative and
executive authority under this Guaranty, thus making its enforcement a political question, the Court plainly implied that the political
question barrier was no absolute: "Unquestionably a military government, established as the permanent government of the State, would
not be a republican government, and it would be the duty of Congress to overthrow it." 7 How., at 45. Of course, it does not necessarily follow that if Congress did not act, the Court would. For while
the judiciary might be able to decide the limits of the meaning of
"republican form," and thus the factor of lack of criteria might fall
away, there would remain other possible barriers to decision because
of primary commitment to another branch, which would have to be
considered in the particular fact setting presented.

That was not the only occasion on which this Court indicated that
lack of criteria does not obliterate the Guaranty's extreme limits:
"The guaranty is of a republican form of government. No particular government is designated as republican, neither is the exact form
to be guaranteed, in any manner especially designated. Here, as in
other parts of the instrument, we are compelled to resort elsewhere
to ascertain what was intended.

"The guaranty necessarily implies a duty on the part of the
States themselves to provide such a government. All the States had
governments when the Constitution was adopted. In all the people
participated to some extent, through their representatives elected in
the manner specially provided. These governments the Constitution
did not change. They were accepted precisely as they were, and it

BAKER v. CARR.

But the only significance that *Luther* could have for our immediate purposes is in its holding that the Guaranty Clause is not a repository of judicially manageable standards which a court could utilize independently in order to identify a State's lawful government. The Court has since refused to resort to the Guaranty Clause—which alone had been invoked for the purpose—as the source of a constitutional standard for invalidating state action. See *Taylor & Marshall* v. *Beckham (No. 1)*, 178 U. S. 548 (claim that Kentucky's resolution of contested gubernatorial election deprived voters of republican government held nonjusticiable); *Pacific States Tel. Co.* v. *Oregon,* 223 U. S. 118 (claim that initiative and referendum negated republican government held nonjusticiable); *Kiernan* v. *Portland,* 223 U. S. 151 (claim that municipal charter amendment *per* municipal initiative and referendum negated republican government held non-

is, therefore, to be presumed that they were such as it was the duty of the States to provide. Thus we have unmistakable evidence of what was republican in form, within the meaning of that term as employed in the Constitution." *Minor* v. *Happersett,* 21 Wall. 162, 175–176. There, the question was whether a government republican in form could deny the vote to women.

In re Duncan, 139 U. S. 449, upheld a murder conviction against a claim that the relevant codes had been invalidly enacted. The Court there said:

"By the Constitution, a republican form of government is guaranteed to every State in the Union, and the distinguishing feature of that form is the right of the people to choose their own officers for governmental administration, and pass their own laws in virtue of the legislative power reposed in representative bodies, whose legitimate acts may be said to be those of the people themselves; but, while the people are thus the source of political power, their governments, National and State, have been limited by written constitutions, and they have themselves thereby set bounds to their own power, as against the sudden impulses of mere majorities." 139 U. S., at 461. But the Court did not find any of these fundamental principles violated.

justiciable); *Marshall* v. *Dye,* 231 U. S. 250 (claim that Indiana's constitutional amendment procedure negated republican government held nonjusticiable); *O'Neill* v. *Leamer,* 239 U. S. 244 (claim that delegation to court of power to form drainage districts negated republican government held "futile"); *Ohio ex rel. Davis* v. *Hildebrant,* 241 U. S. 565 (claim that invalidation of state reapportionment statute *per* referendum negates republican government held nonjusticiable); [49] *Mountain Timber Co.* v. *Washington,* 243 U. S. 219 (claim that workmen's compensation violates republican government held nonjusticiable); *Ohio ex rel. Bryant* v. *Akron Metropolitan Park District,* 281 U. S. 74 (claim that rule requiring invalidation of statute by all but one justice of state court negated republican government held nonjusticiable); *Highland Farms Dairy* v. *Agnew,* 300 U. S. 608 (claim that delegation to agency of power to control milk prices violated republican government, rejected).

Just as the Court has consistently held that a challenge to state action based on the Guaranty Clause presents no justiciable question so has it held, and for the same reasons, that challenges to congressional action on the ground of inconsistency with that clause present no justiciable question. In *Georgia* v. *Stanton,* 6 Wall. 50, the State sought by an original bill to enjoin execution of the Reconstruction Acts, claiming that it already possessed "A republican State, in every political, legal, constitutional, and juridical sense," and that enforcement of the new Acts "Instead of keeping the guaranty against a forcible overthrow of its government by foreign invaders or domestic insurgents, . . . is destroying that very government by force." [50] Congress had clearly refused to

---

[49] But cf. *Hawke* v. *Smith* (*No. 1*), 253 U. S. 221; *National Prohibition Cases,* 253 U. S. 350.

[50] 6 Wall., at 65, 66.

BAKER v. CARR.

recognize the republican character of the government of the suing State.[51]   It seemed to the Court that the only constitutional claim that could be presented was under the Guaranty Clause, and Congress having determined that the effects of the recent hostilities required extraordinary measures to restore governments of a republican form, this Court refused to interfere with Congress' action at the behest of a claimant relying on that very guaranty.[52]

In only a few other cases has the Court considered Art. IV, § 4, in relation to congressional action. It has refused to pass on a claim relying on the Guaranty Clause to establish that Congress lacked power to allow the States to employ the referendum in passing on legislation redistricting for congressional seats. *Ohio ex rel. Davis* v. *Hildebrant, supra.* And it has pointed out that Congress is not required to establish republican government in the territories before they become States, and before they have attained a sufficient population to warrant a

---

[51] The First Reconstruction Act opened: "Whereas no legal State governments . . . now exists [*sic*] in the rebel States of . . . Georgia [and] Mississippi . . . ; and whereas it is necessary that peace and good order should be enforced in said States until loyal and republican State governments can be legally established: . . ." 14 Stat. 428. And see 15 Stat. 2, 14.

[52] In *Mississippi* v. *Johnson*, 4 Wall. 475, the State sought to enjoin the President from executing the Acts, alleging that his role was purely ministerial. The Court held that the duties were in no sense ministerial, and that although the State sought to compel inaction rather than action, the absolute lack of precedent for any such distinction left the case one in which "general principles . . . forbid judicial interference with the exercise of Executive discretion." 4 Wall., at 499. See also *Mississippi* v. *Stanton*, 154 U. S. 554; and see 2 Warren, The Supreme Court in United States History (Rev. ed.), 463.

For another instance of congressional action challenged as transgressing the Guaranty Clause, see *The Collector* v. *Day*, 11 Wall. 113, 125–126, overruled, *Graves* v. *O'Keefe*, 306 U. S. 466.

popularly elected legislature. *Downes* v. *Bidwell*, 182 U. S. 244, 278–279 (dictum).[53]

We come, finally, to the ultimate inquiry whether our precedents as to what constitutes a nonjusticiable "political question" bring the case before us under the umbrella of that doctrine. A natural beginning is to note whether any of the common characteristics which we have been able to identify and label descriptively are present. We find none: The question here is the consistency of state action with the Federal Constitution. We have no question decided, or to be decided, by a political branch of government coequal with this Court. Nor do we risk embarrassment of our government abroad, or grave disturbance at home [54] if we take issue with Tennessee as to the constitutionality of her action here challenged. Nor need the appellants, in order to succeed in this action, ask the Court to enter upon policy determinations for which judicially manageable standards are lacking. Judicial standards under the Equal Protection Clause are well developed and familiar, and it has been open to courts since the enactment of the Fourteenth Amendment to determine, if on the particular facts they must, that a discrimination reflects *no* policy, but simply arbitrary and capricious action.

This case does, in one sense, involve the allocation of political power within a State, and the appellants

---

[53] On the other hand, the implication of the Guaranty Clause in a case concerning congressional action does not always preclude judicial action. It has been held that the clause gives Congress no power to impose restrictions upon a State's admission which would undercut the constitutional mandate that the States be on an equal footing. *Coyle* v. *Smith*, 221 U. S. 559. And in *Texas* v. *White*, 7 Wall. 700, although Congress had determined that the State's government was not republican in form, the State's standing to bring an original action in this Court was sustained.

[54] See, *infra*, p. 235, considering *Kidd* v. *McCanless*, 352 U. S. 920.

might conceivably have added a claim under the Guaranty Clause. Of course, as we have seen, any reliance on that clause would be futile. But because any reliance on the Guaranty Clause could not have succeeded it does not follow that appellants may not be heard on the equal protection claim which in fact they tender. True, it must be clear that the Fourteenth Amendment claim is not so enmeshed with those political question elements which render Guaranty Clause claims nonjusticiable as actually to present a political question itself. But we have found that not to be the case here.

In this connection special attention is due *Pacific States Tel. Co.* v. *Oregon,* 223 U. S. 118. In that case a corporation tax statute enacted by the initiative was attacked ostensibly on three grounds: (1) due process; (2) equal protection; and (3) the Guaranty Clause. But it was clear that the first two grounds were invoked solely in aid of the contention that the tax was invalid by reason of its passage:

> "The defendant company does not contend here that it could not have been required to pay a license tax. It does not assert that it was denied an opportunity to be heard as to the amount for which it was taxed, or that there was anything inhering in the tax or involved intrinsically in the law which violated any of its constitutional rights. If such questions had been raised they would have been justiciable, and therefore would have required the calling into operation of judicial power. Instead, however, of doing any of these things, the attack on the statute here made is of a wholly different character. Its essentially political nature is at once made manifest by understanding that the assault which the contention here advanced makes it [*sic*] not on the tax as a tax, but on the State as a State. It is addressed to the

211

framework and political character of the government by which the statute levying the tax was passed. It is the government, the political entity, which (reducing the case to its essence) is called to the bar of this court, not for the purpose of testing judicially some exercise of power assailed, on the ground that its exertion has injuriously affected the rights of an individual because of repugnancy to some constitutional limitation, but to demand of the State that it establish its right to exist as a State, republican in form." 223 U. S., at 150–151.

The due process and equal protection claims were held nonjusticiable in *Pacific States* not because they happened to be joined with a Guaranty Clause claim, or because they sought to place before the Court a subject matter which might conceivably have been dealt with through the Guaranty Clause, but because the Court believed that they were invoked merely in verbal aid of the resolution of issues which, in its view, entailed political questions. *Pacific States* may be compared with cases such as *Mountain Timber Co.* v. *Washington,* 243 U. S. 219, wherein the Court refused to consider whether a workmen's compensation act violated the Guaranty Clause but considered at length, and rejected, due process and equal protection arguments advanced against it; and *O'Neill* v. *Leamer,* 239 U. S. 244, wherein the Court refused to consider whether Nebraska's delegation of power to form drainage districts violated the Guaranty Clause, but went on to consider and reject the contention that the action against which an injunction was sought was not a taking for a public purpose.

We conclude then that the nonjusticiability of claims resting on the Guaranty Clause which arises from their embodiment of questions that were thought "political," can have no bearing upon the justiciability of the equal protection claim presented in this case. Finally, we emphasize that it is the involvement in Guaranty Clause claims of the elements thought to define "political questions," and no other feature, which could render them nonjusticiable. Specifically, we have said that such claims are not held nonjusticiable because they touch matters of state governmental organization. Brief examination of a few cases demonstrates this.

When challenges to state action respecting matters of "the administration of the affairs of the State and the officers through whom they are conducted" [55] have rested on claims of constitutional deprivation which are amenable to judicial correction, this Court has acted upon its view of the merits of the claim. For example, in *Boyd* v. *Nebraska ex rel. Thayer,* 143 U. S. 135, we reversed the Nebraska Supreme Court's decision that Nebraska's Governor was not a citizen of the United States or of the State and therefore could not continue in office. In *Kennard* v. *Louisiana ex rel. Morgan,* 92 U. S. 480, and *Foster* v. *Kansas ex rel. Johnston,* 112 U. S. 201, we considered whether persons had been removed from public office by procedures consistent with the Fourteenth Amendment's due process guaranty, and held on the merits that they had. And only last Term, in *Gomillion* v. *Lightfoot,* 364 U. S. 339, we applied the Fifteenth Amendment to strike down a redrafting of municipal boundaries which effected a discriminatory impairment of voting rights, in the face of what a majority of the Court of Appeals thought to be a sweeping commitment to state legislatures of the power to draw and redraw such boundaries.[56]

Gomillion was brought by a Negro who had been a resident of the City of Tuskegee, Alabama, until the municipal boundaries were so recast by the State Legis-

---

[55] *Boyd* v. *Nebraska ex rel. Thayer,* 143 U. S. 135, 183 (Field, J., dissenting).

[56] *Gomillion* v. *Lightfoot,* 270 F. 2d 594, relying upon, *inter alia, Hunter* v. *Pittsburgh,* 207 U. S. 161.

lature as to exclude practically all Negroes. The plaintiff claimed deprivation of the right to vote in municipal elections. The District Court's dismissal for want of jurisdiction and failure to state a claim upon which relief could be granted was affirmed by the Court of Appeals. This Court unanimously reversed. This Court's answer to the argument that States enjoyed unrestricted control over municipal boundaries was:

> "Legislative control of municipalities, no less than other state power, lies within the scope of relevant limitations imposed by the United States Constitution. . . . The opposite conclusion, urged upon us by respondents, would sanction the achievement by a State of any impairment of voting rights whatever so long as it was cloaked in the garb of the realignment of political subdivisions. 'It is inconceivable that guaranties embedded in the Constitution of the United States may thus be manipulated out of existence.'" 364 U. S., at 344–345.

To a second argument, that *Colegrove* v. *Green, supra,* was a barrier to hearing the merits of the case, the Court responded that *Gomillion* was lifted "out of the so-called 'political' arena and into the conventional sphere of constitutional litigation" because here was discriminatory treatment of a racial minority violating the Fifteenth Amendment.

> "A statute which is alleged to have worked unconstitutional deprivations of petitioners' rights is not immune to attack simply because the mechanism employed by the legislature is a redefinition of municipal boundaries. . . . While in form this is merely an act redefining metes and bounds, if the allegations are established, the inescapable human effect of this essay in geometry and geography is to despoil colored citizens, and only colored citizens, of

214

BAKER *v.* CARR.

their theretofore enjoyed voting rights.   That was not *Colegrove* v. *Green.*

"When a State exercises power wholly within the domain of state interest, it is insulated from federal judicial review.   But such insulation is not carried over when state power is used as an instrument for circumventing a federally protected right."   364 U. S., at 347.[57]

We have not overlooked such cases as *In re Sawyer,* 124 U. S. 200, and *Walton* v. *House of Representatives,* 265 U. S. 487, which held that federal equity power could not be exercised to enjoin a state proceeding to remove a public officer.   But these decisions explicitly reflect only a traditional limit upon equity jurisdiction, and not upon federal courts' power to inquire into matters of state governmental organization.   This is clear not only from the opinions in those cases, but also from *White* v. *Berry,* 171 U. S. 366, which, relying on *Sawyer,* withheld federal equity from staying removal of a *federal* officer.   *Wilson* v. *North Carolina,* 169 U. S. 586, simply dismissed an appeal from an unsuccessful suit to upset a State's removal procedure, on the ground that the constitutional claim presented—that a jury trial was necessary if the removal procedure was to comport with due process requirements—was frivolous.   Finally, in *Taylor and Marshall* v. *Beckham (No. 1),* 178 U. S. 548, where losing candidates attacked the constitutionality of Kentucky's resolution of a contested gubernatorial election, the Court refused to consider the merits of a claim posited upon

---

[57] The Court's opinion was joined by MR. JUSTICE DOUGLAS, noting his adherence to the dissents in *Colegrove* and *South* v. *Peters, supra;* and the judgment was concurred in by MR. JUSTICE WHITTAKER, who wrote that the decision should rest on the Equal Protection Clause rather than on the Fifteenth Amendment, since there had been not solely a denial of the vote (if there had been that at all) but also a "fencing out" of a racial group.

the Guaranty Clause, holding it presented a political question, but also held on the merits that the ousted candidates had suffered no deprivation of property without due process of law.[58]

Since, as has been established, the equal protection claim tendered in this case does not require decision of any political question, and since the presence of a matter affecting state government does not render the case non-justiciable, it seems appropriate to examine again the reasoning by which the District Court reached its conclusion that the case was nonjusticiable.

We have already noted that the District Court's holding that the subject matter of this complaint was non-justiciable relied upon *Colegrove* v. *Green, supra,* and later cases. Some of those concerned the choice of members of a state legislature, as in this case; others, like *Colegrove* itself and earlier precedents, *Smiley* v. *Holm,* 285 U. S. 355, *Koenig* v. *Flynn,* 285 U. S. 375, and *Carroll* v. *Becker,* 285 U. S. 380, concerned the choice of Representatives in the Federal Congress. *Smiley, Koenig* and *Carroll* settled the issue in favor of justiciability of questions of congressional redistricting. The Court followed these precedents in *Colegrove* although over the dissent of three of the seven Justices who participated in that decision. On the issue of justiciability, all four Justices comprising a majority relied upon *Smiley* v. *Holm,* but in two opinions, one for three Justices, 328 U. S., at 566, 568, and a separate one by Mr. Justice Rutledge, 328 U. S., at 564. The argument that congressional redistricting problems presented a "political question" the resolution of which was confided to Congress might have been rested upon Art. I, § 4, Art. I, § 5, Art. I, § 2, and Amendment

---

[58] No holding to the contrary is to be found in *Cave* v. *Newell,* 246 U. S. 650, dismissing a writ of error to the Supreme Court of Missouri, 272 Mo. 653, 199 S. W. 1014; or in *Snowden* v. *Hughes,* 321 U. S. 1.

XIV, § 2. Mr. Justice Rutledge said: "But for the ruling in *Smiley* v. *Holm,* 285 U. S. 355, I should have supposed that the provisions of the Constitution, Art. I, § 4, that 'The Times, Places and Manner of holding Elections for . . . Representatives, shall be prescribed in each State by the Legislature thereof; but the Congress may at any time by Law make or alter such Regulations . . .'; Art. I, § 2 [but see Amendment XIV, § 2], vesting in Congress the duty of apportionment of representatives among the several states 'according to their respective Numbers'; and Art. I, § 5, making each House the sole judge of the qualifications of its own members, would remove the issues in this case from justiciable cognizance. But, in my judgment, the *Smiley* case rules squarely to the contrary, save only in the matter of degree. . . . Assuming that that decision is to stand, I think . . . that its effect is to rule that this Court has power to afford relief in a case of this type as against the objection that the issues are not justiciable." 328 U. S., at 564–565. Accordingly, Mr. Justice Rutledge joined in the conclusion that the case was justiciable, although he held that the dismissal of the complaint should be affirmed. His view was that "The shortness of the time remaining [before forthcoming elections] makes it doubtful whether action could, or would, be taken in time to secure for petitioners the effective relief they seek. . . . I think, therefore, the case is one in which the Court may properly, and should, decline to exercise its jurisdiction. Accordingly, the judgment should be affirmed and I join in that disposition of the cause." 328 U. S., at 565–566.[59]

---

[59] The ground of Mr. Justice Rutledge's vote to affirm is further explained in his footnote 3, 328 U. S., at 566: " 'The power of a court of equity to act is a discretionary one. . . . Where a federal court of equity is asked to interfere with the enforcement of state laws, it should do so only "to prevent irreparable injury which is clear and

Article I, §§ 2, 4, and 5, and Amendment XIV, § 2, relate only to congressional elections and obviously do not govern apportionment of state legislatures. However, our decisions in favor of justiciability even in light of those provisions plainly afford no support for the District Court's conclusion that the subject matter of this controversy presents a political question. Indeed, the refusal to award relief in *Colegrove* resulted only from the controlling view of a want of equity. Nor is anything contrary to be found in those *per curiams* that came after *Colegrove*. This Court dismissed the appeals in *Cook* v. *Fortson* and *Turman* v. *Duckworth*, 329 U. S. 675, as moot. *MacDougall* v. *Green*, 335 U. S. 281, held only that in that case equity would not act to void the State's requirement that there be at least a minimum of support for nom-

---

imminent." ' *American Federation of Labor* v. *Watson*, 327 U. S. 582, 593 and cases cited."

No constitutional questions, including the question whether voters have a judicially enforceable constitutional right to vote at elections of congressmen from districts of equal population, were decided in *Colegrove*. Six of the participating Justices reached the questions but divided three to three on their merits. Mr. Justice Rutledge believed that it was not necessary to decide them. He said: "There is [an alternative to constitutional decision] in this case. And I think the gravity of the constitutional questions raised so great, together with the possibilities for collision [with the political departments of the Government], that the admonition [against avoidable constitutional decision] is appropriate to be followed here. Other reasons support this view, including the fact that, in my opinion, the basic ruling and less important ones in *Smiley* v. *Holm, supra*, would otherwise be brought into question." 328 U. S., at 564–565. He also joined with his brethren who shared his view that the issues were justiciable in considering that *Wood* v. *Broom*, 287 U. S. 1, decided no constitutional questions but "the Court disposed of the cause on the ground that the 1929 Reapportionment Act, 46 Stat. 21, did not carry forward the requirements of the 1911 Act, 37 Stat. 13, and declined to decide whether there was equity in the bill." 328 U. S., at 565; see also, *id.*, at 573. We agree with this view of *Wood* v. *Broom*.

inees for state-wide office, over at least a minimal area of the State.   Problems of timing were critical in *Remmey v. Smith,* 342 U. S. 916, dismissing for want of a substantial federal question a three-judge court's dismissal of the suit as prematurely brought, 102 F. Supp. 708; and in *Hartsfield* v. *Sloan,* 357 U. S. 916, denying mandamus sought to compel the convening of a three-judge court— movants urged the Court to advance consideration of their case, "Inasmuch as the mere lapse of time before this case can be reached in the normal course of . . . business may defeat the cause, and inasmuch as the time problem is due to the inherent nature of the case . . . ."   *South* v. *Peters,* 339 U. S. 276, like *Colegrove* appears to be a refusal to exercise equity's powers; see the statement of the holding, quoted, *supra,* p. 203.   And *Cox* v. *Peters,* 342 U. S. 936, dismissed for want of a substantial federal question the appeal from the state court's holding that their primary elections implicated no "state action."   See 208 Ga. 498, 67 S. E. 2d 579.   But compare *Terry* v. *Adams,* 345 U. S. 461.

Tedesco v. *Board of Supervisors,* 339 U. S. 940, indicates solely that no substantial federal question was raised by a state court's refusal to upset the districting of city council seats, especially as it was urged that there was a rational justification for the challenged districting.   See 43 So. 2d 514.   Similarly, in *Anderson* v. *Jordan,* 343 U. S. 912, it was certain only that the state court had refused to issue a discretionary writ, original mandamus in the Supreme Court.   That had been denied without opinion, and of course it was urged here that an adequate state ground barred this Court's review.   And in *Kidd* v. *McCanless,* 200 Tenn. 273, 292 S. W. 2d 40, the Supreme Court of Tennessee held that it could not invalidate the very statute at issue in the case at bar, but its holding rested on its state law of remedies, *i. e.,* the state view of *de facto* officers,[60] and not on any view that the norm for legislative apportionment in Tennessee is not numbers of qualified voters resident in the several counties. Of course this Court was there precluded by the adequate state ground, and in dismissing the appeal, 352 U. S. 920, we cited *Anderson, supra,* as well as *Colegrove.* Nor does the Tennessee court's decision in that case bear upon this, for just as in *Smith* v. *Holm,* 220 Minn. 486, 19 N. W. 2d 914, and *Magraw* v. *Donovan,* 163 F. Supp. 184, 177 F. Supp. 803, a state court's inability to grant relief does not bar a federal court's assuming jurisdiction to inquire into alleged deprivation of federal constitutional rights. Problems of relief also controlled in *Radford* v. *Gary,* 352 U. S. 991, affirming the District Court's refusal to mandamus the Governor to call a session of the legislature, to mandamus the legislature then to apportion, and if they did not comply, to mandamus the State Supreme Court to do so. And *Matthews* v. *Handley,* 361 U. S. 127, affirmed a refusal to strike down the State's gross income tax statute—urged on the ground that the legislature was malapportioned—that had rested on the adequacy of available state legal remedies for suits involving that tax, including challenges to its constitutionality. Lastly, *Colegrove* v. *Barrett,* 330 U. S. 804, in which Mr. Justice Rutledge concurred in this Court's refusal to note the appeal from a dismissal for want of equity, is sufficiently explained by his statement in *Cook* v. *Fortson, supra:* "The discretionary exercise or non-exercise of equitable or declaratory judgment jurisdiction . . . in one case is not precedent in another case

---

[60] See also *Buford* v. *State Board of Elections,* 206 Tenn. 480, 334 S. W. 2d 726; *State ex rel. Sanborn* v. *Davidson County Board of Election Comm'rs,* No. 36,391 Tenn. Sup. Ct., Oct. 29, 1954 (unreported); 8 Vand. L. Rev. 501 (1955).

where the facts differ." 329 U. S., at 678, n. 8. (Citations omitted.)

We conclude that the complaint's allegations of a denial of equal protection present a justiciable constitutional cause of action upon which appellants are entitled to a trial and a decision. The right asserted is within the reach of judicial protection under the Fourteenth Amendment.

The judgment of the District Court is reversed and the cause is remanded for further proceedings consistent with this opinion.

Reversed and remanded.

MR. JUSTICE WHITTAKER did not participate in the decision of this case.

APPENDIX TO OPINION OF THE COURT.

The Tennessee Code Annotated provides for representation in the General Assembly as follows:

"3–101. *Composition—Counties electing one representative each.*—The general assembly of the state of Tennessee shall be composed of thirty-three (33) senators and ninety-nine (99) representatives, to be apportioned among the qualified voters of the state as follows: Until the next enumeration and apportionment of voters each of the following counties shall elect one (1) representative, to wit: Bedford, Blount, Cannon, Carroll, Chester, Cocke, Claiborne, Coffee, Crockett, DeKalb, Dickson, Dyer, Fayette, Franklin, Giles, Greene, Hardeman, Hardin, Henry, Hickman, Hawkins, Haywood, Jackson, Lake, Lauderdale, Lawrence, Lincoln, Marion, Marshall, Maury, Monroe, Montgomery, Moore, McMinn, McNairy, Obion, Overton, Putnam, Roane, Robertson, Rutherford, Sevier, Smith, Stewart, Sullivan, Sumner, Tipton, Warren, Washington, White, Weakley, Williamson and Wilson. [Acts 1881 (E. S.), ch. 5, § 1; 1881 (E. S.), ch. 6, § 1; 1901, ch. 122, § 2; 1907, ch. 178, §§ 1, 2; 1915, ch. 145; Shan., § 123; Acts 1919, ch. 147, §§ 1, 2; 1925 Private, ch. 472, § 1; Code 1932, § 140; Acts 1935, ch. 150, § 1; 1941, ch. 58, § 1; 1945, ch. 68, § 1; C. Supp. 1950, § 140.]

"3–102. *Counties electing two representatives each.*— The following counties shall elect two (2) representatives each, to wit: Gibson and Madison. [Acts 1901, ch. 122, § 3; Shan., § 124; mod. Code 1932, § 141.]

"3–103. *Counties electing three representatives each.*— The following counties shall elect three (3) representatives each, to wit: Knox and Hamilton. [Acts 1901, ch. 122, § 4; Shan., § 125; Code 1932, § 142.]

"3–104. *Davidson County.*—Davidson county shall elect six (6) representatives. [Acts 1901, ch. 122, § 5; Shan., § 126; Code 1932, § 143.]

"3–105. *Shelby county.*—Shelby county shall elect eight (8) representatives. Said county shall consist of eight (8) representative districts, numbered one (1) through eight (8), each district co-extensive with the county, with one (1) representative to be elected from each district. [Acts 1901, ch. 122, § 6; Shan., § 126a1; Code 1932, § 144; Acts 1957, ch. 220, § 1; 1959, ch. 213, § 1.]

"3–106. *Joint representatives.*—The following counties jointly, shall elect one representative, as follows, to wit:

"First district—Johnson and Carter.

"Second district—Sullivan and Hawkins.

"Third district—Washington, Greene and Unicoi.

"Fourth district—Jefferson and Hamblen.

"Fifth district—Hancock and Grainger.

"Sixth district—Scott, Campbell, and Union.

"Seventh district—Anderson and Morgan.

"Eighth district—Knox and Loudon.

BAKER v. CARR.

"Ninth district—Polk and Bradley.

"Tenth district—Meigs and Rhea.

"Eleventh district—Cumberland, Bledsoe, Sequatchie, Van Buren and Grundy.

"Twelfth district—Fentress, Pickett, Overton, Clay and Putnam.

"Fourteenth district—Sumner, Trousdale and Macon.

"Fifteenth district—Davidson and Wilson.

"Seventeenth district — Giles, Lewis, Maury and Wayne.

"Eighteenth district—Williamson, Cheatham and Robertson.

"Nineteenth district—Montgomery and Houston.

"Twentieth district—Humphreys and Perry.

"Twenty-first district—Benton and Decatur.

"Twenty-second district—Henry, Weakley and Carroll.

"Twenty-third district—Madison and Henderson.

"Twenty-sixth district—Tipton and Lauderdale. [Acts 1901, ch. 122, § 7; 1907, ch. 178, §§ 1, 2; 1915, ch. 145, §§ 1, 2; Shan., § 127; Acts 1919, ch. 147, § 1; 1925 Private, ch. 472, § 2; Code 1932, § 145; Acts 1933, ch. 167, § 1; 1935, ch. 150, § 2; 1941, ch. 58, § 2; 1945, ch. 68, § 2; C. Supp. 1950, § 145; Acts 1957, ch. 220, § 2.]

"3–107. *State senatorial districts.*—Until the next enumeration and apportionment of voters, the following counties shall comprise the senatorial districts, to wit:

"First district—Johnson, Carter, Unicoi, Greene, and Washington.

"Second district—Sullivan and Hawkins.

"Third district—Hancock, Morgan, Grainger, Claiborne, Union, Campbell, and Scott.

"Fourth district—Cocke, Hamblen, Jefferson, Sevier, and Blount.

"Fifth district—Knox.

"Sixth district—Knox, Loudon, Anderson, and Roane.

223

"Seventh district—McMinn, Bradley, Monroe, and Polk.

"Eighth district—Hamilton.

"Ninth district—Rhea, Meigs, Bledsoe, Sequatchie, Van Buren, White, and Cumberland.

"Tenth district—Fentress, Pickett, Clay, Overton, Putnam, and Jackson.

"Eleventh district—Marion, Franklin, Grundy and Warren.

"Twelfth district—Rutherford, Cannon, and DeKalb.

"Thirteenth district—Wilson and Smith.

"Fourteenth district—Sumner, Trousdale and Macon.

"Fifteenth district—Montgomery and Robertson.

"Sixteenth district—Davidson.

"Seventeenth district—Davidson.

"Eighteenth district—Bedford, Coffee and Moore.

"Nineteenth district—Lincoln and Marshall.

"Twentieth district—Maury, Perry and Lewis.

"Twenty-first district—Hickman, Williamson and Cheatham.

"Twenty-second district—Giles, Lawrence and Wayne.

"Twenty-third district—Dickson, Humphreys, Houston and Stewart.

"Twenty-fourth district—Henry and Carroll.

"Twenty-fifth district—Madison, Henderson and Chester.

"Twenty-sixth district—Hardeman, McNairy, Hardin, Decatur and Benton.

"Twenty-seventh district—Gibson.

"Twenty-eighth district—Lake, Obion and Weakley.

"Twenty-ninth district — Dyer, Lauderdale and Crockett.

"Thirtieth district—Tipton and Shelby.

"Thirty-first district—Haywood and Fayette.

"Thirty-second district—Shelby.

"Thirty-third district—Shelby. [Acts 1901, ch. 122, § 1; 1907, ch. 3, § 1; Shan., § 128; Code 1932, § 146; Acts 1945, ch. 11, § 1; C. Supp. 1950, § 146.]"

Today's apportionment statute is as enacted in 1901, with minor changes. For example:

(1) In 1957, Shelby County was raised from 7½ to 8 representatives. Acts of 1957, c. 220. See also Acts of 1959, c. 213. The 1957 Act, § 2, abolished the Twenty-seventh Joint Representative District, which had included Shelby and Fayette Counties.

(2) In 1907, Marion County was given a whole House seat instead of sharing a joint seat with Franklin County. Acts of 1907, c. 178. Acts of 1915, c. 145, repealed that change, restoring the *status quo ante*. And that reversal was itself reversed, Acts of 1919, c. 147.

(3) James County was in 1901 one of five counties in the Seventh State Senate District and one of the three in the Ninth House District. It appears that James County no longer exists but we are not advised when or how it was dissolved.

(4) In 1945, Anderson and Roane Counties were shifted to the Sixth State Senate District from the Seventh, and Monroe and Polk Counties were shifted to the Seventh from the Sixth. Acts of 1945, c. 11.

BROWN v. BOARD OF EDUCATION.

BROWN ET AL. v. BOARD OF EDUCATION
OF TOPEKA ET AL.

NO. 1. APPEAL FROM THE UNITED STATES DISTRICT COURT FOR THE DISTRICT OF KANSAS.*

Argued December 9, 1952.—Reargued December 8, 1953.—
Decided May 17, 1954.

Segregation of white and Negro children in the public schools of a State solely on the basis of race, pursuant to state laws permitting or requiring such segregation, denies to Negro children the equal protection of the laws guaranteed by the Fourteenth Amendment— even though the physical facilities and other "tangible" factors of white and Negro schools may be equal.

(a) The history of the Fourteenth Amendment is inconclusive as to its intended effect on public education.

(b) The question presented in these cases must be determined, not on the basis of conditions existing when the Fourteenth Amendment was adopted, but in the light of the full development of public education and its present place in American life throughout the Nation.

(c) Where a State has undertaken to provide an opportunity for an education in its public schools, such an opportunity is a right which must be made available to all on equal terms.

(d) Segregation of children in public schools solely on the basis of race deprives children of the minority group of equal educational opportunities, even though the physical facilities and other "tangible" factors may be equal.

(e) The "separate but equal" doctrine adopted in *Plessy* v. *Ferguson*, 163 U. S. 537, has no place in the field of public education.

---

*Together with No. 2, *Briggs et al.* v. *Elliott et al.*, on appeal from the United States District Court for the Eastern District of South Carolina, argued December 9–10, 1952, reargued December 7–8, 1953; No. 4, *Davis et al.* v. *County School Board of Prince Edward County, Virginia, et al.*, on appeal from the United States District Court for the Eastern District of Virginia, argued December 10, 1952, reargued December 7–8, 1953; and No. 10, *Gebhart et al.* v. *Belton et al.*, on certiorari to the Supreme Court of Delaware, argued December 11, 1952, reargued December 9, 1953.

226

(f) The cases are restored to the docket for further argument on specified questions relating to the forms of the decrees. Pp. 495–496.

Robert L. Carter argued the cause for appellants in No. 1 on the original argument and on the reargument. *Thurgood Marshall* argued the cause for appellants in No. 2 on the original argument and *Spottswood W. Robinson, III,* for appellants in No. 4 on the original argument, and both argued the causes for appellants in Nos. 2 and 4 on the reargument. *Louis L. Redding* and *Jack Greenberg* argued the cause for respondents in No. 10 on the original argument and *Jack Greenberg* and *Thurgood Marshall* on the reargument.

On the briefs were *Robert L. Carter, Thurgood Marshall, Spottswood W. Robinson, III, Louis L. Redding, Jack Greenberg, George E. C. Hayes, William R. Ming, Jr., Constance Baker Motley, James M. Nabrit, Jr., Charles S. Scott, Frank D. Reeves, Harold R. Boulware* and *Oliver W. Hill* for appellants in Nos. 1, 2 and 4 and respondents in No. 10; *George M. Johnson* for appellants in Nos. 1, 2 and 4; and *Loren Miller* for appellants in Nos. 2 and 4. *Arthur D. Shores* and *A. T. Walden* were on the Statement as to Jurisdiction and a brief opposing a Motion to Dismiss or Affirm in No. 2.

Paul E. Wilson, Assistant Attorney General of Kansas, argued the cause for appellees in No. 1 on the original argument and on the reargument. With him on the briefs was *Harold R. Fatzer,* Attorney General.

John W. Davis argued the cause for appellees in No. 2 on the original argument and for appellees in Nos. 2 and 4 on the reargument. With him on the briefs in No. 2 were *T. C. Callison,* Attorney General of South Carolina, *Robert McC. Figg, Jr., S. E. Rogers, William R. Meagher* and *Taggart Whipple.*

227

J. Lindsay Almond, Jr., Attorney General of Virginia, and *T. Justin Moore* argued the cause for appellees in No. 4 on the original argument and for appellees in Nos. 2 and 4 on the reargument. On the briefs in No. 4 were *J. Lindsay Almond, Jr.,* Attorney General, and *Henry T. Wickham,* Special Assistant Attorney General, for the State of Virginia, and *T. Justin Moore, Archibald G. Robertson, John W. Riely* and *T. Justin Moore, Jr.* for the Prince Edward County School Authorities, appellees.

H. Albert Young, Attorney General of Delaware, argued the cause for petitioners in No. 10 on the original argument and on the reargument. With him on the briefs was *Louis J. Finger,* Special Deputy Attorney General.

By special leave of Court, *Assistant Attorney General Rankin* argued the cause for the United States on the reargument, as *amicus curiae,* urging reversal in Nos. 1, 2 and 4 and affirmance in No. 10. With him on the brief were *Attorney General Brownell, Philip Elman, Leon Ulman, William J. Lamont* and *M. Magdelena Schoch. James P. McGranery,* then Attorney General, and *Philip Elman* filed a brief for the United States on the original argument, as *amicus curiae,* urging reversal in Nos. 1, 2 and 4 and affirmance in No. 10.

Briefs of *amici curiae* supporting appellants in No. 1 were filed by *Shad Polier, Will Maslow* and *Joseph B. Robison* for the American Jewish Congress; by *Edwin J. Lukas, Arnold Forster, Arthur Garfield Hays, Frank E. Karelsen, Leonard Haas, Saburo Kido* and *Theodore Leskes* for the American Civil Liberties Union et al.; and by *John Ligtenberg* and *Selma M. Borchardt* for the American Federation of Teachers. Briefs of *amici curiae* supporting appellants in No. 1 and respondents in No. 10 were filed by *Arthur J. Goldberg* and *Thomas E. Harris*

228

for the Congress of Industrial Organizations and by
Phineas Indritz for the American Veterans Committee,
Inc.

MR. CHIEF JUSTICE WARREN delivered the opinion of
the Court.

These cases come to us from the States of Kansas,
South Carolina, Virginia, and Delaware. They are pre-
mised on different facts and different local conditions,
but a common legal question justifies their consideration
together in this consolidated opinion.[1]

_____

[1] In the Kansas case, *Brown* v. *Board of Education,* the plaintiffs
are Negro children of elementary school age residing in Topeka.
They brought this action in the United States District Court for the
District of Kansas to enjoin enforcement of a Kansas statute which
permits, but does not require, cities of more than 15,000 population
to maintain separate school facilities for Negro and white students.
Kan. Gen. Stat. § 72–1724 (1949). Pursuant to that authority, the
Topeka Board of Education elected to establish segregated elementary
schools. Other public schools in the community, however, are oper-
ated on a nonsegregated basis. The three-judge District Court, convened under 28 U. S. C. §§ 2281 and 2284, found that segregation
in public education has a detrimental effect upon Negro children,
but denied relief on the ground that the Negro and white schools
were substantially equal with respect to buildings, transportation,
curricula, and educational qualifications of teachers. 98 F. Supp. 797.
The case is here on direct appeal under 28 U. S. C. § 1253.

In the South Carolina case, *Briggs* v. *Elliott,* the plaintiffs are Negro
children of both elementary and high school age residing in Clarendon
County. They brought this action in the United States District
Court for the Eastern District of South Carolina to enjoin enforcement of provisions in the state constitution and statutory code which
require the segregation of Negroes and whites in public schools.
S. C. Const., Art. XI, § 7; S. C. Code § 5377 (1942). The three-
judge District Court, convened under 28 U. S. C. §§ 2281 and 2284,
denied the requested relief. The court found that the Negro schools
were inferior to the white schools and ordered the defendants to begin
immediately to equalize the facilities. But the court sustained the
validity of the contested provisions and denied the plaintiffs admis-

229

BROWN *v.* BOARD OF EDUCATION.

In each of the cases, minors of the Negro race, through their legal representatives, seek the aid of the courts in obtaining admission to the public schools of their community on a nonsegregated basis. In each instance,

---

sion to the white schools during the equalization program. 98 F. Supp. 529. This Court vacated the District Court's judgment and remanded the case for the purpose of obtaining the court's views on a report filed by the defendants concerning the progress made in the equalization program. 342 U. S. 350. On remand, the District Court found that substantial equality had been achieved except for buildings and that the defendants were proceeding to rectify this inequality as well. 103 F. Supp. 920. The case is again here on direct appeal under 28 U. S. C. § 1253.

In the Virginia case, *Davis* v. *County School Board,* the plaintiffs are Negro children of high school age residing in Prince Edward County. They brought this action in the United States District Court for the Eastern District of Virginia to enjoin enforcement of provisions in the state constitution and statutory code which require the segregation of Negroes and whites in public schools. Va. Const., § 140; Va. Code § 22–221 (1950). The three-judge District Court, convened under 28 U. S. C. §§ 2281 and 2284, denied the requested relief. The court found the Negro school inferior in physical plant, curricula, and transportation, and ordered the defendants forthwith to provide substantially equal curricula and transportation and to "proceed with all reasonable diligence and dispatch to remove" the inequality in physical plant. But, as in the South Carolina case, the court sustained the validity of the contested provisions and denied the plaintiffs admission to the white schools during the equalization program. 103 F. Supp. 337. The case is here on direct appeal under 28 U. S. C. § 1253.

In the Delaware case, *Gebhart* v. *Belton,* the plaintiffs are Negro children of both elementary and high school age residing in New Castle County. They brought this action in the Delaware Court of Chancery to enjoin enforcement of provisions in the state constitution and statutory code which require the segregation of Negroes and whites in public schools. Del. Const., Art. X, § 2; Del. Rev. Code § 2631 (1935). The Chancellor gave judgment for the plaintiffs and ordered their immediate admission to schools previously attended only by white children, on the ground that the Negro schools were inferior with respect to teacher training, pupil-teacher ratio, extracurricular activities, physical plant, and time and distance in-they had been denied admission to schools attended by white children under laws requiring or permitting segregation according to race.   This segregation was alleged to deprive the plaintiffs of the equal protection of the laws under the Fourteenth Amendment.   In each of the cases other than the Delaware case, a three-judge federal district court denied relief to the plaintiffs on the so-called "separate but equal" doctrine announced by this Court in *Plessy* v. *Ferguson,* 163 U. S. 537.   Under that doctrine, equality of treatment is accorded when the races are provided substantially equal facilities, even though these facilities be separate.   In the Delaware case, the Supreme Court of Delaware adhered to that doctrine, but ordered that the plaintiffs be admitted to the white schools because of their superiority to the Negro schools.

The plaintiffs contend that segregated public schools are not "equal" and cannot be made "equal," and that hence they are deprived of the equal protection of the laws.   Because of the obvious importance of the question presented, the Court took jurisdiction.[2]   Argument was heard in the 1952 Term, and reargument was heard this Term on certain questions propounded by the Court.[3]

---

volved in travel. 87 A. 2d 862. The Chancellor also found that segregation itself results in an inferior education for Negro children (see note 10, *infra*), but did not rest his decision on that ground. *Id.,* at 865. The Chancellor's decree was affirmed by the Supreme Court of Delaware, which intimated, however, that the defendants might be able to obtain a modification of the decree after equalization of the Negro and white schools had been accomplished. 91 A. 2d 137, 152. The defendants, contending only that the Delaware courts had erred in ordering the immediate admission of the Negro plaintiffs to the white schools, applied to this Court for certiorari. The writ was granted, 344 U. S. 891. The plaintiffs, who were successful below, did not submit a cross-petition.

[2] 344 U. S. 1, 141, 891.

[3] 345 U. S. 972. The Attorney General of the United States participated both Terms as *amicus curiae.*

BROWN v. BOARD OF EDUCATION.

Reargument was largely devoted to the circumstances surrounding the adoption of the Fourteenth Amendment in 1868. It covered exhaustively consideration of the Amendment in Congress, ratification by the states, then existing practices in racial segregation, and the views of proponents and opponents of the Amendment. This discussion and our own investigation convince us that, although these sources cast some light, it is not enough to resolve the problem with which we are faced. At best, they are inconclusive. The most avid proponents of the post-War Amendments undoubtedly intended them to remove all legal distinctions among "all persons born or naturalized in the United States." Their opponents, just as certainly, were antagonistic to both the letter and the spirit of the Amendments and wished them to have the most limited effect. What others in Congress and the state legislatures had in mind cannot be determined with any degree of certainty.

An additional reason for the inconclusive nature of the Amendment's history, with respect to segregated schools, is the status of public education at that time.[4] In the South, the movement toward free common schools, sup-

---

[4] For a general study of the development of public education prior to the Amendment, see Butts and Cremin, A History of Education in American Culture (1953), Pts. I, II; Cubberley, Public Education in the United States (1934 ed.), cc. II–XII. School practices current at the time of the adoption of the Fourteenth Amendment are described in Butts and Cremin, supra, at 269–275; Cubberley, supra, at 288–339, 408–431; Knight, Public Education in the South (1922), cc. VIII, IX. See also H. Ex. Doc. No. 315, 41st Cong., 2d Sess. (1871). Although the demand for free public schools followed substantially the same pattern in both the North and the South, the development in the South did not begin to gain momentum until about 1850, some twenty years after that in the North. The reasons for the somewhat slower development in the South (e. g., the rural character of the South and the different regional attitudes toward state assistance) are well explained in Cubberley, supra, at 408–423. In the country as a whole, but particularly in the South, the War

ported by general taxation, had not yet taken hold. Education of white children was largely in the hands of private groups. Education of Negroes was almost nonexistent, and practically all of the race were illiterate. In fact, any education of Negroes was forbidden by law in some states. Today, in contrast, many Negroes have achieved outstanding success in the arts and sciences as well as in the business and professional world. It is true that public school education at the time of the Amendment had advanced further in the North, but the effect of the Amendment on Northern States was generally ignored in the congressional debates. Even in the North, the conditions of public education did not approximate those existing today. The curriculum was usually rudimentary; ungraded schools were common in rural areas; the school term was but three months a year in many states; and compulsory school attendance was virtually unknown. As a consequence, it is not surprising that there should be so little in the history of the Fourteenth Amendment relating to its intended effect on public education.

In the first cases in this Court construing the Fourteenth Amendment, decided shortly after its adoption, the Court interpreted it as proscribing all state-imposed discriminations against the Negro race.[5] The doctrine of

---

virtually stopped all progress in public education. *Id.*, at 427–428. The low status of Negro education in all sections of the country, both before and immediately after the War, is described in Beale, A History of Freedom of Teaching in American Schools (1941), 112–132, 175–195. Compulsory school attendance laws were not generally adopted until after the ratification of the Fourteenth Amendment, and it was not until 1918 that such laws were in force in all the states. Cubberley, *supra*, at 563–565.

[5] *Slaughter-House Cases*, 16 Wall. 36, 67–72 (1873); *Strauder* v. *West Virginia*, 100 U. S. 303, 307–308 (1880):

"It ordains that no State shall deprive any person of life, liberty, or property, without due process of law, or deny to any person within its jurisdiction the equal protection of the laws. What is this but

BROWN *v.* BOARD OF EDUCATION.

"separate but equal" did not make its appearance in this Court until 1896 in the case of *Plessy* v. *Ferguson, supra,* involving not education but transportation.[6] American courts have since labored with the doctrine for over half a century. In this Court, there have been six cases involving the "separate but equal" doctrine in the field of public education.[7] In *Cumming* v. *County Board of Education,* 175 U. S. 528, and *Gong Lum* v. *Rice,* 275 U. S. 78, the validity of the doctrine itself was not challenged.[8] In more recent cases, all on the graduate school

---

declaring that the law in the States shall be the same for the black as for the white; that all persons, whether colored or white, shall stand equal before the laws of the States, and, in regard to the colored race, for whose protection the amendment was primarily designed, that no discrimination shall be made against them by law because of their color? The words of the amendment, it is true, are prohibitory, but they contain a necessary implication of a positive immunity, or right, most valuable to the colored race,—the right to exemption from unfriendly legislation against them distinctively as colored,—exemption from legal discriminations, implying inferiority in civil society, lessening the security of their enjoyment of the rights which others enjoy, and discriminations which are steps towards reducing them to the condition of a subject race."
See also *Virginia* v. *Rives,* 100 U. S. 313, 318 (1880); *Ex parte Virginia,* 100 U. S. 339, 344–345 (1880).

[6] The doctrine apparently originated in *Roberts* v. *City of Boston,* 59 Mass. 198, 206 (1850), upholding school segregation against attack as being violative of a state constitutional guarantee of equality. Segregation in Boston public schools was eliminated in 1855. Mass. Acts 1855, c. 256. But elsewhere in the North segregation in public education has persisted in some communities until recent years. It is apparent that such segregation has long been a nationwide problem, not merely one of sectional concern.

[7] See also *Berea College* v. *Kentucky,* 211 U. S. 45 (1908).

[8] In the *Cumming* case, Negro taxpayers sought an injunction requiring the defendant school board to discontinue the operation of a high school for white children until the board resumed operation of a high school for Negro children. Similarly, in the *Gong Lum* case, the plaintiff, a child of Chinese descent, contended only that state authorities had misapplied the doctrine by classifying him with Negro children and requiring him to attend a Negro school.

level, inequality was found in that specific benefits enjoyed by white students were denied to Negro students of the same educational qualifications. *Missouri ex rel. Gaines* v. *Canada,* 305 U. S. 337; *Sipuel* v. *Oklahoma,* 332 U. S. 631; *Sweatt* v. *Painter,* 339 U. S. 629; *McLaurin* v. *Oklahoma State Regents,* 339 U. S. 637. In none of these cases was it necessary to re-examine the doctrine to grant relief to the Negro plaintiff. And in *Sweatt* v. *Painter, supra,* the Court expressly reserved decision on the question whether *Plessy* v. *Ferguson* should be held inapplicable to public education.

In the instant cases, that question is directly presented. Here, unlike *Sweatt* v. *Painter,* there are findings below that the Negro and white schools involved have been equalized, or are being equalized, with respect to buildings, curricula, qualifications and salaries of teachers, and other "tangible" factors.[9] Our decision, therefore, cannot turn on merely a comparison of these tangible factors in the Negro and white schools involved in each of the cases. We must look instead to the effect of segregation itself on public education.

In approaching this problem, we cannot turn the clock back to 1868 when the Amendment was adopted, or even to 1896 when *Plessy* v. *Ferguson* was written. We must consider public education in the light of its full development and its present place in American life throughout

---

[9] In the Kansas case, the court below found substantial equality as to all such factors. 98 F. Supp. 797, 798. In the South Carolina case, the court below found that the defendants were proceeding "promptly and in good faith to comply with the court's decree." 103 F. Supp. 920, 921. In the Virginia case, the court below noted that the equalization program was already "afoot and progressing" (103 F. Supp. 337, 341); since then, we have been advised, in the Virginia Attorney General's brief on reargument, that the program has now been completed. In the Delaware case, the court below similarly noted that the state's equalization program was well under way. 91 A. 2d 137, 149.

the Nation. Only in this way can it be determined if segregation in public schools deprives these plaintiffs of the equal protection of the laws.

Today, education is perhaps the most important function of state and local governments. Compulsory school attendance laws and the great expenditures for education both demonstrate our recognition of the importance of education to our democratic society. It is required in the performance of our most basic public responsibilities, even service in the armed forces. It is the very foundation of good citizenship. Today it is a principal instrument in awakening the child to cultural values, in preparing him for later professional training, and in helping him to adjust normally to his environment. In these days, it is doubtful that any child may reasonably be expected to succeed in life if he is denied the opportunity of an education. Such an opportunity, where the state has undertaken to provide it, is a right which must be made available to all on equal terms.

We come then to the question presented: Does segregation of children in public schools solely on the basis of race, even though the physical facilities and other "tangible" factors may be equal, deprive the children of the minority group of equal educational opportunities? We believe that it does.

In *Sweatt* v. *Painter, supra,* in finding that a segregated law school for Negroes could not provide them equal educational opportunities, this Court relied in large part on "those qualities which are incapable of objective measurement but which make for greatness in a law school." In *McLaurin* v. *Oklahoma State Regents, supra,* the Court, in requiring that a Negro admitted to a white graduate school be treated like all other students, again resorted to intangible considerations: ". . . his ability to study, to engage in discussions and exchange views with other students, and, in general, to learn his profession."

Such considerations apply with added force to children in grade and high schools. To separate them from others of similar age and qualifications solely because of their race generates a feeling of inferiority as to their status in the community that may affect their hearts and minds in a way unlikely ever to be undone. The effect of this separation on their educational opportunities was well stated by a finding in the Kansas case by a court which nevertheless felt compelled to rule against the Negro plaintiffs:

> "Segregation of white and colored children in public schools has a detrimental effect upon the colored children. The impact is greater when it has the sanction of the law; for the policy of separating the races is usually interpreted as denoting the inferiority of the negro group. A sense of inferiority affects the motivation of a child to learn. Segregation with the sanction of law, therefore, has a tendency to [retard] the educational and mental development of negro children and to deprive them of some of the benefits they would receive in a racial[ly] integrated school system." [10]

Whatever may have been the extent of psychological knowledge at the time of *Plessy* v. *Ferguson,* this finding is amply supported by modern authority.[11] Any lan-

---

[10] A similar finding was made in the Delaware case: "I conclude from the testimony that in our Delaware society, State-imposed segregation in education itself results in the Negro children, as a class, receiving educational opportunities which are substantially inferior to those available to white children otherwise similarly situated." 87 A. 2d 862, 865.

[11] K. B. Clark, Effect of Prejudice and Discrimination on Personality Development (Midcentury White House Conference on Children and Youth, 1950); Witmer and Kotinsky, Personality in the Making (1952), c. VI; Deutscher and Chein, The Psychological Effects of Enforced Segregation: A Survey of Social Science Opinion, 26 J. Psychol. 259 (1948); Chein, What are the Psychological Effects of

BROWN v. BOARD OF EDUCATION.

guage in *Plessy* v. *Ferguson* contrary to this finding is rejected.

We conclude that in the field of public education the doctrine of "separate but equal" has no place. Separate educational facilities are inherently unequal. Therefore, we hold that the plaintiffs and others similarly situated for whom the actions have been brought are, by reason of the segregation complained of, deprived of the equal protection of the laws guaranteed by the Fourteenth Amendment. This disposition makes unnecessary any discussion whether such segregation also violates the Due Process Clause of the Fourteenth Amendment.[12]

Because these are class actions, because of the wide applicability of this decision, and because of the great variety of local conditions, the formulation of decrees in these cases presents problems of considerable complexity. On reargument, the consideration of appropriate relief was necessarily subordinated to the primary question—the constitutionality of segregation in public education. We have now announced that such segregation is a denial of the equal protection of the laws. In order that we may have the full assistance of the parties in formulating decrees, the cases will be restored to the docket, and the parties are requested to present further argument on Questions 4 and 5 previously propounded by the Court for the reargument this Term.[13]   The Attorney General

---

Segregation Under Conditions of Equal Facilities?, 3 Int. J. Opinion and Attitude Res. 229 (1949); Brameld, Educational Costs, in Discrimination and National Welfare (MacIver, ed., 1949), 44–48; Frazier, The Negro in the United States (1949), 674–681. And see generally Myrdal, An American Dilemma (1944).

[12] See *Bolling* v. *Sharpe, post*, p. 497, concerning the Due Process Clause of the Fifth Amendment.

[13] "4. Assuming it is decided that segregation in public schools violates the Fourteenth Amendment

"(a) would a decree necessarily follow providing that, within the

of the United States is again invited to participate.   The Attorneys General of the states requiring or permitting segregation in public education will also be permitted to appear as *amici curiae* upon request to do so by September 15, 1954, and submission of briefs by October 1, 1954.[14]

It is so ordered.

---

limits set by normal geographic school districting, Negro children should forthwith be admitted to schools of their choice, or

"(*b*) may this Court, in the exercise of its equity powers, permit an effective gradual adjustment to be brought about from existing segregated systems to a system not based on color distinctions?

"5. On the assumption on which questions 4 (*a*) and (*b*) are based, and assuming further that this Court will exercise its equity powers to the end described in question 4 (*b*),

"(*a*) should this Court formulate detailed decrees in these cases;

"(*b*) if so, what specific issues should the decrees reach;

"(*c*) should this Court appoint a special master to hear evidence with a view to recommending specific terms for such decrees;

"(*d*) should this Court remand to the courts of first instance with directions to frame decrees in these cases, and if so what general directions should the decrees of this Court include and what procedures should the courts of first instance follow in arriving at the specific terms of more detailed decrees?"

[14] See Rule 42, Revised Rules of this Court (effective July 1, 1954).

GIDEON v. WAINWRIGHT.

GIDEON v. WAINWRIGHT, CORRECTIONS DIRECTOR.

CERTIORARI TO THE SUPREME COURT OF FLORIDA.

No. 155. Argued January 15, 1963.—Decided March 18, 1963.

Charged in a Florida State Court with a noncapital felony, petitioner appeared without funds and without counsel and asked the Court to appoint counsel for him; but this was denied on the ground that the state law permitted appointment of counsel for indigent defendants in capital cases only. Petitioner conducted his own defense about as well as could be expected of a layman; but he was convicted and sentenced to imprisonment. Subsequently, he applied to the State Supreme Court for a writ of habeas corpus, on the ground that his conviction violated his rights under the Federal Constitution. The State Supreme Court denied all relief. *Held:* The right of an indigent defendant in a criminal trial to have the assistance of counsel is a fundamental right essential to a fair trial, and petitioner's trial and conviction without the assistance of counsel violated the Fourteenth Amendment. *Betts* v. *Brady,* 316 U. S. 455, overruled.

Reversed and cause remanded.

Abe Fortas, by appointment of the Court, 370 U. S. 932, argued the cause for petitioner. With him on the brief were *Abe Krash* and *Ralph Temple.*

Bruce R. Jacob, Assistant Attorney General of Florida, argued the cause for respondent. With him on the brief were *Richard W. Ervin,* Attorney General, and *A. G. Spicola, Jr.,* Assistant Attorney General.

J. Lee Rankin, by special leave of Court, argued the cause for the American Civil Liberties Union et al., as *amici curiae,* urging reversal. With him on the brief were *Norman Dorsen, John Dwight Evans, Jr., Melvin L. Wulf, Richard J. Medalie, Howard W. Dixon* and *Richard Yale Feder.*

George D. Mentz, Assistant Attorney General of Alabama, argued the cause for the State of Alabama, as *amicus curiae,* urging affirmance. With him on the brief were *MacDonald Gallion,* Attorney General of Alabama, *T. W. Bruton,* Attorney General of North Carolina, and *Ralph Moody,* Assistant Attorney General of North Carolina.

A brief for the state governments of twenty-two States and Commonwealths, as *amici curiae,* urging reversal, was filed by *Edward J. McCormack, Jr.,* Attorney General of Massachusetts, *Walter F. Mondale,* Attorney General of Minnesota, *Duke W. Dunbar,* Attorney General of Colorado, *Albert L. Coles,* Attorney General of Connecticut, *Eugene Cook,* Attorney General of Georgia, *Shiro Kashiwa,* Attorney General of Hawaii, *Frank Benson,* Attorney General of Idaho, *William G. Clark,* Attorney General of Illinois, *Evan L. Hultman,* Attorney General of Iowa, *John B. Breckinridge,* Attorney General of Kentucky, *Frank E. Hancock,* Attorney General of Maine, *Frank J. Kelley,* Attorney General of Michigan, *Thomas F. Eagleton,* Attorney General of Missouri, *Charles E. Springer,* Attorney General of Nevada, *Mark McElroy,* Attorney General of Ohio, *Leslie R. Burgum,* Attorney General of North Dakota, *Robert Y. Thornton,* Attorney General of Oregon, *J. Joseph Nugent,* Attorney General of Rhode Island, *A. C. Miller,* Attorney General of South Dakota, *John J. O'Connell,* Attorney General of Washington, *C. Donald Robertson,* Attorney General of West Virginia, and *George N. Hayes,* Attorney General of Alaska.

Robert Y. Thornton, Attorney General of Oregon, and *Harold W. Adams,* Assistant Attorney General, filed a separate brief for the State of Oregon, as *amicus curiae.*

MR. JUSTICE BLACK delivered the opinion of the Court.

Petitioner was charged in a Florida state court with having broken and entered a poolroom with intent to commit a misdemeanor. This offense is a felony under

241

Florida law.   Appearing in court without funds and without a lawyer, petitioner asked the court to appoint counsel for him, whereupon the following colloquy took place:

> "The COURT: Mr. Gideon, I am sorry, but I cannot appoint Counsel to represent you in this case. Under the laws of the State of Florida, the only time the Court can appoint Counsel to represent a Defendant is when that person is charged with a capital offense.   I am sorry, but I will have to deny your request to appoint Counsel to defend you in this case.
>
> "The DEFENDANT: The United States Supreme Court says I am entitled to be represented by Counsel."

Put to trial before a jury, Gideon conducted his defense about as well as could be expected from a layman.   He made an opening statement to the jury, cross-examined the State's witnesses, presented witnesses in his own defense, declined to testify himself, and made a short argument "emphasizing his innocence to the charge contained in the Information filed in this case."   The jury returned a verdict of guilty, and petitioner was sentenced to serve five years in the state prison.   Later, petitioner filed in the Florida Supreme Court this habeas corpus petition attacking his conviction and sentence on the ground that the trial court's refusal to appoint counsel for him denied him rights "guaranteed by the Constitution and the Bill of Rights by the United States Government." [1]   Treating the petition for habeas corpus as properly before it, the State Supreme Court, "upon consideration thereof" but without an opinion, denied all relief.   Since 1942, when *Betts* v. *Brady,* 316 U. S. 455, was decided by a divided

---

[1] Later in the petition for habeas corpus, signed and apparently prepared by petitioner himself, he stated, "I, Clarence Earl Gideon, claim that I was denied the rights of the 4th, 5th and 14th amendments of the Bill of Rights."

Court, the problem of a defendant's federal constitutional right to counsel in a state court has been a continuing source of controversy and litigation in both state and federal courts.[2] To give this problem another review here, we granted certiorari. 370 U. S. 908. Since Gideon was proceeding *in forma pauperis,* we appointed counsel to represent him and requested both sides to discuss in their briefs and oral arguments the following: "Should this Court's holding in *Betts* v. *Brady,* 316 U. S. 455, be reconsidered?"

I.

The facts upon which Betts claimed that he had been unconstitutionally denied the right to have counsel appointed to assist him are strikingly like the facts upon which Gideon here bases his federal constitutional claim. Betts was indicted for robbery in a Maryland state court. On arraignment, he told the trial judge of his lack of funds to hire a lawyer and asked the court to appoint one for him. Betts was advised that it was not the practice in that county to appoint counsel for indigent defendants except in murder and rape cases. He then pleaded not guilty, had witnesses summoned, cross-examined the State's witnesses, examined his own, and chose not to testify himself. He was found guilty by the judge, sitting without a jury, and sentenced to eight years in prison.

---

[2] Of the many such cases to reach this Court, recent examples are *Carnley* v. *Cochran,* 369 U. S. 506 (1962); *Hudson* v. *North Carolina,* 363 U. S. 697 (1960); *Moore* v. *Michigan,* 355 U. S. 155 (1957). Illustrative cases in the state courts are *Artrip* v. *State,* 136 So. 2d 574 (Ct. App. Ala. 1962); *Shaffer* v. *Warden,* 211 Md. 635, 126 A. 2d 573 (1956). For examples of commentary, see Allen, The Supreme Court, Federalism, and State Systems of Criminal Justice, 8 De Paul L. Rev. 213 (1959); Kamisar, The Right to Counsel and the Fourteenth Amendment: A Dialogue on "The Most Pervasive Right" of an Accused, 30 U. of Chi. L. Rev. 1 (1962); The Right to Counsel, 45 Minn. L. Rev. 693 (1961).

Like Gideon, Betts sought release by habeas corpus, alleging that he had been denied the right to assistance of counsel in violation of the Fourteenth Amendment. Betts was denied any relief, and on review this Court affirmed. It was held that a refusal to appoint counsel for an indigent defendant charged with a felony did not necessarily violate the Due Process Clause of the Fourteenth Amendment, which for reasons given the Court deemed to be the only applicable federal constitutional provision. The Court said:

> "Asserted denial [of due process] is to be tested by an appraisal of the totality of facts in a given case. That which may, in one setting, constitute a denial of fundamental fairness, shocking to the universal sense of justice, may, in other circumstances, and in the light of other considerations, fall short of such denial." 316 U. S., at 462.

Treating due process as "a concept less rigid and more fluid than those envisaged in other specific and particular provisions of the Bill of Rights," the Court held that refusal to appoint counsel under the particular facts and circumstances in the *Betts* case was not so "offensive to the common and fundamental ideas of fairness" as to amount to a denial of due process. Since the facts and circumstances of the two cases are so nearly indistinguishable, we think the *Betts* v. *Brady* holding if left standing would require us to reject Gideon's claim that the Constitution guarantees him the assistance of counsel. Upon full reconsideration we conclude that *Betts* v. *Brady* should be overruled.

II.

The Sixth Amendment provides, "In all criminal prosecutions, the accused shall enjoy the right . . . to have the Assistance of Counsel for his defence." We have construed this to mean that in federal courts counsel must be provided for defendants unable to employ counsel unless the right is competently and intelligently waived.[3] Betts argued that this right is extended to indigent defendants in state courts by the Fourteenth Amendment. In response the Court stated that, while the Sixth Amendment laid down "no rule for the conduct of the States, the question recurs whether the constraint laid by the Amendment upon the national courts expresses a rule so fundamental and essential to a fair trial, and so, to due process of law, that it is made obligatory upon the States by the Fourteenth Amendment." 316 U. S., at 465. In order to decide whether the Sixth Amendment's guarantee of counsel is of this fundamental nature, the Court in *Betts* set out and considered "[r]elevant data on the subject . . . afforded by constitutional and statutory provisions subsisting in the colonies and the States prior to the inclusion of the Bill of Rights in the national Constitution, and in the constitutional, legislative, and judicial history of the States to the present date." 316 U. S., at 465. On the basis of this historical data the Court concluded that "appointment of counsel is not a fundamental right, essential to a fair trial." 316 U. S., at 471. It was for this reason the *Betts* Court refused to accept the contention that the Sixth Amendment's guarantee of counsel for indigent federal defendants was extended to or, in the words of that Court, "made obligatory upon the States by the Fourteenth Amendment." Plainly, had the Court concluded that appointment of counsel for an indigent criminal defendant was "a fundamental right, essential to a fair trial," it would have held that the Fourteenth Amendment requires appointment of counsel in a state court, just as the Sixth Amendment requires in a federal court.

---

[3] *Johnson* v. *Zerbst*, 304 U. S. 458 (1938).

We think the Court in *Betts* had ample precedent for acknowledging that those guarantees of the Bill of Rights which are fundamental safeguards of liberty immune from federal abridgment are equally protected against state invasion by the Due Process Clause of the Fourteenth Amendment.   This same principle was recognized, explained, and applied in *Powell* v. *Alabama,* 287 U. S. 45 (1932), a case upholding the right of counsel, where the Court held that despite sweeping language to the contrary in *Hurtado* v. *California,* 110 U. S. 516 (1884), the Fourteenth Amendment "embraced" those " 'fundamental principles of liberty and justice which lie at the base of all our civil and political institutions,' " even though they had been "specifically dealt with in another part of the federal Constitution."   287 U. S., at 67.   In many cases other than *Powell* and *Betts,* this Court has looked to the fundamental nature of original Bill of Rights guarantees to decide whether the Fourteenth Amendment makes them obligatory on the States.   Explicitly recognized to be of this "fundamental nature" and therefore made immune from state invasion by the Fourteenth, or some part of it, are the First Amendment's freedoms of speech, press, religion, assembly, association, and petition for redress of grievances.[4]   For the same reason, though not always in precisely the same terminology, the Court has made obligatory on the States the Fifth Amendment's command that

---

[4] *E. g., Gitlow* v. *New York,* 268 U. S. 652, 666 (1925) (speech and press); *Lovell* v. *City of Griffin,* 303 U. S. 444, 450 (1938) (speech and press); *Staub* v. *City of Baxley,* 355 U. S. 313, 321 (1958) (speech); *Grosjean* v. *American Press Co.,* 297 U. S. 233, 244 (1936) (press); *Cantwell* v. *Connecticut,* 310 U. S. 296, 303 (1940) (religion); *De Jonge* v. *Oregon,* 299 U. S. 353, 364 (1937) (assembly); *Shelton* v. *Tucker,* 364 U. S. 479, 486, 488 (1960) (association); *Louisiana ex rel. Gremillion* v. *NAACP,* 366 U. S. 293, 296 (1961) (association); *Edwards* v. *South Carolina,* 372 U. S. 229 (1963) (speech, assembly, petition for redress of grievances).

private property shall not be taken for public use without just compensation,[5] the Fourth Amendment's prohibition of unreasonable searches and seizures,[6] and the Eighth's ban on cruel and unusual punishment.[7] On the other hand, this Court in *Palko* v. *Connecticut,* 302 U. S. 319 (1937), refused to hold that the Fourteenth Amendment made the double jeopardy provision of the Fifth Amendment obligatory on the States. In so refusing, however, the Court, speaking through Mr. Justice Cardozo, was careful to emphasize that "immunities that are valid as against the federal government by force of the specific pledges of particular amendments have been found to be implicit in the concept of ordered liberty, and thus, through the Fourteenth Amendment, become valid as against the states" and that guarantees "in their origin . . . effective against the federal government alone" had by prior cases "been taken over from the earlier articles of the federal bill of rights and brought within the Fourteenth Amendment by a process of absorption." 302 U. S., at 324–325, 326.

We accept *Betts* v. *Brady's* assumption, based as it was on our prior cases, that a provision of the Bill of Rights which is "fundamental and essential to a fair trial" is made obligatory upon the States by the Fourteenth Amendment. We think the Court in *Betts* was wrong, however, in concluding that the Sixth Amendment's guarantee of counsel is not one of these fundamental rights. Ten years before *Betts* v. *Brady,* this Court, after full consideration of all the historical data examined in *Betts,* had unequivocally declared that "the right to the aid of

---

[5] *E. g., Chicago, B. & Q. R. Co.* v. *Chicago,* 166 U. S. 226, 235–241 (1897); *Smyth* v. *Ames,* 169 U. S. 466, 522–526 (1898).

[6] *E. g., Wolf* v. *Colorado,* 338 U. S. 25, 27–28 (1949); *Elkins* v. *United States,* 364 U. S. 206, 213 (1960); *Mapp* v. *Ohio,* 367 U. S. 643, 655 (1961).

[7] *Robinson* v. *California,* 370 U. S. 660, 666 (1962).

counsel is of this fundamental character." *Powell* v. *Alabama,* 287 U. S. 45, 68 (1932). While the Court at the close of its *Powell* opinion did by its language, as this Court frequently does, limit its holding to the particular facts and circumstances of that case, its conclusions about the fundamental nature of the right to counsel are unmistakable. Several years later, in 1936, the Court reemphasized what it had said about the fundamental nature of the right to counsel in this language:

> "We concluded that certain fundamental rights, safeguarded by the first eight amendments against federal action, were also safeguarded against state action by the due process of law clause of the Fourteenth Amendment, and among them the fundamental right of the accused to the aid of counsel in a criminal prosecution." *Grosjean* v. *American Press Co.,* 297 U. S. 233, 243–244 (1936).

And again in 1938 this Court said:

> "[The assistance of counsel] is one of the safeguards of the Sixth Amendment deemed necessary to insure fundamental human rights of life and liberty. . . . The Sixth Amendment stands as a constant admonition that if the constitutional safeguards it provides be lost, justice will not 'still be done.'" *Johnson* v. *Zerbst,* 304 U. S. 458, 462 (1938). To the same effect, see *Avery* v. *Alabama,* 308 U. S. 444 (1940), and *Smith* v. *O'Grady,* 312 U. S. 329 (1941).

In light of these and many other prior decisions of this Court, it is not surprising that the *Betts* Court, when faced with the contention that "one charged with crime, who is unable to obtain counsel, must be furnished counsel by the State," conceded that "[e]xpressions in the opinions of this court lend color to the argument . . . ." 316 U. S., at 462–463. The fact is that in deciding as it did— that "appointment of counsel is not a fundamental right,

248

essential to a fair trial"—the Court in *Betts* v. *Brady* made
an abrupt break with its own well-considered precedents.
In returning to these old precedents, sounder we believe
than the new, we but restore constitutional principles
established to achieve a fair system of justice.   Not only
these precedents but also reason and reflection require
us to recognize that in our adversary system of criminal
justice, any person haled into court, who is too poor to
hire a lawyer, cannot be assured a fair trial unless counsel is provided for him.   This seems to us to be an
obvious truth.   Governments, both state and federal,
quite properly spend vast sums of money to establish
machinery to try defendants accused of crime.   Lawyers
to prosecute are everywhere deemed essential to protect
the public's interest in an orderly society.   Similarly,
there are few defendants charged with crime, few indeed,
who fail to hire the best lawyers they can get to prepare
and present their defenses.   That government hires
lawyers to prosecute and defendants who have the money
hire lawyers to defend are the strongest indications of
the widespread belief that lawyers in criminal courts are
necessities, not luxuries.   The right of one charged with
crime to counsel may not be deemed fundamental and
essential to fair trials in some countries, but it is in ours.
From the very beginning, our state and national constitutions and laws have laid great emphasis on procedural
and substantive safeguards designed to assure fair trials
before impartial tribunals in which every defendant stands
equal before the law.   This noble ideal cannot be realized
if the poor man charged with crime has to face his accusers without a lawyer to assist him.   A defendant's need
for a lawyer is nowhere better stated than in the moving
words of Mr. Justice Sutherland in *Powell* v. *Alabama:*

> "The right to be heard would be, in many cases, of
> little avail if it did not comprehend the right to be

heard by counsel. Even the intelligent and educated layman has small and sometimes no skill in the science of law. If charged with crime, he is incapable, generally, of determining for himself whether the indictment is good or bad. He is unfamiliar with the rules of evidence. Left without the aid of counsel he may be put on trial without a proper charge, and convicted upon incompetent evidence, or evidence irrelevant to the issue or otherwise inadmissible. He lacks both the skill and knowledge adequately to prepare his defense, even though he have a perfect one. He requires the guiding hand of counsel at every step in the proceedings against him. Without it, though he be not guilty, he faces the danger of conviction because he does not know how to establish his innocence." 287 U. S., at 68–69.

The Court in *Betts* v. *Brady* departed from the sound wisdom upon which the Court's holding in *Powell* v. *Alabama* rested. Florida, supported by two other States, has asked that *Betts* v. *Brady* be left intact. Twenty-two States, as friends of the Court, argue that *Betts* was "an anachronism when handed down" and that it should now be overruled. We agree.

The judgment is reversed and the cause is remanded to the Supreme Court of Florida for further action not inconsistent with this opinion.

Reversed.

JUSTICES SERVING WITH CHIEF JUSTICE WARREN

NAME	PARTY	APPOINTED	SERVICE TERMINATED	PRIOR OFFICES
Hugo L. Black	Democrat	1937	—	U.S. Senate
Stanley F. Reed	Democrat	1938	1957	U.S. Solicitor General
Felix Frankfurter	Democrat	1939	1962	Professor of Law, Harvard
William O. Douglas	Democrat	1939	—	Chairman, Securities & Exchange Commission
Robert H. Jackson	Democrat	1941	1954	U.S. Attorney General
Harold H. Burton	Republican	1945	1958	U.S. Senate; Mayor of Cleveland
Tom C. Clark	Democrat	1949	1967	U.S. Attorney General
Sherman Minton	Democrat	1949	1956	U.S. Senate; Circuit Court Judge
John M. Harlan	Republican	1955	—	Circuit Court Judge
William J. Brennan, Jr.	Democrat	1956	—	New Jersey Supreme Court Judge
Charles E. Whittaker	Republican	1957	1962	Circuit Court Judge
Potter Stewart	Republican	1958	—	Circuit Court Judge
Byron R. White	Democrat	1962	—	Deputy Attorney General
Arthur J. Goldberg	Democrat	1962	1965	Secretary of Labor
Abe Fortas	Democrat	1965	—	Private practice
Thurgood Marshall	Democrat	1967	—	U.S. Solicitor General; Circuit Court Judge

251

INDEX

Certiorari, petitions for, 49, 114–17
Chafee, Zechariah, 105
character, assassination of, 4; evidence of, 60; witnesses, 69
chart, statistical, 164
church and state related activities and problems, 79, 86–88, 94, 166
Cicenia v. *Lagay,* 357 U.S. 504 (1958), 76
cities, problems in, 39–40, 167
citizens, freedom to criticize, 1; law abiding, 40, 66; privacy of, 13, 16; rights of, 21, 62
citizenship, privileges of, 5, 130
civil rights, litigation and struggle for, 29, 39, 48–49, 65, 118, 126, 143, 156;
Civil Rights Act, violation of, 13; of 1963, 160; of 1964, 48, 50, 54; of 1968, 52
Clark, Justice Tom C., opinions of, 17, 19, 35–36, 88, 90–92, 97, 101–02, 155
Clayton Act, 134–35, 137, 141, 144, 150
codes, legal, 99; police, 25
coercion, 48, 72; freedom from, 82, 92; of dissenters, 81; economic, 142; police, 23; psychological, 122; trade, 149–50
Colegrove v. *Green,* 328 U.S. 549 (1946), 30, 35, 43
collective bargaining agreements, 129, 131–33
communications, 106, 108, 116, 122, 155; failure of, 123; industry, 115
Communism and communists, 13–15, 18, 21, 158, 161
Communist associations, 17, 25
Communist Party, 11, 18–19, 156
Communist Party v. *Subversive Activities Control Board,* 367 U.S. (1961), 18
compulsory package arrangement sales, 136
confessions, extorting, 25, 163; involuntary, 23; need for, 24, 63–64, 72–73, 119–120; traditional, 23; use of, 178; voluntary, 59–60, 64, 74
confrontation, constitutional right of, 6, 14, 58
Congress, 3, 14–15, 24, 27, 29, 32–33, 52, 70, 87, 121, 126, 145, 159–60; Acts of, 5, 12, 154; on civil rights, 160; and labor movement, 129; limitations on, 88; responsibilities, 130, 148, 152; on reapportionment, 37–38, 40; Southern members of, 158
congressional investigations, 16, 18, 109, 154
Connecticut, 39

conscientious objectors, 81, 83
conservative philosophy, 123
conspiratorial conduct, 3, 135, 140
Constitution, the, interpretation of, 2, 20, 33, 37–38, 55, 87, 152–53; language of, 4
Constitutional principles, 35, 69, 157; rights of, 23, 52, 58, 67
Constitutional Rights and Liberties, 105
consumer protection, 39, 139
contract, breach of, 132–33
contracts, collective, 130; consignment, 149; enforcement, 132; federal, 131; labor, 129, 131
contractual arrangements and restraints, 136, 142, 150
convictions, rate of, 61
Cooper v. *Aaron,* 358 U.S. 1 (1958), 29
counsel, assistance of, 58, 60–61, 73, 119; right to, 22, 33, 67, 163
courts, attitude toward, 4, 12; criminal, 63; district, 129–30, 148; federal, 23, 34, 37, 44, 54, 63, 73–74, 128, 132; lower, 151; state, 34, 49, 62–64, 68, 74, 86, 120, 127–29, 132; trial, 68
Cox, Archibald, 102, 111
Cox v. *Louisiana,* 379 U.S. 536 (1965), 105
crime, rate of, 8, 10, 61, 65–66, 70, 72, 75, 77, 158
criminality, cases, 11, 22, 64–65, 77, 118, 124, 143; justice, 1, 33, 40, 59, 61, 63, 65–66, 156, 159; law, 8, 23–24, 26, 51, 118, 123; processes and procedures, 24–25, 58, 63, 73, 165–66
criminals, safeguards for, 22, 24, 74, 122, 157, 159
Crooker v. *California,* 357 U.S. 433 (1958), 24, 76
Cuba, missile crisis over, 21; right to travel to, 21
cynicism, and antitrust cases, 134, 144–147, 151

D

De Gregory v. *Attorney General of New Hampshire,* 383 U.S. 825 (1966), 104, 110
Debs v. *United States,* 249 U.S. 211 (1919), 99–101
"Decision Monday," and press releases, 114
Declaration of Independence, 160
defamation, 129
defendants, impecunious, 69; rights of, 67, 75, 77

255

Japanese-Americans, resettlement of, 9, 163

Jefferson, Thomas, 2, 79, 166

Jehovah's Witnesses, and religious principles, 79, 85, 104, 155

Jencks v. *United States*, 353 U.S. 657 (1957), 15

Jews, orthodox, 83; seminary of, 5

John Birch Society, 1, 28

Johnson, President Lyndon B., 2, 32, 159–160, 162

Johnson v. *New Jersey*, 384 U.S. 719 (1966), 120

Joint Anti-Fascist Refugee Committee, 13

Jones v. *Falcey*, 48 N.J. 25, 40, 222 (1966), 42

judges rules, English practice under, 25

judicial valor and integrity, 22, 126, 130, 154–55

jury, the, 60, 67, 70, 85, 100–01; common-law, 58; local, 128; stacked, 123

Justice, Department of, 15, 27, 113, 135, 144, 148, 151

K

Kalven, Harry, Jr., 98

Kamisar, Yale, 71, 105

Kansas, 40, 85

Kansas v. *Garber*, 197 Kansas 567, 419, 896 (1966), 85

Katz v. *United States*, 389 U.S. 347 (1967), 4, 26

Kauper, Paul G., 78

Kauper, Thomas E., 134

Kennedy, President John F., 2–3, 32, 159, 160

Kilbourn v. *Thompson*, 103 U.S. 168 (1881), 104

Kingsley Pictures Corporation v. *Regents*, 360 U.S. 684 (1959), 98, 109

Korean War, 156

Kreshik v. *St. Nicholas Cathedral of the Russian Orthodox Church*, 363 U.S. 190 (1960), 81–82

Kurland, Philip B., 91–92, 109, 162

L

labor, child, 1; contracts, 131; decisions on, 118, 126–28; industry relations with, 126; laws, 129, 131, 133; practices, 127, 132, 137; unions, 19

Lady Chatterly's Lover, and censorship, 98

Lamont v. *Postmaster*, 381 U.S. 301 (1965), 18

Landrum-Griffin Act of 1959, 129

law enforcement agencies and officials, 1, 4, 22, 24–25, 66, 71, 74–75, 131–32, 134–35, 144, 156, 158

"Law and order," 122

Lawrence, David, 17

lawyers, 24, 28, 59, 62, 67, 126; antitrust, 138–39; common-law, 140; consultive 116, 119; court appointed, 116; government, 145–46

"Les Amants," 20

Levellers, the, 166

Lewis, Anthony, 1

libel, constitutional law on, 104; common-law, 128; judgments, 112; malicious and harmful, 133; plaintiffs, 113; seditious, 105; state law on, 100

liberalism, 4, 7, 9

libertarian philosophy, 96, 132, 156, 158–59

liberty, civil, 6; individual, 16, 19, 108; intellectual, 79; pretrial, 69; religious, 78–79, 81–85, 90–91, 93, 96–97; safeguards of, 119

Lincoln, President Abraham, 153

Little Rock, Arkansas, and segregation, 29

lobbying, practice of, 146

local government, 34, 36, 40–41, 154

Long, Senator Russell B., 120

Los Angeles Times, 113

Loving v. *Virginia*, 388 U.S. 1 (1967), 29

loyalty security program, 14

Lynumn v. *Illinois*, 372 U.S. 528 (1963), 23

M

Madison, James, 152

malapportionment, pattern of, 34, 39, 42

Mallory v. *United States*, 354 U.S. 449 (1957), 70

Manual Enterprises v. *Day*, 370 U.S. 478 (1962), 110

Mapp v. *Ohio*, 367 U.S. 643 (1961), 22, 71, 121

Marbury v. *Madison*, 5 U.S. (1 Cranch) 49 (1803), 32

Marchetti v. *United States*, 390 U.S. 39 (1968), 22

markets, 147; definition of, 140–41, 148; free and unrestricted, 134–35, 141–42; self-regulatory, 134

Marshall, Chief Justice John, 1–2, 32, 117, 153, 163, 166

Martin v. *Hunter's Lessee*, 14 U.S. (1 Wheat), 304 (1816), 32

Pollock, Sir Frederick, 133
polls, public opinion, 75
pollution, curbs on, 40
population, inequality of distribution, 35, 42
Populism, 134, 138
post office, 18
prayer, school, 78, 86, 89–92, 94, 96, 118, 158–60
pre-emption, doctrine of, 126–29
preferred-position, concept of, 155
Preisler v. *Heinkel*, 390 U.S. 939 (1968), 44
Preisler v. *Kirkpatrick*, 390 U.S. 939 (1968), 44
presidency, the, powers of, 21, 37, 152–53, 160
press, the, 107, 112–13, 115–19, 121, 123–25
price controls, 134–36, 140, 149–50
prisoners, 25
progressivism, 16, 153
property, tax exempt, 36
prosecutor, restrictions on, 22
protection, disparity in, 66
"provincialism," 127
public domain, 106
public facilities, and racism, 29, 47, 50, 55, 118
public issues, debates on, 98
public office, religious tests for, 89
public opinion, 7, 33, 118, 123, 158–61
purchasers and dealers, transactions of, 140
Pye, A. Kenneth, 58

R

race relations, problems of, 1, 6, 8, 14, 26, 28, 33, 46–50, 55–57, 118, 158–59
See also segregation
Radin, Max, 9
radio coverage, 119, 125
Railway Labor Act, 133
reapportionment and redistricting, 3, 11, 14, 31, 37, 39–40, 42, 44, 78, 118, 126, 159, 161–64, 166–67
red-baiting, 16, 163
Reed, Justice Stanley F., 102, 155
Rees v. *Peyton*, 384 U.S. 312 (1966), 116
reform, social, 75, 153
rehabilitation, 62
religion, aid to, 93; definition of, 83; hostility to, 86; instructions in, 80; practice of, 81, 86, 92, 97, 118; precepts of, 99; tests required in, 82

reporters, 113–14, 118–20, 123–24. *See also* newspapers
Republican Party, 9, 26, 39, 157
resale price maintenance, 135–36, 140
restraints, governmental, 14, 21; contractual, 136; trade, 150; vertical, 135, 142
retailers, 149
Reynolds v. *Sims*, 377 U.S. 533 (1964), 31, 35–38, 41
Rhode Island, 86
rich, the, opportunities of, 63, 65
rights, individual, 22, 59, 65–67, 72, 132
riots, 8, 75–76
Roberts, Justice Owen J., 5
Rochin v. *California*, 342 U.S. 165 (1952), 12
Rogers v. *Paul*, 382 U.S. 198 (1965), 55
Roosevelt, President Franklin D., 153
Roth v. *United States*, 354 U.S. 476 (1957), 20, 104, 109
Rumely v. *United States*, 345 U.S. (1953), 104
rural areas, 1, 39, 42, 167
Russian Orthodox Church, 81–82
Rutledge, Justice Wiley B., 155

S

sabbatarian convictions, 81, 84–85
St. Antoine, Theodore J., 126
St. Louis Post Dispatch, 40
San Diego Building Trades Council v. *Garmon*, 359 U.S. 236 (1959), 128
Saturday Evening Post, 9
Saturday, work on, 84
Scales v. *United States*, 367 U.S. 203 (1961), 18
Schempp v. *School District of Abington Township*, 374 U.S. 203 (1963), 86–87, 89–95, 97, 100
Schenck v. *United States*, 249 U.S. 99–100
Schneider v. *New Jersey*, 308 U.S. 147 (1939), 108
schools, biracial, 55; boards for, 40; lunches in, 94; parochial, 79, 86–87, 90, 94–95; private, 87, 94; public, 54, 80, 86–87, 90
Schware v. *Board of Examiners*, 353 U.S. (1957), 13
search and seizure, unlawful, 22, 33, 58, 60, 63–64, 67, 71, 163
secular purpose doctrine, 79–80, 83–84, 87, 91, 94–96
segregation, and racism, 3, 27–28, 47, 52, 118, 123

Selective Service, 81
self-organization, federal rights of, 127
sellers and buyers, 135–36, 141–42
Senate Judiciary Committee, 72, 74, 124
"Separate but equal" facilities, doctrine of, 26, 28, 46, 50, 156
Seventh Day Adventists, 84, 93
Shelly v. *Kraemer*, 334 U.S. 1 (1948), 49
Shelton v. *Tucker*, 364 U.S. 479 (1960), 108
Sherbert v. *Verner*, 374 U.S. 398 (1963), 81, 83–85, 93, 96
Sherman Act, 134–37
Simpson Oil Company v. *Union Oil Company*, 377 U.S. 13 (1964), 136, 142, 149–151
sit-in demonstrations, 49, 51, 158
slavery issue, 153, 166
small businesses, protection of, 138–39, 142–43, 147
Smith Act of 1940, 15, 18
Smith v. *California*, 361 U.S. 147 (1959), 107, 110
social responsibility, 1, 9, 22, 32, 66, 107, 153, 161
Socialism and socialists, 99–100
Solicitor-General, Office of, 147
South, the, 47, 49, 52–55, 157–58
South Carolina, 81, 84, 93, 119
Soviet Union, 156
Spano v. *New York*, 360 U.S. 315, 320 (1959), 23
Speck, Richard, 123
Speiser v. *Randall*, 357 U.S. 513 (1958), 107
Spencerian economic theories, 8
sports, professional, 10, 137
Stanley, Governor Thomas B., 28
State Chief Justices, Conference of, 159
State government, 1, 23, 28, 30, 34, 36–38, 40, 42, 62, 81, 152, 154, 159, 167
States' rights, doctrine of, 9, 159
statute of limitations, 131
Stewart, Justice Potter, 17, 19–20, 35–36, 84–85, 98, 101–02, 108, 147, 155
Stone, Chief Justice Harlan F., 154, 163–164
strikes, 127–28, 132
substantive rules, 126–27, 129–30, 132
suburbia, 39, 42, 167
subversion, inquiry into, 16, 49, 103
Subversive Activities Control Act, 18–19
Sunday Closing laws, 81, 83–86, 89, 95–96
supply and demand, elasticity of, 138

Sutherland, Arthur E., 155
Swann v. *Adams*, 384 U.S. 440 (1967), 42
Sweatt v. *Painter*, 339 U.S. 629 (1950), 26
Sweezy v. *New Hampshire*, 354 U.S. 234 (1957), 16, 18, 104

T

Taft-Hartley Labor Act, 15, 126, 129, 132
Tampa Electric Company v. *Nashville Coal Company*, 365 U.S. 320 (1961), 136, 141, 146
Taney, Chief Justice Roger, 166
taxation, exemptions from, 86, 107; regulations covering, 22, 93, 153; and taxpayer, 86–87
technological developments, problems created by, 134
television coverage, 119, 123, 125
Tennessee, 39
Textile Workers Union v. *Lincoln Mills*, 353 U.S. 448 (1957), 130–32
Thayer, James B., 154–55
theistic concepts, 83
Thornhill v. *Alabama*, 310 U.S. 88 (1940), 156
Three Hour Bill, 70
Thurmond, Senator James S., 119
tie-in arrangements, 136, 140–42
Time Inc. v. *Hill, Butts*, 385 U.S. 374 (1967), 106–07
Times Film v. *Chicago*, 365 U.S. 43 (1961), 20
Torcaso v. *Watkins*, 367 U.S. 488 (1961), 81, 83, 88
transportation, 79, 90, 94
Traynor, Justice, 62
Trop v. *Dulles*, 356 U.S. 86 (1958), 5, 12
Truman, President Harry S., 14, 156
Tydings, Senator Millard, 121

U

Ulysses, and censorship, 109
unemployment compensation benefits, 81, 84–85, 93
unions, affairs of, 6, 129–30; agents for, 127; railroad, 133; security provisions of, 133; shop agreement of, 133; strikes by, 132
United Press International, 113, 115
United States v. *Aluminum Company of America*, 377 U.S. 271 (1964), 148, 151

261